D1626181

Discovering Theory in Clinical Practice

Rhonda Peterson Dealey • Michelle R. Evans
Editors

Discovering Theory in Clinical Practice

A Casebook for Clinical Counseling and Social Work Practice

 Springer

Editors
Rhonda Peterson Dealey
Department of Social Work
Washburn University
Topeka, KS, USA

Michelle R. Evans
School of Social Work
Aurora University
Aurora, IL, USA

ISBN 978-3-030-57309-6   ISBN 978-3-030-57310-2   (eBook)
https://doi.org/10.1007/978-3-030-57310-2

This Springer imprint is published by the registered company Springer Nature Switzerland AG
The registered company address is: Gewerbestrasse 11, 6330 Cham, Switzerland

To my students who inspired this book
To my teachers, especially Fred, who
nurtured my enthusiasm for clinical theory
To my clients who taught me more than a
million books ever could
And to my family and colleagues for their
endless patience and encouragement

—Rhonda Peterson Dealey

To the many people that have taken time to
show me a different perspective—colleagues,
mentors, students, and clients—and to the
social workers and clinicians that come after
me, this book is for you.

—Michelle R. Evans

Preface

The idea for this book originated several years ago when we were part of a cohort of clinical doctoral students studying together for our oral and written comprehensive exams. The idea had merit at the time, but trying to add a book project while doing full-time social work, adjunct teaching, and preparing for examinations and dissertation proposals was not realistic. The idea, like many other grand ideas of overzealous doctoral students, was set aside with little expectation of its eventual realization. However, the true passion for the book came as a result of years of teaching graduate social work students interested in clinical practice and trying to help them make the connection between the theories in their textbooks and their real-world clients. How could we facilitate integration of the ideas that students were analyzing into their experiences with the clients they were hoping to serve? We returned to that original idea and decided the time was right to pursue this text.

The study of theory related to clinical practice can be cumbersome and confusing. A recent graduate student in a course which provides an overview of clinical theory remarked, "It feels like when I go to the eye doctor and they ask me, 'Which is better, #1 or #2? Now which is better, #2 or #3?' I read about one theoretical model and think, 'This is really interesting.' And then I read the next thing and think, 'I really like this, too.' How am I supposed to decide which one fits me?"

Our students expressed a desire to be able to visualize how those theories described in textbooks and lectures, some of which were conceptualized decades ago, were being applied in the here and now. They wanted even more examples and contexts than they were already being given. As instructors we suspected that other instructors were experiencing the same phenomenon and having difficulty finding current cases to satisfy their students' needs.

We also recognized from our recent graduates that they were craving ways to continue their learning and apply the knowledge they had gained in their beginning clinical practice. They were looking for models that could help them understand their clients better and expand their clinical skills. Likewise, their clinical supervisors were always on the lookout for resources that could aid in the supervision process.

In thinking about this book, we asked ourselves these questions: How can we help students gain a greater connection to the use of theory to inform practice decisions? How can we assist educators to bring theory to life for their students? How can we aid newly-minted clinicians to expand their understanding of the use of clinical theory in practice?

It is our hope that this text will serve as a resource for students, instructors, and practitioners, for both those who get excited about theory as well as for those less inclined to enjoy the practice of theoretical contemplation yet desire to engage in best practices. We recommend beginning with Chap. 1, which invites the reader to consider valuable ways that theory informs clinical approaches, briefly reviews the historical evolution of clinical theory, and demonstrates how theory guides the clinical process. With this foundation, we suggest the reader then proceed with whatever theory or case seems most intriguing. Each chapter presents with the same format, but there is no need to read the chapters sequentially. A section on cultural considerations and discussion questions are provided in each chapter to aid the reader in thinking further about the theory and case. The cases represent a variety of clients, children and adults, of varying ethnic, racial, and gender identities, who present with a variety of concerns. All cases represent actual clients, some as a composite of cases, and all have been anonymized to protect the clients' privacy. Hence some cases resolve with exceptional outcomes and some end prematurely. But all represent a clinician's fullest efforts to provide thoughtful, theory-based practice for their client.

Topeka, KS, USA   Rhonda Peterson Dealey
Aurora, IL, USA   Michelle R. Evans

Contents

About the Editors

Rhonda Peterson Dealey, DSW, LSCSW is an assistant professor of social work and the Master of Social Work Program Director at Washburn University in Topeka, Kansas. She has been a licensed clinical social work practitioner for more than 25 years, working with individuals and families across the lifespan in the arenas of child welfare, health care, and school social work. Her research interests include children's mental health and well-being and particularly the role of play, and some of her favorite people call her Nanna. She is eternally grateful for the lessons her clients and students teach her every day. Dr. Dealey earned a BA in social work and psychology from Bethany College in Lindsborg, Kansas; a Master of Social Work degree from University of Arkansas at Little Rock; and a Doctor of Social Work degree from Aurora University in Aurora, Illinois.

Michelle R. Evans, DSW, LCSW, CADC is a Licensed Clinical Social Worker, Certified Alcohol and Drug Counselor, and Licensed Sex Offender Treatment Provider and Evaluator with experience in micro-, mezzo-, and macro-level social work. She has worked primarily with the Latino population throughout her career as a bilingual and bicultural social worker. She is currently the Hospital Administrator for Elgin Mental Health Center in Elgin, Illinois. She is in private practice at Nickerson & Associates, PC as a bilingual therapist where she treats adults and adolescents with mental health issues, substance abuse issues, and sex addictions. She also teaches on these topics at Aurora University and University of Chicago in Illinois. Throughout her career, she has worked to increase equity, justice, and cultural awareness at these institutions. Dr. Evans earned a Doctor of Social Work and a Master of Social Work degree from Aurora University in Aurora, Illinois.

About the Contributors

Gladis Anaya completed her Bachelor's in Social Work at the University of Saint Joseph in West Hartford, Connecticut. Gladis completed a year-long practicum in an urban high school where she provided individual support to Latinx urban youth. At the Enfield Food Shelf, she assisted families in enrolling in the SNAP program, organized social activities and meals for children, and participated in the Hunger Action coalition. Gladis is in the process of applying to Masters of Social Work programs to receive advanced training to pursue her goal of supporting recently arrived immigrant families with navigating systems in the United States.

Jennifer Anderson, PhD, MSW, LCSW earned her MSW from Southern Illinois University at Carbondale, and her PhD from Indiana University School of Social Work. Jennifer is a licensed clinical social worker with nearly 20 years of clinical experience in mental health and addictions and has an extensive background in working with the LGBT community. She teaches practice and theory courses for the University of Wisconsin at Whitewater social work program. She serves on the Editorial Board of the Journal for Social Services Research and is a council member for the Council for Social Work Education (CSWE). Her area of research is in interprofessional education (IPE) program design. She has received multiple awards and recognitions for her service. Most recently, Dr. Anderson received the Chancellor's Award for her support of individuals with disabilities on campus. When Jennifer is not teaching, you will find her playing with her two dogs—one of which serves as a therapy dog for a support group on campus.

Nina Aronoff, PhD, MSW, LICSW is a Clinical Associate Professor of Social Work in the Master of Social Work program at Boston University in Massachusetts, with a focus on clinical social work and racial justice. She has over 30 years of clinical and administrative practice experience working with individuals, families, and organizations, particularly around the issues of diversity and inclusion, anti-oppressive practice, collaborative practice, and leadership. In addition to these areas, her scholarship has also focused on justice-based practice and curriculum development, and girls' and women's development and empowerment through sports.

Rachel M. Bailey, MSW, LCSW is an Assistant Clinical Professor at the University of Missouri Columbia School of Social Work, where she teaches in both the Graduate and Undergraduate programs. She is trained in evidence-based practices including Dialectical Behavioral Therapy, Trauma Focused Cognitive Behavioral Therapy, Eye Movement Desensitization Reprocessing, and Prolonged Exposure. Rachel has extensive training and experience in assessment and treatment of suicidal clients. She is a co-founding member of DBT Vitality, and treats suicidal clients in her private practice.

Jessica D. Cless, PhD, LMFT received her Master's and PhD degrees in Marriage and Family Therapy from Kansas State University in Manhattan, KS. She is a proud Kansan, and believes the capacity for love and change resides in every person. Jessica is a Licensed Marriage and Family Therapist and has worked clinically with a diverse population of children, couples, and families. She has developed a clinical specialization in treating childhood traumatic stress and regularly uses a blend of Cognitive Behavioral Therapy and Narrative Therapy, and Play Therapy methods to treat clients. Jessica is currently an Assistant Professor at Washburn University in Topeka, serving as the program coordinator for the Master of Arts in Addiction Counseling in the Family and Human Services Department.

Ashley Davis, PhD, MSW is Clinical Associate Professor at the Boston University School of Social Work in Massachusetts. She earned a B.A. from Wellesley College in Massachusetts, and both an MSW and PhD from Simmons University in Boston. She teaches courses in clinical practice and social work research to MSW students. Her research interests include white privilege, microaggressions, and racial justice in social work education and practice. She maintains a private practice of individuals, couples, and families in Arlington, Massachusetts.

Joan Fedota, EdD, MSW, LCSW earned her MSW from Loyola University of Chicago in Illinois, and her Doctorate in Educational Leadership from National Louis University in Chicago. Joan is a licensed clinical social worker with over 25 years of experience and has an extensive clinical background. Joan has been a leader in the field of school social work where she has received numerous regional and state awards. Joan has served on many boards, conference committees, and has served as the former President of the Illinois Association of School Social Workers. Joan holds the rank of Associate Professor and serves as the Assistant Dean of the Social Work Program at George Williams College at Aurora University in Williams Bay, Wisconsin. When Joan is not teaching and mentoring the next generation of social work leaders, she often volunteers her time towards civic-centered fundraising.

So' Nia L. Gilkey, PhD, LCSW-BACS is Core PhD/DSW faculty in the Barbara Solomon School of Social Work at Walden University in Minneapolis, Minnesota. She is also former Program Director for the Bachelor of Social Work Program at Texas A&M University-Kingsville. Dr. Gilkey has been a social work educator and licensed clinical social worker since 2004. She is actively engaged in social work research as a scholar-practitioner and maintains a small private practice. Dr. Gilkey specializes in child and family trauma and mental health/mental illness. Dr. Gilkey has taught state-side and internationally, presented at state, national and international conferences, and is a peer-reviewed published scholar with journal articles, book chapters, other scholarly reports. Dr. Gilkey currently serves as a cultural competency consultant for the Oregon Center for Brain Injury and has served as a consultant for the Department of Defense, UNICEF, USAID, and CARES-International.

Neil Gorman, DSW, LCSW is an assistant professor at the Aurora University School of Social Work in Aurora, Illinois, where he teaches classes on theory and psychotherapy practice. In addition to teaching Neil is also a member of the American Association of Psychoanalytic Clinical Social Workers (AAPCSW), he provides psychoanalytic psychotherapy at SamaraCare Counseling. Neil first became interested in psychoanalysis when early on in his doctoral program he read Freud's Introductory Lectures to Psychoanalysis and his interest in psychoanalysis continues to deepen the more he learns about it. http://neilgorman.com.

Philip Miller, DSW is an Assistant Professor at Keuka College, Division of Social Work, in Keuka Park, New York, and is a licensed clinical social worker with 25 years of social work experience. He completed a Doctorate of Social Work from Rutgers University in New Brunswick, New Jersey, and a Master of Social Work degree from Washington University in St. Louis, Missouri, with a concentration in mental health and specialization in family therapy. He is a certified Gottman Marital Therapist and spent 8 years active duty in the United States Air Force as a clinical social worker. Dr. Miller's research interests include couples, military social work, and experiential learning.

Alison Smith Mitchell, PhD, LCSW earned her PhD from the Smith College School for Social Work in Northampton, Massachusetts. Her research focuses on supporting opioid-exposed children and families, particularly those living in rural areas. Dr. Mitchell combines practical experience with research expertise, measuring the impact of service provision for clients and staff alike, using findings to guide future programming or undertakings for agencies and research partners. She volunteers as a Court Appointed Special Advocates for children (CASA) guardian ad litem for children in protection cases and was formerly a K-12 educator and administrator. She currently serves as adjunct faculty at the University of Maine School of Social Work in Orono and the Smith College School for Social Work, and is a mental health practitioner in central Maine.

Madeline Pérez De Jesus, PhD is an Associate Professor in the Department of Social Work at the University of Saint Joseph in West Hartford, Connecticut. She earned her doctorate from the City University of New York and her Masters from the Hunter College School of Social Work in New York City. She is a co-author of the book *Theory & Educational Research* (Routledge Press), where she writes about her relationship with theory. Her other publications include articles in *Social Work with Groups* and *Reflections: Narrative of Professional Helping.*

Enitzaida Rodríguez, MSW is a social in a public school in New England. Prior to this role, she worked for 21 years as a probation officer for juveniles. She earned her Master's in Social Work at the University of Connecticut in Hartford and her Bachelor's in Social Work from the University of Saint Joseph (USJ) in West Hartford, Connecticut. In 2009, Enitzaida returned to USJ to complete a post-graduate certificate in Latino Community Practice, where she engaged in community-based participatory research with Puerto Rican youth and developed a bilingual/bicultural curriculum around self-esteem. She is a social work field instructor, adjunct instructor, and mentor to emerging social workers.

Wendy Seerup, MSW, LCSW earned her BS and MSW degrees from University of Illinois at Champaign-Urbana. Wendy is a licensed clinical social worker with nearly 20 years of experience in mental health treatment, play therapy, and family therapy. Wendy has a wealth of experience in the field of experiential therapy which includes direct practice, teaching, program development, community outreach, and clinical supervision. She teaches practice and theory courses at George Williams College in Williams Bay, Wisconsin, and is a council member for the Council for Social Work Education (CSWE). Her area of research is in animal assisted therapy. She serves on the board of directors for a community non-profit and is an avid water-ski performer. When she is not on the water performing at local events, you will find Wendy on challenge by choice courses helping to co-facilitate team building activities and empowerment experiences at the local outdoor leadership program.

Robin Shultz, DSW, LCSW, LMFT, CADC is in private practice where she works with individuals, couples, and families from a systems perspective. Robin received post-graduate training in Bowen Family Systems Theory at the Center for Consultation in Evanston, Illinois and enjoys helping interested clinicians learn about its principles and how it might effectively be used in therapy.

Angela Song, PhD, LCSW is a board-certified psychodynamic clinician in private practice in Honolulu, Hawaii. Her training was done primarily in Chicago, Illinois. Her research interests include chronic pain treatment and attachment theory, as a supplement of relational theory. She has presented about diversity in clinical practice, and about cultural considerations in attachment theory. She teaches courses on trauma and neurobiology, and psychodynamic perspectives on bereavement.

Ann F. Trettin, PhD, LISW-S earned her MSW degree at Ohio State University in Columbus and completed her PhD at the University of Toledo in Higher Education Administration. She currently serves as an Adjunct Instructor at Ohio University, Saint Louis University, and the University of Chicago, teaching play therapy and courses focused on the care of children, adolescents, and families. Ann also serves as the MSW Program Coordinator at Saint Louis University @ Lourdes. She continues in clinical practice at Trettin Play Therapy Center, in Toledo, Ohio, where she works primarily with younger children using child-centered play therapy techniques.

Chapter 1
Theory in Practice

Michelle R. Evans and Rhonda Peterson Dealey

The Essence of Theory for Clinical Practice

"I just don't understand why we are spending so much time studying theory," remarked the clinical graduate student frankly. "Who cares what a bunch of dead white guys think! I just want to know how to do therapy the right way." Her remarks likely express the thoughts of many other students who have felt exasperated by Freud's adherence to the psychosexual stages or by the dense yet ambiguous writings of object relations theorists. Why can't students just learn the "skills" of effective therapy without exploration of theoretical history and metacognitive exercises into the why's and how's of therapeutic efficacy and effectiveness? Is theory really that important? This chapter explores the notion of theory and its importance for clinical practice, provides a brief overview of the evolution of clinical theory, and describes a framework for how theory directly informs day-to-day clinical practice.

Practitioners of any scientific discipline are fundamentally theoretical problem-solvers (Kuhn, 2012). Theory allows for explanation of what is observed in one's world, in essence a "symbolic model" (Ford & Urban, 1998, p. 6) of one's experience and environment. It provides a structure or systemization of ideas and thoughts to answer important questions about what has been observed and what remains supposition. It allows for possibility and hypothesis testing, for analysis and deduction. Theory supplies explanation and meaning and affords the theorist with a mechanism for identification and for prediction. Applied theory attempts to "describe aspects of the natural world that can be applied to create a benefit or reduce a cost" (Heesacker & Lichtenberg, 2012. p. 72). In clinical practice, theory helps explain

M. R. Evans (✉)
School of Social Work, Aurora University, Aurora, IL, USA
e-mail: mevans@aurora.edu

R. P. Dealey
Social Work, Washburn University, Topeka, KS, USA
e-mail: Rhonda.PetersonDealey@washburn.edu

what is seen and heard, ascribes meaning to client experiences, behaviors and problems, and suggests methodology and mechanisms for intervention. Clinical practice theory answers the questions: *What is the problem and how did it arise? What needs to happen now in order for change to occur?* and *What constitutes meaningful change?*

So how does theory inform clinical practice? Theory serves a multitude of functions for the clinician, four of which are offered here as contribution to the argument that being theoretically informed is corequisite with ethical and competent practice: *(1) theoretical adherence lays a foundation for professional skill development; (2) theoretical knowledge establishes the context for theoretical relationship and interaction; (3) study of theory provokes practitioners to gain a deeper understanding of themselves,* and *(4) theory serves to define and connect evidence-informed practice and practice-informed evidence.* Specific instances of where theory informs the day-to-day practice of the clinician and client will be examined later in this chapter.

Theoretical adherence lays a foundation for professional skill development. The student asks why one cannot simply be trained in the necessary skills to provide therapeutic intervention without having to study and think about the philosophical and esoteric concepts of clinical theory. The answer is that it is theory itself that suggests what skills are needed. Clinical theory informs the understanding of pathology and wellness, how problems evolve and change occurs. A theoretical framework which purports insight as the key mechanism of change will demand a different set of skills than a framework which suggests that behavior is altered through environmental reinforcement and aversion avoidance. A theoretical paradigm which asserts that problems develop as a result of intrapsychic forces and internal conflicts will likely require different forms of intervention than a theoretical paradigm which maintains that problems develop as a consequence of external injustices and disparities. Assessment of childhood experiences and early familial relationships is highly valued by adherents of Adler's Individual Psychology (Adler, 1969). Assessment for proponents of solution-focused brief therapy, on the other hand, looks very different, and rarely encompasses details from the distant past (De Shazer, 1985). Honing the skills of one's craft, then, is largely dependent upon the understanding of what one's craft is and does. Theory helps the practitioner know what to look for and what steps to take when intervening.

Theoretical knowledge establishes the context for theoretical relationship and interaction. Nearly all contemporary approaches to clinical psychotherapeutic processes acknowledge that a working alliance is a critical component to effective intervention. Quantitative research and meta-analysis (Wampold, 2001, 2010) suggest that contextual factors such as therapeutic relationship and alliance, and the personal and interpersonal skills of the therapist are primary determinants of therapeutic outcome, and that technique has significantly less effect. Even so, theory informs the understanding of relationship within the therapeutic context. Is therapeutic relationship necessary and sufficient for change (Rogers, 1961, 1967) or is it a necessary collaborative effort, but a non-causal factor in client change (Dattilio & Hanna, 2012)? What considerations are given to power structures in the therapeutic environment (Brown, 2010)? Is the therapeutic relationship a focus of communication in the therapy setting or an irrelevant topic that distracts from the function of therapy? Theory seeks to answer such questions and aids the clinician in developing a therapeutic context conducive to client success.

Study of theory provokes practitioners to gain a deeper understanding of themselves. Who the therapist is and how that enters the therapeutic context is key to ethical practice and positive client outcomes (Baldwin, 2013.) Attention to one's own inner woundedness allows a therapist to embrace one's own vulnerability and prepare for boundary-appropriate joining with clients (Miller & Baldwin Jr, 2013; Piercy & Bao, 2013). Such inward reflection may even reduce a practitioner's risk of burnout (Miller & Baldwin Jr, 2013). Inner self-exploration can be sparked through a variety of means: the clinician's own experience in therapy and/or supervision; spontaneous awareness of countertransference triggered in provision of services; or an intentional effort to practice reflectively and reflexively. The theoretical understanding a clinician has of clients is essentially the same understanding the clinician has of oneself (Stedmon & Dallos, 2009). The study of theory in practice affords the practitioner an avenue for searching one's own values, beliefs, experiences, and worldview, to challenge uncovered bias and prejudice, and to consider new ways of understanding oneself and others. Theory can even inform one's approach to studying theory and practicing reflection.

Theory serves to define and connect evidence-informed practice and practice-informed evidence. Theory informs the work of both scientific researchers and practitioners of clinical psychotherapy and may, in fact, function as a bridge between the two (Heesacker & Lichtenberg, 2012). Researchers and practitioners are interested in causal effects and correlations which give insight into client experiences and outcomes. Both scientists and clinicians are interested in the operationalization of concepts of theory into observable processes, that is, the transformation of thought constructs into actionable interventions and/or tools of outcome evaluation. In the era of managed care and quality outcomes reimbursement models, practitioners and payor sources are forced to consider the effectiveness of treatment modalities. A case could be made that the experience of each client system is in essence a research venture. A hypothesis is formulated and tested, conclusions are drawn, and future implications are noted. These pseudo-experiments in aggregate serve as the building blocks of clinical wisdom for practitioners and are the practice-informed evidence which guides future work with new client systems. Such practice-informed evidence, grounded in theory, should be the guiding force for scientific inquiry. Without the guidance of practice-based inquiry, scientific-based inquiry risks privileging theoretical influence in ways that may be detrimental to understanding what is best practice and most helpful to clients. Some theories by nature are easier to operationalize and therefore study. Popularity of a modality and/or connectedness of a theoretical proponent to sources of power and resource, e.g., research funding, may privilege what research is done and for whom. It is via a pathway of theoretical dialogue that practice and research can come together to inform the evolution of theory and treatment.

The Evolution of Clinical Theory

Sigmund Freud (1989) is often credited as being the first to theorize that mental illness could be understood and treated using talk therapy. Freud proposed a model of personality structure, pathology development, and methodology for treatment based on the premise that neuroses exist as a result of internal drive and conflicts. Freud's structure of the clinical hour in which exchange of language between a paying client and a trained therapist still informs clinical work to this day. While Freud's ideas became widely accepted worldwide and dominated approaches to mental illness treatment for decades, even in his own time Freud was not without critics. Contemporaries of Freud who challenged his ideas and hypothesized differently the determinants of mental illness and the motivations of human beings are often referred to as Neo-Freudians. Carl Jung (1961), once a valued colleague of Freud's, challenged his friend's psychosexual theories and ventured off to theorize a spiritual approach which emphasized a quest for meaning as a motivating force. Jung suggested that not only is a person's past determinant of the present state, but so, too, is the future aspiration. Jung's contributions, including the collective unconscious, dream functions, and the notion of individuation as integration of conscious and unconscious material, are still helpful to clinical therapists today (Harris, 1996). Alfred Adler (1969), also once an esteemed colleague of Freud's, theorized concepts such as the inferiority complex and importance of birth order which inform clinical practice and the common vernacular yet today.

Next-generation clinicians, often referred to as the Ego Psychologists, were less concerned about the drives and more concerned about the development of the ego. Anna Freud's (1936) ego defense mechanisms are an important part of clinical education and have made their way into everyday language. Hartmann's (1939) hypothesis that aspects of ego development occur outside of conflict was an important evolution of understanding human experience. Erikson's (1950) optimistic framework of crisis and mastery of stages across the entire lifespan continues to inform understanding of human development.

Psychoanalytic theory continued to evolve during the 1940s and 1950s when several American and British practitioners diverged from Freud's theory that human motivation is driven by satisfaction of sexual and aggressive needs and suggested that human relationship is central to formation of the psyche and motivates human behavior. Their theories are categorized as object relations theories and focus on the internalized images of self in relation to significant others, referred to as objects, namely the mother. While they all focused on how early relationships create mental representations of self and others which inform relationships in later life, the ideas of individual object relations theorists varied widely. Melanie Klein, who is often credited with founding the object relations approach to psychoanalysis, developed her ideas from her work with infants and young children and suggested that experiences in the first months of life were critical. Ronald Fairbairn's conceptualization of a splitting defense to create good objects and bad objects continues to inform psychoanalytic understanding and practice. D. W. Winnicott, a British pediatrician who trained in psychoanalysis, conceptualized a child's developing capacity to separate me and not-me and the symbolic use of an object, which led to an understanding of the significance of transitional objects in self-soothing. These and other object relations theorists contributed much more which continues to inform clinical practice. The evolution of psychoanalytic understanding diverged further into an understanding of the concept of self, including such matters as self-esteem, self-regulation, and self-cohesion (Goldstein, 2001).

While much of clinical theory evolved as a progression from early psychoanalytic thoughts, a great deal of clinical theory developed as a rejection of psychoanalytic understanding and particularly the deterministic understanding of human experience. Existential and humanistic approaches to clinical work beginning in the 1940s and 1950s provided a new philosophy related to human suffering and human potential. Existential therapy, based on a way of thinking rather than a subscribed modality of treatment, arose following the devastation of World Wars I and II and emphasized the difficult issues of suffering, anxiety, isolation, and tragedy. Existential thinkers suggest that individuals are free to choose their actions and reactions to circumstances. Finding meaning and accepting responsibility and power for change are key tasks in an existential approach (Frankl, 1963; Yalom, 2003). Humanistic theorist, Abraham Maslow (1943), argued that people are basically good and are capable of growth and healing, and that the function of therapy is to help clients remove the obstacles that interfere with their self-actualizing tendencies. Carl Rogers' (1961) non-directive approach, which placed the client as expert of their own experience, was a radical departure from psychoanalytic models. The non-judgmental stance of the therapist, the focus on the here-and-now, and the emphasis on empathic understanding of Rogers' person-centered approach garnered a very different therapy experience for client and practitioner.

Different yet, behavioral approaches to therapy applied principles of classical and operant conditioning to the treatment of psychological problems and behavioral functioning. By the 1970s behavioral models, such as Bandura's (1977) theory of social modeling, significantly impacted psychotherapy as well as education and other forms of social work practice. Behavioral approaches quickly broadened to encompass cognition as the site of distress and the locus for change. Rational emotive behavior therapy (Ellis, 1997) suggested that people's beliefs about events and circumstances contribute to their emotional distress and symptoms. Beck's (1963, 1976) early depression research suggested that clients' cognitive distortions resulted in negative biases for how they interpreted life events. According to cognitive behavioral theorists, automatic and maladaptive thoughts and feelings impact individuals more than actual events, and psychoeducational approaches to behavioral change can be used to change maladaptive thinking (Beck & Haigh, 2014). A "third wave" of cognitive behavioral approaches has changed the landscape of therapy by valuing holism and health and emphasizing context, acceptance, relationships, and goals. Mindfulness-based therapies, dialectical behavioral therapy, and acceptance and commitment therapy are examples of this third wave of behavioral theory (Hayes & Hofmann, 2017).

Feminist theories inform much of contemporary psychotherapy. Growing out of the women's movement of the 1960s and 1970s, feminist theorists sought to move away from the perspective of internalized psychopathology and toward a focus on understanding the impact of social, political, and cultural factors which marginalize and constrain women. Clinicians began to integrate feminist ideologies and values with existing therapeutic modalities, challenging the patriarchal systems which previously defined the therapy experience. The feminist perspective continued to evolve, challenging not only gender roles and stereotypes, but calling out other forms of oppression, analyzing power structures in society and within the therapeutic relationship, and utilizing a sociocultural perspective to understand and address client problems (Enns, 2004).

Postmodernist perspectives have influenced clinical theory and practice dramatically in recent decades. Suggesting that truth is subjective and contextual, postmodern theorists privilege language systems as the basis of construction of meaning. Social constructionists suggest that knowledge of reality is constructed and influenced by the historical social context and dominant language. Practitioners who subscribe to a postmodern, social constructionist viewpoint disavow the idea of therapist as expert and elect a more collaborative interaction with clients (De Shazer & Berg, 1988). Solution-focused brief therapy and narrative therapy are two popular forms of clinical therapy which are informed by postmodern perspectives.

Theoretical evolution and paradigmatic shifts occur as a result of a changed worldview (Kuhn, 2012). Clinical theory in the past 100 years has changed markedly as the world in which it exists has changed markedly. It is difficult to know exactly how many forms of clinical therapy are actually being utilized currently. The Psychology Today website, which is designed to assist individuals in finding a local therapist who would be a good match, describes 66 different common types of therapy. Herink (1980) identified more than 200 forms of therapy. And certainly, anyone form of therapy is practiced somewhat uniquely by individual adherents.

Theoretical approaches are based on underlying philosophical assumptions about human nature, mental health, and pathology which inform methods and processes in clinical practice. Since the days of Freud and Jung, arguments of theoretical superiority have existed. All forms of therapy have been scientifically shown to be effective, and some research suggests that the level of allegiance of the clinician to the treatment model, that is, the belief that their theoretical approach is superior to other approaches, accounted for any variance between outcomes in differing approaches (Wampold, 2001, 2010). Debates have arisen as to the value of theoretical singularity versus theoretical plurality and integration. A newer orientation toward process-based therapy over traditional methods-based approaches may emerge as the next standard of evaluation (Hayes & Hofmann, 2017). Regardless, the overall interpretation of the body of research suggests that therapy, executed with fidelity and competence, is beneficial to patients (Lambert, 2013).

Creating a Clinical Framework Using Theory

Theory provides us with the basis to understand the complex lives of our clients in an orderly way. Concepts about the person, human behavior in the environment, and the person's resiliency, among other topics, must be fully considered in order to be able to understand what interventions might be useful to help the client achieve their goal. Theories provide the clinician with a foundational base to understand why problems occur for humans and what needs to change to help the person enhance their wellbeing. In the best interventions, theory, research, and practice are combined in a meaningful way that allows the clinician to understand the interpersonal and environmental factors that are impacting the client. The experience that the clinician gains while in practice and the knowledge from research and training provide the clinician with a base to continue to develop knowledge on an ongoing basis that benefits the field of practice.

It is important to understand the difference between a theory and a therapy. Clinical theory incorporates the held beliefs that explain some aspects of human phenomenon, pathology, and cure. A clinical therapy is a more specific treatment modality that provides an explanation of specific interventions that should be used to correct a specific impairment. Therapies are created from theory. These terms are often used interchangeably but there is a difference between the two. A therapy has specific interventions and protocols that are recommended and which may provide the clinician with guidance for activities, interventions, and clinician behaviors, while a theory may encompass a larger scope and may be less prescriptive.

Many clinicians use evidence-based practices (EBP) which are therapies that have gone through peer-reviewed research to prove their efficacy with specific populations. Using a proven EBP is considered best practice; however, there is still research lacking for many populations and therapies. As more research is completed, additional EBPs will be identified. Clinicians often work with individuals from populations that are under-researched. Therefore, the clinician must use the best available knowledge and experience to make appropriate treatment decisions for that individual's needs. Beginning clinicians should seek supervision when choosing a theory or therapy for a client that may be under-researched for that population.

Using theory to understand how to help clients has many advantages. It gives the clinician an opportunity to organize principles to assess the client accurately. It minimizes the bias of the clinician's experience as it provides a framework that the clinician can focus on, instead of focusing only on their own experiences. The theory can also provide a basis for rationale for making clinical decisions. Evidence-based practices, especially, provide clear researched evidence for why a specific intervention is chosen to help a client.

A clinical framework is a structural plan or basis for action based on clinical theory or therapy. This framework is based upon the theory or therapy that the clinician is using to understand the client. To build this clinical framework, the clinician must first choose a theory or therapy that is aligned with the client's reason for seeking treatment. For instance, cognitive behavioral therapy (CBT) is an evidence-based practice to treat substance use disorders. If a clinician is seeing a client with a substance use disorder, they may consider using this therapy as a basis for their clinical framework. Once the clinician decides on the therapy that they will use in their work, they will develop a hypothesis of the presenting problem based on the therapy. The term hypothesis is being used here as a tentative assumption or working idea as to what may be causing the client's presenting problem. Using the example of the clinician that has chosen to use CBT to work with their client, they would examine the client's thinking patterns during the initial assessment to identify problematic thought patterns and core beliefs, for instance. This theory-based assessment would allow the clinician to identify what thoughts or behaviors are most problematic for the client. Once these thoughts and behaviors are identified, the clinician will create a hypothesis of what thoughts and behaviors will need to change to help the client. This hypothesis would be supported by the evidence of the client's thoughts, behaviors, internal and external experiences reported during the assessment process. The hypothesis will be instrumental in helping the clinician set and evaluate goals and interventions for the client during the treatment process.

Developing Client Goals Using Theory

Once the clinician has identified the hypothesis that will be guiding their work, they will use this information to set client goals. Many of the theories encourage the clinician to work with the client to set goals collaboratively. These goals are guided by the theory's explanation of the problem and how people change. For instance, using the example above, a clinician using CBT would collaboratively set goals with the client that are related to addressing cognitive distortions or maladaptive behaviors as CBT promotes client psychoeducation and collaboration as an intervention. Other theories might not value the collaboration or psychoeducation as highly and thus a different approach might be taken.

The clinician may create goals that are specific or more general depending on the nature of the services that are being provided and the theory in use. If a goal is too vague or does not align with the theory, the clinician and client may find themselves unclear as to the therapeutic work that needs to be accomplished. If the clinician and client find that they are not moving forward, the clinician should review the hypothesis and realign the goals with the original understanding of the reason for requesting services to help the client achieve a good outcome from treatment.

Planning and Implementing Change Strategies

Once the clinician has identified theory-based goals that will help the client, they will design interventions that are supported by the theory. For instance, if the clinician has been using CBT to create their clinical framework, the interventions should directly address the goals created within this framework. A client with the goal of reducing cognitive distortions might initially participate in the intervention of receiving psychoeducation to help them identify cognitive distortions.

Interventions are chosen based on the client's readiness to engage in change and their willingness to participate. Clients that are hesitant about change may benefit from the use of change strategy models such as the stages of change or motivational interviewing. These two models can provide clinicians with tools to help a client move forward in their commitment for change and can often be used in conjunction with many theories and therapies to help the client move toward their goals.

In addition to using change models, clinicians can integrate other theories or therapies to better meet client needs. When doing this, the clinician needs to ensure that the interventions align with the goals and current needs of a client. This can be very helpful for both the clinician and client, especially when working with clients from under-researched populations. A clinician may choose to use a few techniques from the alternate therapy to meet the needs of the client, or they may choose to use another theory altogether when working with one specific problem that the client has. For instance, if the client with a substance use disorder also has unresolved grief from a childhood incident that has been impacting their mental health, the clinician may use a narrative model to help the client process and "re-author" this incident (White, 2007). The clinician and client may return to using CBT regarding the current use of substances, but they may find that a different approach is more helpful for this particular issue that the client is facing. However, integrating other therapies should be done with caution to avoid losing focus on the goals of the clients.

Using the Clinical Framework to Develop a Plan for Termination

A clinician begins to plan for termination during the initial assessment. As the clinician assesses the individual, they must develop an idea of what the client will need to achieve to allow them to feel that they have resolved the presenting problem. From that picture of what the client should have achieved at termination, the clinician is able to consider the client's need for change from where they are at initial intake to termination within the framework of the theory. For instance, using the client described above, the picture that the clinician using CBT might develop is a client that is able to avoid cognitive distortions and utilize coping skills consistently to manage urges and thoughts to use substances. If the clinician develops a solid hypothesis, the goals and interventions that are based on the hypothesis will lead the client to that picture of success at termination.

The evaluation for termination is ongoing as the client participates in ongoing goal evaluations. When the client has achieved all goals and there are not any additional goals that the client wishes to address, termination can be considered. This is typically done collaboratively.

Summary

Theory is the foundation of all clinical work. It provides an understanding for why clients develop problems and how change can happen. Four arguments were presented regarding the contribution of theory to ethical and competent practice: *(1) theoretical adherence lays a foundation for professional skill development; (2) theoretical knowledge establishes the context for theoretical relationship and interaction; (3) study of theory provokes practitioners to gain a deeper understanding of themselves, and (4) theory serves to define and connect evidence-informed practice and practice-informed evidence.* In this chapter, the history of the development of clinical practice theory was discussed. The use of clinical theory with clients was reviewed with a discussion of how theory guides clinical interventions to help clients meet their goals. In each of the following chapters, a specific clinical practice theory will be reviewed with an application to a case. The reader is encouraged to peruse the chapters in whatever sequence seems most relevant and interesting.

References

Adler, A. (1969). *The practice and theory of individual psychology*. Totowa, NJ: Littlefield, Adams, & Co. (2nd rev. ed. published 1929).

Baldwin, M. (Ed.). (2013). *The use of self in therapy* (3rd ed.). New York: Routledge.

Bandura, A. (1977). *Social learning theory*. Englewood Cliffs, NJ: Prentice-Hall.

Beck, A. T. (1963). Thinking and depression: Idiosyncratic content and cognitive distortions. *Archives of General Psychiatry, 9*, 324–333.

Beck, A. T. (1976). *Cognitive therapy and emotional disorders*. New York: New American Library.

Beck, A. T., & Haigh, E. A. P. (2014). Advances in cognitive theory and therapy: The generic cognitive model. *Annual Review of Clinical Psychology, 10*, 1–24.

Brown, L. S. (2010). *Feminist therapy*. Washington, DC: American Psychological Association.

Dattilio, F. M., & Hanna, M. A. (2012). Collaboration in cognitive-behavior therapy. *Journal of Clinical Psychology, 68*(2), 146–158.

De Shazer, S. (1985). *Keys to solutions in brief therapy*. New York: Norton.

De Shazer, S., & Berg, I. (1988). Doing therapy: A post-structural revision. *Journal of Marital and Family Therapy, 18*, 71–81.

Ellis, A. (1997). The evolution of Albert Ellis and rational emotive behavior therapy. In J. K. Zeig (Ed.), *The evolution of psychotherapy: The third conference* (pp. 69–82). New York: Brunner/Mazel.

Enns, C. Z. (2004). *Feminist theories and feminist psychotherapies: Origins, themes, and diversity* (2nd ed.). New York: Haworth.

Erikson, E. H. (1950). *Childhood and society*. New York: Norton.

Ford, D. H., & Urban, H. B. (1998). *Contemporary models of psychotherapy: A comparative analysis* (2nd ed.). Hoboken, NJ: John Wiley & Sons.

Frankl, V. (1963). *Man's search for meaning*. Boston, MA: Beacon.

Freud, A. (1936). *The ego and the mechanisms of defense* (The writings of Anna Freud) (Vol. 2). New York: International Universities Press.

Freud, S. (1989). *An outline of psychoanalysis*. New York: Norton.

Goldstein, E. (2001). *Object relations theory and self psychology in social work practice*. New York: The Free Press.

Harris, A. S. (1996). *Living with paradox: An introduction to Jungian psychology*. Belmont, CA: Brooks/Cole Cengage.

Hartmann, H. (1939). Ego psychology and the problem of adaptation. (D. Rappaport, Trans., 14th ed.). New York: International Universities Press. (Original work published 1939)

Hayes, S. C., & Hofmann, S. G. (2017). The third wave of cognitive behavioral therapy and the rise of process-based care. *World Psychiatry, 16*(3), 245–246. https://doi.org/10.1002/wps.20442.

Heesacker, M., & Lichtenberg, J. W. (2012). Theory and research for counseling interventions. In E. M. Altmaier & J. C. Hansen (Eds.), *The Oxford handbook of counseling psychology*. Oxford: Oxford University Press.

Herink, R. (1980). *The psychotherapy handbook: The A to Z guide to more than 250 different therapies in use today*. New York: New American Library.

Jung, C. G. (1961). *Memories, dreams, reflections*. New York: Vintage.

Kuhn, T. S. (2012). *The structure of scientific revolutions*. Chicago, IL: University of Chicago Press.

Lambert, M. J. (2013). The efficacy and effectiveness of psychotherapy. In M. J. Lambert (Ed.), *Bergin & Garfield's handbook of psychotherapy and behavior change* (6th ed.). Amsterdam: Wiley.

Maslow, A. H. (1943). A theory of human motivation. *Psychological Review, 50*(4), 370–396. https://doi.org/10.1037/h0054346.

Miller, G. D., & Baldwin, D. C., Jr. (2013). The implication of the wounded-healer archetype for the use of self in psychotherapy. In M. Baldwin (Ed.), *The use of self in therapy* (3rd ed.). New York: Routledge.

Piercy, F. P., & Bao, A. K. (2013). In M. Baldwin (Ed.), *The use of self in therapy* (3rd ed.). New York: Routledge.

Psychology Today. (n.d.). Types of therapy. Retrieved from https://www.psychologytoday.com/us/types-of-therapy

Rogers, C. (1961). *On becoming a person*. Boston: Houghton Mifflin.

Rogers, C. (1967). The conditions of change from a client-centered viewpoint. In B. Berenson & R. Carkhuff (Eds.), *Sources of gain in counseling and psychotherapy*. New York: Hold, Rinehart & Winston.

Stedmon, J., & Dallos, R. (2009). *Reflective practice in psychotherapy and counselling*. Berkshire, England: Open University Press.

Wampold, B. E. (2001). *The great psychotherapy debate: Models, methods, and findings*. Hillsdale, NJ: Erlbaum.

Wampold, B. E. (2010). The research evidence for the common factors models: A historical situated perspective. In B. L. Duncan, S. D. Miller, B. E. Wampold, & M. A. Hubble (Eds.), *The heart and soul of change: Delivering what works in therapy* (2nd ed.). Washington, DC: American Psychological Association.

White, M. (2007). *Maps of narrative practice*. New York: W.W. Norton.

Yalom, I. D. (2003). *The gift of therapy: An open letter to a new generation of therapists and their patients*. New York: Harper Collins.

Chapter 2
Interpersonal Theory: The Case of Lisa

Angela Song

Introduction to Interpersonal Theory

Students of social work use the *person-in-environment* (PIE) approach for each treatment. The person-in-environment framework endorses the idea that individuals are engaged in an ongoing transactional process that facilitates or blocks one's ability to experience satisfactory social functioning (Corcoran & Walsh, 2006). The quality of how a person functions depends on the biological, psychological, and social (*biopsychosocial*) factors of their life. This differs from the medical perspective, in which individuals are classified as abnormal or disordered. Social workers analyze histories and also think about current conditions. They find ways to enter the patient's world and try their best to understand what the patient's experience is like, all the while constructing a comprehensive, biopsychosocial framework. An essential element in understanding the patient's environment is having an awareness of relational dynamic themes. What is the nature of the patient's relationships? How do they get their needs met, especially when they are needs that require a separate human being? What kind of attachment styles are commonly used by the patient? Attachment styles specifically pertain to how the patient relates to the significant people in their lives. How do they communicate? How do they make their choices? How do they manage stress in the relationship? Not only does the exploration nudge the therapist to think about the patient's relationships, but it also starts to reveal the impact of anxiety that is present in the patient's relational world.

In addition to these questions, is the question of who the therapist is to the patient. How does the patient experience the therapist? Therapists are not without influence. Often, this area is overlooked or underestimated. Some therapists see themselves only as observers and a blank slate. However, it is hard to imagine that to be true. Humans have perception. Harry Stack Sullivan's Interpersonal Theory provides

A. Song (✉)
Honolulu, HI, USA
e-mail: angela@songpsychotherapy.com

© Springer Nature Switzerland AG 2021
R. P. Dealey, M. R. Evans (eds.), *Discovering Theory in Clinical Practice*,
https://doi.org/10.1007/978-3-030-57310-2_2

a way for a therapist to be an observer and an active participant in the therapeutic process.

Sullivan is known as the founder of Interpersonal Theory. As an only child who did not have consistent access to his mother, Sullivan formulated some critical ideas of what a healthy childhood experience required (Palombo et al., 2009). Drawing from his own experiences, Sullivan believed that interpersonal experiences have an impact on how personality is developed. He acknowledged that humans have a need for relatedness and that the way a person navigates their relationships in fulfilling this need is reflective of the characteristics of their personality (Palombo et al., 2009). Therapeutic relationships are ones that fit this description of a significant relationship—a patient seeks treatment to fulfill a human need. While we only have the patient's account of the relational dynamics of their childhood experience, we have information from the therapeutic relationship to gain a clue of what relational dynamics might be like for the patient.

Sullivan constructed a theory of development that depended on interpersonal experiences (Sullivan, 1953). His rubric demonstrates how even the very first human experience of infanthood contributes to the development of one's personality and how they have the ability to impact interpersonal experiences throughout the lifetime. He offered three modes to categorize experiences: the prototaxic mode, the parataxic mode, and the syntaxic mode (Sullivan, 1953).

The **prototaxic** mode refers to the simplest, earliest state of being in which the mind does not perceive a logical sequence (Sullivan, 1953). It is merely a state of being. Imagine the infant, just being. Within that is an experience, i.e., how the caregiver is with the infant. Even in this state, there can be a wide spectrum of affect that the infant experiences, from tension and anxiety to exuberance.

The **parataxic** mode is when one experiences themselves as a separate unit, which indicates awareness of an other (Sullivan, 1953). In this mode, a person interprets everything in terms of how it relates to self.

In the **syntaxic mode**, there is external validation of one's experience from another person (Sullivan, 1953). Language and the experience of communication with a fellow human being are present. Memory has a role, as one starts to develop a pattern built on previous experiences.

While the experiences are constructed from developmental periods, they are not necessarily limited to a specific phase in development. Instead, they are understood as modes. Thus, a person who has had experiences in the syntaxic mode can still have experiences that are prototaxic or parataxic. These modes can be indicators of how a person is functioning. They are the components of a person's self-system, which is central to each person's personality organization (Palombo et al., 2009). Sullivan's self-system begins in infancy and is shaped by responses from the external world. Throughout the process, a set of personality traits would emerge, integrated with the person's self-esteem. The experiences start from the very beginning, such as the first interaction between a mother and an infant.

Personalities are developed from enduring a pattern of recurrent interpersonal situations. One way of organizing the situations is to examine the presence of anxiety. Sullivan believed that humans naturally did this in their interactions with others, with responses eliciting basic categories of response (Palombo et al., 2009). When a caregiver responds to the infant with tenderness, the infant would learn that it was a "good me." For example, if a smiling infant receives a smile back from their mother, they would experience the sensation of "I am good." In contrast, if the baby bites the mother while nursing and the mother becomes anxious and communicates disfavor, the baby has the sensation of "I am bad, I am causing this discomfort." A "bad me" would increase the mother's anxiety. If the mother has an intense reaction that the baby cannot process, then the baby's sense of self disorganizes. A response of severe anxiety would incur a "not me" sensation. Anxieties are generated when the fulfillment of the need for relationship is threatened. Disruptive symptoms begin to emerge when the anxieties are not managed well (Sullivan, 1953).

Healthy development is dependent on healthy relationships. However, healthy relationships do not guarantee an anxiety-free life. Anxiety is a part of human existence. When an anxious situation presents itself, healthy relationships are less perceived to be under threat. In other words, if a relationship is healthy, those involved are less concerned about losing the other person when a stressful circumstance arises.

One way of assessing health in a relationship is observing a person's attachment patterns. Think about it like body temperature. Everyone has a temperature. Temperature provides information on how the body is functioning while meeting cellular needs. Temperatures that are higher or lower than average indicate that the body may be functioning under stress. Likewise, attachment patterns reflect how people are functioning in their significant relationships, in which they are trying to get their needs met. There are four general classifications of attachment: secure, avoidant-dismissive, ambivalent-preoccupied, and disorganized (Wallin, 2007). The last three constitute the insecure category. These designations reflect the degree of anxiety and avoidance exhibited in the relationship (Brennan, Clark, & Shaver, 1998). A secure attachment reflects flexibility and resilience in the interactions of that relationship, and is built through sensitivity, acceptance, cooperation, and emotional availability. An avoidant-dismissive attachment pattern can lack visible distress, but possesses cellular signals of distress, such as a rise in cortisol levels. This superficial indifference present in avoidant-dismissive attachment reflects a defensive accommodation to detachment—essentially, the person has learned that visible distress is of no use and they have given up communicating their affect to the other person. The ambivalent-preoccupied attachment pattern features a sense of preoccupation that prevents the person from freely accessing their genuine experience, leaving the person angry or passive. These patterns are a byproduct of early experiences that may have been unpredictable and occasionally available at best. Finally, disorganized attachment patterns look bizarre, contradictory, and inexplicable. They can reflect early experiences with caregivers that had been frightening, frightened, or dissociated. The caregiver may have been simultaneously the safe haven and also the source of danger. The difficult, contradictory space lends itself to the disorganized display.

A person with secure attachments will feel some confidence and resilience in their relationships, compared to someone who may have insecure attachments. Mental health problems arise when anxiety is not managed in healthy ways. The "not me" category of sudden, intense, adverse emotional reaction can lead to awe, dread, loathing, and horror in later life, including dissociation (Sullivan, 1953). It is possible for states of dissociation to trigger the emergence of pathologies such as schizophrenia.

Treatment using Sullivan's Interpersonal Theory is an organic process of inquiry, exploration, and examination. Sullivan described a process in which the therapist is an active participant. He believed that in order to understand someone, it was critical to know how they dealt with the essential people in their lives (Cooper, 1995).

Sullivan drew on his colleagues' ideas to shape his theory. He felt it was important to learn who the patients were and what caused them to develop as they did (Cooper, 1995). Freud's ideas of dynamic and descriptive unconscious led Sullivan to think about selectively unattended aspects of earlier relationships (Cooper, 1995). **Selective inattention** became one of the central organizing ideas of how Sullivan believed information was included or excluded from a person's consciousness (Sullivan, 1956). While Freud may have believed the exclusion to be an act of repression, Sullivan would suggest that the information could be accessed with the right question. If the therapist asked about material that the patient did not bring up themselves, they could both focus on what had been selectively overlooked (Cooper, 1995). Thus, the therapist starts to actively participate by bringing in areas that might not have been previously considered by the patient.

The therapist's participation goes beyond taking patients to places that they themselves had not previously considered. Sullivan believed that the exploration should not be limited to the contents of the individual mind, but expanded to the individual in relation to others (Cooper, 1995). Using detailed inquiry, the therapist would learn who the other people were, and what situations would evoke specific dynamics, such as feelings of inadequacy or low self-esteem. It is through this kind of active exploration that the therapist could find out about the patient's underlying psychological structure. Who makes the patient feel valuable? Who brings them down? What topics lead to the emergence of such experiences?

Sullivan proposed four parts to his interview process: inception, reconnaissance, detailed inquiry, and termination (Cooper, 1995). Inception pertains to introductions, such as building rapport and establishing the relationship. Building rapport is commonly the first step in many theories and is not unique to Interpersonal Theory. Therapists track the patient's affect and comfort level, orienting them to the fact that venturing into difficult spaces requires a combination of trust and comfort in the relationship.

Reconnaissance describes the process of developing an overview of the patient's internal structure. The therapist gathers what has been told by the patient and constructs a framework of how the patient functions. Furthermore, it is possible to observe what impacts how the patient functions (Cooper, 1995). Reconnaissance is not to be confused with an initial diagnosis. Sullivan thought this would process take about 7.5–15 h. It is more than history taking, a process that brings something new to what the patient has known all of their life. It is a new and vital part of the treatment that has the potential to shift the patient's perspective. As such, it can be a psychologically meaningful discovery for the patient. The facts of what they had always known have not changed, but their *experience* of those very same facts has, in a significant way. They bring to light "underlying attitudes and feelings that the patient absorbed without ever realizing it" (Cooper, 1995). What is also compelling about this approach is that no behaviors are pathologized as the therapist learns about the patient's character. The therapist simply tries to know what it feels like to be them in ordinary aspects of living. It is then also essential to check in with the patient to see if the therapist is constructing an accurate picture of the patient's experience. Questions like, "Is it like _____?" are a safe way to clarify. The therapist as an expert does not mean always knowing, but rather, knowing where to look and how to ask (Cooper, 1995).

The detailed inquiry is the actual process of information gathering. It looks at common aspects of everyday living that can "elicit information about important invisible forces within a family, such as loyalties, beliefs, passions, and pretenses" (Cooper, 1995, p. 681). In addition to providing the dynamics of the patient's mind, the information gives guidance on what is acknowledged. Focusing on information that was unnoticed can help integrate and make sense of the patient's feelings (Cooper, 1995). Integrating and making sense helps manage the anxiety that the patient has about those areas.

These components describe an approach that shifts the patient's focus from their symptoms and shortcomings to the impact of their relationships (Cooper, 1995). There is more of a comprehensive understanding of the person's environment. When disruptive symptoms are viewed in light of the environment, they usually make more sense. There is understanding. The issues feel approachable. Anxiety decreases because the symptoms do not feel like they appear out of nowhere. There is a sound, understandable reason for how they came to be. Even more, there is a way to address those symptoms with less shame, embarrassment, and other anxiety-provoking aspects. The idea that actual experience shapes personality development becomes more likely to be the case, rather than the belief that the patient is a "bad me" or a "not me."

The nature of relational dynamics can be reasonably consistent. For example, when a person's attachment style is assessed, it is not uncommon to find that one has a general attachment pattern that is evident in multiple significant relationships. Thus, a person with a general anxiously insecure attachment would most likely exhibit those anxious patterns in many of their relationships. This finding aligns with Sullivan's belief that transference is always present in treatment, so the focus ought to be on one's character. The work is not about pinpointing a flaw or a wrong, but about understanding one's character. It is a collaboration between the therapist and the patient. Some of the work returns to traditional psychodynamic therapy, such as examining the dynamisms of fear and lust (Sullivan, 1953). The goal of the collaboration is to develop a resolution that makes sense to the patient and the therapist. Reeducation is part of that process. In this shifted, biopsychosocial state of understanding, the patient and therapist are then able to acknowledge dysfunction in their relationships (Palombo et al., 2009). The insights uncovered can be used to take steps in improving the relational dynamics, such as practicing healthy boundaries and communication skills.

Introduction to the Case of Lisa

Lisa is an Asian American woman in her thirties. She enjoys a highly successful career as a healthcare provider. She and her fiancé are newly engaged after dating seriously for 3 years. They live together in a highly desired neighborhood. All names and identifiers of this case have been changed to protect the confidentiality of the client.

This neighborhood happens to be thousands of miles away from her family. During her intake, she remarked that her family is very close, but that she needs to be as far as possible. This theme has become evident in her significant relationships.

Lisa's parents immigrated to the United States a year before she was born. Her father was in graduate school, her brother was three, and her mother left behind a successful career in their home country. Her parents were unfamiliar with cultural norms in the new country. When a fellow graduate student offered to help the family, they welcomed him. At first, he was helping with matters like setting up a bank account and applying for a mortgage. Then he was helping with her mother's small side business while also teaching Lisa domestic skills, like cooking and cleaning. She would say that he raised her while her parents were too busy with work and school. When she was sick or injured, he would be the one to take care of her and nurse her back to health. He became a part of the household, living just a few blocks away. He had created such an integral role for himself that it would be hard for the family to know how to function without him. As such, Lisa's mother would detest his presence, yell and scream at him, but the family did not make concrete decisions to part ways with him.

The family friend introduced Lisa's father to what he would call other "cultural practices," including viewing child pornography. He went as far as telling Lisa's father that it was a common and accepted practice for fathers to have sex with their daughters. Lisa remembers her father masturbating while sitting on the couch with Lisa, one of his hands rubbing her leg. However, the main perpetrator was the family friend, who continuously raped and molested Lisa from age seven to fourteen. When she was fourteen, Lisa told her brother about the abuse and the police were notified. After years of court trials, the ordeal came to an end with the family friend being sentenced to prison. He had other abuse victims, and Lisa even traveled out of state to testify on behalf of those other victims.

Lisa graduated from high school and attended college. After graduating, she spent a year traveling and volunteering abroad. Upon returning home, she knew that she wanted to go to graduate school in a different environment. She only applied to out of state schools and was accepted. Her boyfriend wanted to move with her, but when he discussed moving with Lisa, she felt that he had been putting his life on hold for too long. He had been there to help her end the abuse and had been by her side all along. She felt that he was participating only in her life, and not thinking about how he wanted to evolve in his own experiences. She broke up with him and moved alone.

Lisa's experience of being alone is a significant theme in how she is psychologically organized. When it comes to interpersonal dynamics, she has layers and layers that create a distance. She has a mainly avoidant-dismissive attachment pattern in her close relationships. Distance seems to have been the only way she has been able to find space for herself and her own experiences. In the presence of her family, there is not much space for her. For example, Lisa's mother works diligently in various capacities. She enjoys flipping houses and often lives in them during the renovation. She constantly searches for ways to become rich and famous. She checks in on her husband and son every week, bringing groceries and tending to basic chores, like doing laundry or vacuuming. Lisa finds it difficult to connect with her mother, who feels chaotic and intense to her. Most of their conversations tend to be focused on her mother—about her experiences, her struggles, her sacrifices, as well as her victories and her triumphs.

Lisa's father works from home. She has described him as somewhat of a hoarder, refusing to dispose of anything, including rotten food. He does not leave the house much himself and reacts intensely to change, even with matters such as washing his blankets. Seeing him this way pains Lisa, and loving him from afar makes it more tolerable.

Lisa's brother lives with their father. Lisa believes that revealing her abuse changed him from being a social, popular teenager, to a complete hermit, doing very little outside the home. He bears a tremendous sense of guilt for not protecting his younger sister from the perpetrator. He has difficulty carrying out his own plans and often allows them to fade into the background while their mother dictates what he ought to do. He begrudgingly responds when his mother beckons with projects, but he never says no. Lisa feels responsible for the change in her brother. Guilt and responsibility are general themes, where she feels like she has placed an enormous burden upon her family. Distance, both physical and emotional, has become the most acceptable solution for Lisa. She has built a new life for herself in her new home state. She is well regarded at her workplace. She takes good care of herself physically, staying consistent with a daily workout and sleep routine. She tends to her beauty—she is easily one who can turn heads. She has friendships from different parts of her life. She is adored, but all from a safe distance. The distance also prevents her from feeling genuinely known in her relationships, rendering her in a state of aloneness.

Theoretical Integration

The case poses an interesting challenge—how does one engage with a patient when their central way of organizing is to create distance in their relationships? Lisa's external presence certainly posed a distance. Not only did she look very well put together, but she also exuded an air of confidence. She was kind, articulate, beautiful, competent, and smart. As first impressions go, one might think that there was not much she needed from a therapist. Regardless, the task of Sullivan's inception stage was the same for all patients. It was to figure out how to reach her.

While her external characteristics were genuine and real, there was more to Lisa. On the surface, it was not clear why she wanted to start treatment. She briefly spoke of some pesky anxiety symptoms; issues that sounded like the typical insecurities a 30-year-old might have. As rapport developed, she began to slowly share her internal world. Through Sullivan's inception and reconnaissance stages, the current framework from which she functioned, as well as the foundation that the structure was built upon, was formulated. She talked about her abuse. Her experience was quite pervasive, impacting nearly every portion of her life, then, now, and going forward. True to the features of the avoidantly attached, she appeared fine on the outside, but struggled tremendously on the inside. She felt torn down and naked from the slightest external triggers. Under extreme stress, she lost vision in one eye. These symptoms dominated her on the inside, but were not visible to others.

In a recent session she quietly sat down. Her therapist, who had learned to detect Lisa's slight affect changes, could sense that something was terribly wrong. Lisa began to describe an incident from the past week where she had texted her father a photo of herself in front of a beautiful background. Her father promptly replied, *Wow, sexy*. Lisa hesitantly described how those two words completely disrupted her on the inside.

The therapist felt utter disappointment. It was an empathic feeling about Lisa's bewildered sense of betrayal. The two breathed for a few seconds in silence, processing the intensity of the inner experience. The questions started to form in the therapist's mind. What was the father thinking?!

"I'm so sorry to hear this," the therapist started. She was communicating her inner experience to the patient. Although the therapist spoke in the most careful and thoughtful way possible, the patient just stared straight ahead. She was not there yet. Though the patient said nothing, the therapist felt her acknowledge her words.

"I feel an intensity," the therapist stated. In Sullivan's terms, the intensity they felt was a prototaxic experience, but speaking about it and validating the hurt made it parataxic and syntaxic.

"Yes, you're right," she replied. She worked up the nerve to say her words. "I'm so angry! I don't know what to do."

"What do you want to do?" This was the therapist's way of differentiating what seemed to be tangled within Lisa. It was an attempt to help her define her feeling of anger separately from her fantasy about responding. The therapist was also scanning for possible selective inattention.

"I want to tell him that I'm angry," Lisa muttered. She felt it was safe enough to say this much. "But I don't know why I'm so angry."

"Well, I think it's understandable," the therapist said, referring to the connection of her anger to the event.

"It is?" Lisa seemed surprised since she did not expect her emotion to be understood. It was a new experience that began a reeducation for her about what she could possibly expect from others.

"Absolutely. I know I'm angry on your behalf!" the therapist continued, reaffirming her raw emotion. The statement was a reflection of Lisa, a mirroring of her feelings. She was demonstrating that another person was attuned to Lisa, and that she was worthy of it. "Lisa, this is your dad. Him calling you sexy brings you back to all those earlier memories."

"But it's been years," she insisted.

"It doesn't matter. That word took you back to who you were during the abuse," Lisa started to weep quietly. The therapist struggled between her rage at Lisa's father, and her wanting to console Lisa. She was sure that Lisa could sense the tension. "What happened was truly upsetting and disappointing. It's okay to feel those things. And it's okay to address them, from who you are today. Today, you're not being abused. You're not powerless."

As the session came to a close, Lisa and her therapist discussed what it would be like for Lisa to confront her father about his inappropriate remark. This session illustrates many significant components of Interpersonal Theory. There is a mixture of prototaxic, parataxic, and syntaxic experiences within the dialogue. The two explored the very difficult topic at the center of Lisa's fragile core. The abuse had encompassed all three categories of "good-me," "bad-me," and "not-me," leaving her feeling fractured inside. Lisa could feel the positive affections of "good-me" when she was praised for being obedient, like when she complied to the molestation. At the same time, a different part of her felt a "bad-me," one that felt dirty and used, not only for being molested, but also for bringing the shame of abuse onto the family. Finally, the intensity and confusing responses of her biological parents created the "not-me," disorganized sense of self for Lisa.

Lisa had been in treatment for over a year, and she was slowly opening up, building a secure attachment that was resilient and flexible. Would her father's comment make her retreat back? Would she forget that it was safe to trust another person? The therapist reminded her that there were two of them in the exploration of her experiences and responses. Their syntaxic experience, the element of validating and asking together, helped them recognize that their attachment was secure and trustworthy. They started to organize the information and weave it into a more manageable narrative. The situation stopped being overwhelming. They focused on the areas of selective inattention, paying attention to ways that other significant people in her life had *not* recently failed her. Lisa was able to get her relational needs met through the process of understanding and validation.

In the following session, she appeared calm and collected on the outside. She described how she confronted her father. When the therapist asked how the conversation went, Lisa replied that it was "fine." The therapist suspected the superficial reply. She knew there was more, but she was not certain Lisa would venture there. She was exhibiting the familiar, avoidant-dismissive attachment pattern.

"I wonder what it's like on the inside," the therapist gently opened the discussion. Lisa bravely started to describe how she felt internally at the moment. She reported getting upset with her best friend for making her have a difficult conversation with her father. The therapist wondered about Lisa's displaced anger. A thought emerged as the therapist listened. Hadn't she also encouraged Lisa to confront her father, as her best friend had done? Why was Lisa not upset with her? This omission may have been an area of selective inattention. The therapist asked Lisa about it.

There was a long pause. "Yes. I was mad at you too. I knew you were right, but I didn't want to confront him. It was making me feel angry and vulnerable. But I also knew that you were supposed to be here to help me." Her words resonated. Lisa needed to realize that they could discuss the way she may have been experiencing the therapist in their work. She needed to know that it was okay to talk about it, that there would not be judgment or retaliation.

"Of course, you were mad at me, and it's significant that you were able to say so right now. And I am deeply sorry that you felt so unprotected. I do understand how this is not an easy space to be in." And thus, began the further deepening of their relationship. It was not an actual disagreement, but it was the first time they experienced an uneasy space with each other. This was a significant relational need for Lisa that was being met. This experience allowed her anxiety to dissipate. She was able to address difficult topics with more confidence that their relationship would be able to not only survive the event, but grow through it. It was Sullivan's stated way of being with one another. There was space for Lisa's authentic personality to emerge, and for her self-esteem to grow.

In a subsequent session, Thanksgiving came up as a topic of discussion. In her youth, Thanksgiving, as an American tradition, was relatively unfamiliar. However, residing in a predominantly white neighborhood, Lisa insisted that they celebrate the holiday like the other families did. This was uncharacteristically aggressive for Lisa. However, by then, Lisa was very aware of the difference between her family and the town that they lived in. Lisa would look through magazines at the grocery store and pay attention to the commercials on the television. She worked tirelessly to understand the turkey, stuffing, mashed potatoes, and pumpkin pie. No one was supposed to go to work. Extended families came together. From her perspective, Thanksgiving represented everything her family was not, but what she was longing to have. She was desperate for some sense of likeness and belonging.

Lisa's mother created the dishes as best as she could. Frustrated, tired, and angry, her mother served everything in disposable cups to Lisa as she sat at the table alone. Although Lisa knew that this was not quite the picture she had in mind, she felt obligated to eat everything that her mother put in front of her.

"You know, I've had beautiful Thanksgivings since then, but I don't know why that's the story that comes to mind whenever I think of Thanksgiving," Lisa noted. The therapist wondered if this was another moment of selective inattention.

"Well, that's interesting, isn't it?" the therapist replied. "What are some of the other, 'beautiful' ones that you do remember?"

"My mom never served in disposable cups again. She found places to order the food," she replied. "We tried different places over the years. Supermarkets, restaurants; most places will cater a Thanksgiving meal." As she said this, the therapist also remembered how a social worker brought food to the house the very first year they were in America. The neighborhood thought that Lisa's family was needy because of the frequent wellness checks. Her mother threw out the social worker, feeling completely humiliated and misunderstood.

"Hmmm, you know, I could be wrong, but it sounds like your mother understood what you wanted," the therapist began. Lisa looked up. She seemed to be pleading, to be shown that her mother understood her experience for once.

"That Thanksgiving meal in disposable cups did not go the way you wanted, and it certainly did not go the way she wanted either. She remembered what it was like to feel humiliated and misunderstood. But she didn't stop there. She also understood that you were trying to fit in. She didn't give up. And she didn't say that it wasn't worth it. She found a way to provide what you truly wanted. Maybe she heard you." With that statement, a relational need was being met because it not only gave Lisa a way to appreciate her mother, but it also helped her feel understood by her therapist. It was not so much about Thanksgiving, or any actual events. These were symbols of their relational dynamics, of the overwhelming experience of not being able to manage their anxieties about succeeding in each other's eyes. It was the never-ending search for approval.

Today, Lisa's therapeutic relationship with her therapist continues within their securely attached relationship. They process different, unexplored parts of Lisa's trauma history. The process of detailed inquiry guides them in untying different knots of Lisa's history. When Lisa wants to process new information, they delve into an enriching interchange of "what-ifs," "how abouts," and "I wonders." The process is intimate and real. Her thoughts, now spoken out loud, connect the external to the internal. The experience of having the sustained interest, active listening, and participation of another being facilitates Lisa's transformation.

When she started treatment, Lisa never imagined herself being married. She did not know how to trust that someone could know the real her and still love her the way her fiancé does. Now, Lisa has fewer somatic symptoms. She is aware when she is creating distance, which signals that she is feeling unsafe inside. She also knows when she can be vulnerable so that she can deepen her relationship. She enjoys her secure attachments and she has found a better way to manage the anxieties that arise in her relationships.

Therapists may not be aware of how much of an impact they have on their patients. By the same token, patients may not be aware of the impact that they have on their therapists. That someone close to us is aware of us, our needs, our wishes, our fears—this is a shared human experience that has the potential to bring the change we seek. This is the core idea that is upheld in Sullivan's Interpersonal Theory, and what has brought Lisa's treatment to life.

Cultural Considerations

In terms of the person-in-environment concept, there were several significant cultural influences to be aware of as Lisa and her therapist approached their work. Both Lisa and her therapist were Korean, so there was already a shared understanding of the influences. For example, as the youngest and female child in a Korean family, Lisa's role was nearly nonexistent. It made sense in her parents' culture that no space was being made for her in the family dynamics. When Lisa's abuse came to light, it was indeed a burden to Lisa and her family on many levels. The family made mistakes, which were a significant departure from the expectations of healthy parenting. Not only did they bear the shame of making poor parental choices, but they also bore the cultural shame of being a tainted family. This is the aspect that Lisa prioritizes consciously and subconsciously. She focuses on how her existence brought such shame to the family, and not the fact that she had been a victim. Lisa seemed to be unaware that something tragic and traumatic happened to her. Even now, she has a hard time setting boundaries with her family. She tries to erase her shame and become a vital part of her family structure to avoid feeling disposable. This experience of herself was generated by the way she was treated for much of her early childhood, and has left her feeling exhausted, alone, and worthless.

In addition, seeking psychotherapy itself poses a cultural conflict. At times, it feels like a bit of a betrayal for Lisa to examine and scrutinize her history so carefully. Acknowledging her parents' shortcomings feels like she is being disrespectful to her elders.

Another cultural consideration is the challenge of integrating two different cultures into one's identity. The Thanksgiving example demonstrates Lisa's need to feel "normal," but those norms mean different things between her parents' previous culture and the culture of their new world. The struggle to prioritize between community and individuality is apparent in Lisa's psychological framework.

Discussion Questions

- What were the areas of selective inattention that were used to help broaden Lisa's understanding of her internal psychological organization?
- How did Lisa's general attachment pattern shift as her treatment progressed through the application of Interpersonal Theory?
- Which of the cultural influences may pose a barrier between the therapist and the patient if they had not shared the same societal upbringing?
- Sometimes what people say is not everything that they have on their minds. How would you choose what to share and what not to share as the session progresses?
- What are some examples of prototaxic, parataxic, and syntaxic modes of experiences that you have personally encountered in your own history?
- What are some key detailed inquiry phrases/questions that are familiar to you?
- How would you train your mind to actively scan for areas of selective inattention while listening to the patient?
- What are some things a patient might be surprised to hear in terms of how they impact you?

References

Brennan, K. A., Clark, C. L., & Shaver, P. (1998). Self-report measurement of adult romantic attachment: An integrative overview. In J. A. Simpson & W. S. Rholes (Eds.), *Attachment theory and close relationships* (pp. 46–76). New York: Guilford Press.

Cooper, A. (1995). The detailed inquiry. In M. Lionells, J. Fiscalini, C. H. Mann, & D. B. Stern (Eds.), *Handbook of interpersonal psychoanalysis* (pp. 679–693). Hinsdale, NJ: The Analytic Press.

Corcoran, J., & Walsh, J. (2006). Social work and the DSM: Person-in-environment versus the medical model. In *Clinical assessment and diagnosis in social work practice* (pp. 11–32). New York: Oxford University Press.

Palombo, J., et al. (2009). Interpersonal theory. In *Guide to psychoanalytic developmental theories* (pp. 225–240). New York, NY: Springer.

Sullivan, H. S. (1953). *The interpersonal theory of psychiatry*. New York: W.W. Norton & Company.

Sullivan, H. S. (1956). *Clinical studies in psychiatry*. New York: W.W. Norton & Company.

Wallin, D. (2007). The foundations of attachment theory. In *Attachment in psychotherapy* (pp. 11–24). New York: The Guildford Press.

Chapter 3
Object Relations Theory: The Case of Elyse

Alison Smith Mitchell

Introduction to Object Relations Theory

Elyse, a representative composite of several women, is in her late 20s, mother and step-mother of early adolescents, married to the father of the youngest child. The names and details shared in this case have been altered to protect privacy. Both parents identify as white, cisgender, heterosexual adults according to Elyse. The family is reliant on public assistance and the limited income Elyse's husband earns as a seasonal laborer. Both parents graduated from high school, neither attended college. Elyse has worked in the past, but is currently unemployed, focusing on her recovery from severe opioid addiction.

Elyse's goal in seeking treatment is "I want to deal with my past, with my trauma, before it eats me alive." She has an extensive, intimate trauma history. Details may be challenging to read. The case of Elyse serves as an exemplar in this chapter, which outlines central tenets of object relations theory as proposed by D. W. Winnicott with treatment vignettes to illustrate concepts.

Broadly, object relations theories consider the quality of the individual's relationships, internal and external with self and others, as explanatory of how the individual comes to structure an internal sense of self (Flanagan, 2016; Goldstein, 2001; St. Clair & Wigren, 2004). The source of the relationship—self or other—is the "object" of object relations; the "relations" part includes not only internal and external relationships with self and others, but also the individual's internalized representations of self and other that develop from those interactions (Flanagan, 2016). Object relations theorists expanded upon the study of individual internal psychological development by focusing on relationships, and the process of developing an individuated sense of self in the context of relations with others (Flanagan, 2016).

A. S. Mitchell (✉)
University of Maine, Orono, ME, USA
e-mail: Alison.Mitchell@maine.edu

R. P. Dealey, M. R. Evans (eds.), *Discovering Theory in Clinical Practice*,
https://doi.org/10.1007/978-3-030-57310-2_3

Humans are seen as innately wired for connection (Mitchell & Black, 1995). The individual's developmental environment—the familial or caregiving context, as well as the larger political–social–cultural environment—plays an important role in shaping internal psychological development (Flanagan, 2016; St. Clair & Wigren, 2004). By extension, therapy provides an opportunity for healing through relational "do-over," recognizing and revising unhealthy internal representations or messages formed through the impact of past disruptions in the context of an attuned, healthy therapeutic relationship.

D. W. Winnicott, Object Relations, and Therapy

Winnicottian object relations provide a particularly useful explanatory bridge between individual-relational and system-relational influences. Donald W. Winnicott was a British pediatrician who worked with mothers and children through World War II and beyond, often seeing children with serious mental illnesses (Flanagan, 2016; St. Clair & Wigren, 2004). He developed his conceptualization of how individuals develop an internal sense of self based on his professional practice observations. As a result, much of his language is grounded in the mother–infant dyad. To modernize, one might say "caregiver" in every instance where Winnicott used "mother" and the same processes would still apply (Flanagan, 2016).

For Winnicott, the foundation for the development of psychological capacities and an individual's sense of "self" as unique and different from others is established in infancy within the matrix of a caregiver–infant relationship in a good-enough facilitating or "holding" environment (Flanagan, 2016; St. Clair & Wigren, 2004; Winnicott, 1956b, 1960a, 1960b). Over time, when the caring foundation is attuned and needs are met, the infant and young child builds internal psychological capacity and an increasingly independent sense of self, taking in and incorporating messages received from its external caregiving relationships (Applegate & Bonovitz, 1995). Winnicott conceptualized internal psychological maturational processes as a "me—not me" continuum of individual dependence on and independence from significant caregiving others. The initially totally dependent baby matures both in biological and psychological capacity, still dependent on others for survival but capable of existing independently and tolerating times when needs are not immediately met (Applegate & Bonovitz, 1995; St. Clair & Wigren, 2004; Winnicott, 1945, 1953). Winnicott's formulation of "me—not me" psychological development explicitly assumes the context of relationships with others (Applegate & Bonovitz, 1995; Winnicott, 1956a, 1956b, 1960b).

When an infant is paired with a good enough attuned caregiver who can interpret, contain, manage, and adapt to the infant's gestures or needs in a manner maintaining the infant's developing confidence that needs will be met and disruptions are manageable, this leads the infant toward developing a *true self* (Applegate & Bonovitz, 1995; St. Clair & Wigren, 2004; Winnicott, 1960a). As the infant's sense of true self takes shape, its ego gains strength, and the infant becomes integrated into its body, increasingly able to distinguish between self and other, and able to tolerate experiences of reality and being alone (Applegate & Bonovitz, 1995; St. Clair & Wigren, 2004; Winnicott, 1960a).

On the other hand, if the caregiver cannot protect against environmental impingements, or if as a result of individual innate vulnerabilities, the infant perceives the environment is unsafe, if needs are not met, the infant instead adapts in compliance with external demands, developing a *false self* (Applegate & Bonovitz, 1995; St. Clair & Wigren, 2004; Winnicott, 1960a). The false self is attuned to the needs of the caregiver and environment, protecting the true self, and in the most extreme, may be perceived as the true self (Applegate & Bonovitz, 1995; Winnicott, 1960a). In this view, psychopathologies arise as responses to messages and perceptions about self and other that the individual internalizes in response to environmental impingements.

The caregiving environment can be extended into the therapeutic environment, in which the clinician takes on the role of caregiver. The client can experience repair through the holding environment of the therapy room in the context of an attuned therapeutic relationship. Through a therapeutic relationship responsive to needs the client may recognize and express through words and actions, but also attuned to unexamined, unexpressed dynamics the client conveys, the clinician can act as the caregiver promoting the client's development toward a healthier internalized representation of true self.

A danger of object relations and important point to remember is the client is not infantilized in this process. Rather, a careful assessment through a Winnicottian lens will help the clinician recognize where certain capacities may need strengthening in order to facilitate growth toward the client's sense of true self identification. This will be brought to life through the case of Elyse.

Introduction to the Case of Elyse

Elyse was referred to weekly outpatient mental health therapy by her addiction counselor through a methadone clinic, part of the larger agency where the clinician worked as an adult outpatient mental health provider. Though Elyse and her clinician share several sociocultural identities, they inhabit different educational and economic positions, dynamics that are not deeply explored but which shaped the course of treatment somewhat.

Elyse has a complicated family history. For most of her childhood, Elyse believed her stepfather was her biological father. In fact, she is the child of an incestuous relationship. In her early years, Elyse lived with her grandparents, who Elyse thinks of positively. Elyse thinks of her grandmother fondly due to the strength of their relationship. Though she does not describe this period in her life in great detail, perhaps due to her young age at the time, when Elyse speaks of these family members, there is a softness in her face suggesting she holds positive memories.

Sometime later in childhood, Elyse went back to living with her biological mother. At that point, Elyse's mother had a new man in her life. Shortly after Elyse moved in, he began a pattern of sexual perpetration on Elyse that lasted through her early teen years. Visiting a family member one summer, Elyse revealed what was happening at home.

In the aftermath of her revelations, Elyse bounced between family members. She ended up back with her grandmother and then with the man she thought was her biological father. While living with him, he told her the truth of her parentage. This precipitated a crisis, and child protective services intervened. Elyse then moved through multiple foster settings. Eventually, she was caught smoking an illegal substance and was moved to a drug rehabilitation facility for teens, where she says she learned a lot about drug use.

The rehab facility also attempted to reconnect Elyse and her mother, which resulted in Elyse re-enrolling in high school and moving back in with her mother. She soon realized she was pregnant, carried to term, and delivered a healthy child. Shortly thereafter, she met a new man. Unexpectedly, she became pregnant again, another healthy pregnancy carried to term. Despite all the disruptions and having given birth to two children, Elyse graduated from high school and marched with her class, an accomplishment she shares with pride. She and her partner later married.

She admits to having smoked some marijuana while she was pregnant with the first child but says she did not use substances while she was pregnant with the second. She and her husband began using narcotic painkillers after the children were born, grinding up illicit pills to snort them. Some months later, she tried crack cocaine for the first time, beginning a pattern of periodically layering crack and opioids. Eventually she and her husband began using heroin because they couldn't find the pills anymore and heroin was cheaper anyway.

When Elyse presented for mental health treatment, she was moving from snorting heroin daily to stabilizing on a methadone maintenance dose. At the start of this, her second recovery attempt, her husband was not enrolled in any treatment program, still actively using. She says he was respectful of her efforts and would not use in front of her.

Because Elyse's husband was not enrolled in any treatment program, Elyse could not get take-home doses. The consequence was that she traveled 60–90 min each way daily to check-in and receive her maintenance dose. She was reliant on a public transportation service. Living in a rural area outside the more urban treatment center, there is no mass transit option that serves her community. When the weather is bad, the transportation service does not run, forcing a missed dose, which meant she would experience increasing withdrawal symptoms and cravings by that evening, until she was able to get to the clinic again. Most of the drivers for the transportation service are male, which she found difficult to manage because of her past, so she experienced increased PTSD symptoms while traveling to and from the clinic.

Theoretical Integration

Winnicott (1947) suggested that the client will invoke in the analyst what the client needs for healing. As such, assessing and examining the transference/countertransference dynamic is instructive in beginning to understand Elyse. Her clinician described a mental image of Elyse as a rock perched on a steep slope, barely balanced on the side of a mountain, solid but precarious. The therapist was immediately drawn to Elyse and described her countertransference as maternal. Perhaps in response to her transfer of her sense of fleeting stability, the therapist wanted to provide Elyse solidity and predictability while she gained traction in the methadone program.

Conceptualizing Elyse's substance use as having roots in unmet relational needs was useful for the therapeutic work. Caregiving relationships represent hope for connection and influence expectations of future interactions. Distress results from unpredictable disruptions. Drugs can solve internal dysregulation brought on by disruption, seeming to provide comfort through a release from distressing reality, filling a relational void (Greenberg & Mitchell, 1983; Mitchell, 1984, 2019). Ultimately, however, drugs provide neither care nor comfort, instead often further straining human relationships (Mitchell, 2019).

Knowing that Elyse's rural location likely further highlighted her sense of disconnection (Mitchell, 2019), her clinician began the treatment relationship with an intentional focus on facilitating a reliable, predictable environment for Elyse. Attending to transference and countertransference responses, through supervision, the clinician interpreted her "gut feeling" of providing reliability as clinically appropriate to Elyse's diagnosis of PTSD. Meeting Elyse's unspoken but communicated need to be able to depend upon something and someone as she began her recovery journey seemed a significant first step for Elyse. In Winnicottian terms, the "holding environment" of the therapy space might be an important facilitator of Elyse's early response to treatment.

Unfortunately, the treatment faced a potential barrier. As part of standard first session disclosures, the therapist shared information about her position, explaining that she would be transitioning out of the agency a few months later to complete a professional development opportunity. She was also open about an upcoming week of vacation. Elyse received both, asked some questions, and they worked through Elyse's reactions. The issue of schedule came back a couple of weeks later when creating a treatment plan. Table 3.1 summarizes the treatment goals and objectives in both agency and theoretical language.

The therapist's professional development plans dictated her schedule at the agency. The ensuing conversation allowed the dyad to explore what it might mean to Elyse to form a therapeutic relationship and then be in a situation of transferring to a new clinician. Because they took the time to have the conversation, ultimately, Elyse was able to recognize what she wanted and articulate it, an early statement of her true self desires:

Table 3.1 Treatment goals and objectives in agency and theory language

Treatment goals and objectives			
Agency-language goals and objectives		Theory-language goals and objectives	
Long-term goal in client's words: "I want to deal with my past, with my trauma, before it eats me alive."		Long-term goal in theoretical framing: "I want to be able to express my true self."	
Short-term client objectives	Interventions	Short-term client objectives	Interventions
Elyse will explain family relationships in order to create a genogram representation of those relationships.	Clinician will facilitate creating a genogram, providing a structured, safe environment for client to explain and explore family relationships.	Elyse will experience a therapeutic merger with a good enough therapist.	Good enough clinician will provide a holding environment and therapeutic preoccupation to promote therapeutic merger for the purpose of establishing client's sense of ego relatedness.
Elyse will share her biopsychosocial history in order to create a timeline of life events.	Clinician will provide weekly 45–50 min outpatient therapy	Elyse will experience a therapeutic holding environment and begin to make use of a transitional object (timeline as transitional object).	Good enough clinician will provide a holding environment and transitional object (timeline as transitional object), for the purpose of supporting client's sense of ego relatedness.
Elyse will complete the PCL-5 assessment.	Clinician will provide PCL-5, score, and interpret results with Elyse.	Elyse will experience therapeutic holding environment and begin to experience *true self*-identification through greater understanding of PTSD symptom experience.	Good enough attuned clinician will provide a holding environment in which client can identify true- and false-self experiences.

E: *You know, as we talk about it, I think I get…yeah, I think I'd rather start with the person I can stay with for a long time. Nothing against you. But yeah, you know, I think…I realize that's what I want to do.*

Th: *Ok. I understand and support that decision. That drives our treatment planning process…*

Elyse suggested and her therapist agreed that the therapist's vacation made a natural separation point. In the interim, Elyse asked for help figuring out a way to explain her "messed up wacky family" so she wouldn't have to try to explain those relationships over and over. Her clinician explained the concept of a genogram and suggested creating one.

From a Winnicottian object relations perspective, the activity was a means of establishing and strengthening the therapeutic relationship. Elyse expressed a "need" to be able to explain her family. That need was met with a genogram, a graphic, and tangible representation of her familial relationships. One could theorize that the process might also facilitate rapport, establishing ego relatedness, as Elyse experienced a therapeutic merger that could mimic the maternal preoccupation Winnicott described as the foundation of creating a holding environment. Just as Winnicott theorized infants come to distinguish themselves and their caregivers in the context of a predictable caregiving relationship, through use of supervision, the clinician theorized Elyse might begin to know herself and her therapist as unique individuals within the context of their therapeutic relationship. This is the concept of ego relatedness (Applegate & Bonovitz, 1995).

The second activity was also Elyse's request. She wanted to create a timeline of her life events. Her rationale for this was twofold: first, so she would know that any future therapist she worked with could have access to her story. Second, she admitted in a way that indicated she was bothered by it, that she sometimes felt like she had gaps and wasn't sure of her memories. She thought if she could create a timeline in therapy that might help her put a sense of order to some of her memories. Educating that what she described is a normal trauma response appeared to give Elyse some comfort and confidence. The results of having completed this activity are summarized in her history above.

Through a Winnicott lens, the activity further built Elyse's nascent sense that the therapy environment could reliably provide for her emotional needs. The clinician's ability to receive her history calmly, without judgment or apparent dismay would continue to establish evidence for Elyse that she could risk depending on the therapeutic relationship for "care" in the form of therapeutic interactions. In addition, the physical timeline on paper became a potential transitional object, a means for Elyse to carry with her a reminder of her therapy time, her therapeutic relationship, and her therapist's existence as she moved through her life during the week between sessions.

Finally, as a third objective, Elyse completed the Posttraumatic Checklist 5 [PCL5] (Weathers, Litz, Keane, Palmieri, Marx, & Schnurr, 2013) an assessment tool tied to the Diagnostic and Statistical Manual—fifth edition [DSM-5] (American Psychiatric Association [APA] 2013) that is useful in terms of being able to gain clarity and insight into the individual's unique PTSD symptom experience. The 20-item checklist contains four subscales that align with the four different clusters outlined in the DSM-5 for diagnosing PTSD. Once completed, there is a scoring guide for interpreting the overall score and then the four subscale scores. Elyse's overall score indicated moderate to severe PTSD.

In addition, both client and clinician gained insight into Elyse's symptom experience; she scored most highly in the areas of arousal and intrusions. Using the measure as part of therapy was motivated by a desire to gain clarity into her PTSD symptom experience. Elyse's clinician came to realize later that it also provided the dyad with an initial avenue into facilitating Elyse's development of a sense of true self. She was able to see her symptoms as adaptations related to her trauma history rather than as defining expressions of herself as a person. As Elyse put it, "no wonder I [have trouble] sleeping" and crave drugs before bedtime.

Because of the existence, extent, and nature of Elyse's trauma history, her clinician engaged Elyse in a conversation about how to proceed in a way that would best serve Elyse's needs. The combination of her history and provider's schedule led to the set of decisions made. Deriving out of that conversation, the goals were shaped by the decision not to continue together after the vacation. All of the above were guided by the theory-based proposition that experiencing a predictable holding environment in which Elyse could identify and express her needs, then experience having them met in a manner satisfactory to her, would be a growth-enhancing departure from prior experiences in caregiving relationships. Through the therapeutic process, Elyse might develop or solidify positive internal representations of herself and others.

Treatment

In an effort to establish a safe holding environment, therapy opened by moving carefully and slowly, guided by what Elyse was comfortable sharing. She led with her substance use and her desire to maintain sobriety. Most weeks would start by checking in about her methadone program, such as this early-session excerpt:

Therapist: *Hi! Have you been down to get your dose, or am I seeing you first?*

Elyse*: Nope, I dosed first. I try to get here to dose first, then see you. It doesn't always work because of my ride. But my driver was on time today.*

Th*: Nice when the ride works smoothly. How are you feeling? I know sometimes the dose upsets your stomach.*

E: *I'm ok. It's kind of just starting to hit me.*

Th: *I grabbed some crackers just in case you need something to munch on, they're right there if you want them.*

E: *Oh thank you. That's really nice.*

The intent was simply to facilitate creating some relationship within the therapeutic dyad, allowing Elyse material examples that she could risk depending on the therapeutic "holding environment" and relationship to meet her needs. Though the intent was not explicitly stated to Elyse, it was conveyed through gestures like getting packets of crackers from the break room to have in the office (also an enactment of clinician's maternal countertransference). From a theoretical perspective, these actions promoted Elyse's development of a healthy therapeutic dependence.

As part of the dependence–independence continuum, Winnicott posited there is a developmental move from self-absorbed receipt of care through a period of self-centered ruthless use of the caregiver to attain one's own ends, finally toward a more self-reflective position of concern for the other while also being able to receive care. Developing a capacity for concern requires that the person see others as more complete, whole, and nuanced individuals with needs of their own (Goldstein, 2001; Winnicott, 1945, 1953). In earliest infancy, for example, the baby is not consciously aware of being cared for, at least not in optimal circumstances (St. Clair & Wigren, 2004). As the infant's capacities mature, she becomes increasingly aware of herself as a separate entity able to use external objects, such as the caregiver, for her ends, such as to be fed and soothed. According to Winnicott (1945), the infant is initially ruthlessly intent on need fulfillment and oblivious to the impact of her actions on the other. With good enough caregiving, the infant eventually develops capacity for concern for others, understanding, for example, that her mother is a separate being with her own desires unique from the infant's (St. Clair & Wigren, 2004; Winnicott, 1945).

In treatment, Elyse's decision to move to a different therapist who could be more permanent is symbolic of the care-ruthlessness end of the spectrum, consistent with her initial clinical presentation. During this exchange, Elyse focused on what she wanted, the decision she thought would be best for her needs, with therapist's encouragement.

E: I don't know, I've thought about that a little bit. I mean, I really like you, I'm comfortable with you, and that means a ton to me, you know…? … So, I want to work with you. But I'm also, like, well, you know, it's hard thinking about it. It's not ideal, like, to have to start over again with someone else. I don't want to have to start telling my story all over again to someone else. I mean, I like that you're not all judge-y…I feel like I can talk to you.

Th: I appreciate your honesty, sharing your thoughts, thank you. "It's hard thinking about it." What do you mean? Could you say a little more about that?

Though the clinician could have opted to pursue a line of questions about how it felt for Elyse not to be judged, which would also have been clinically appropriate in terms of developing a sense of true self identity, instead the clinician chose to keep the focus on Elyse's receipt of care by asking her to say more about what was hard to think about. Elyse exhibits a ruthlessness tinged with degrees of mature awareness that the impact of her words might affect her therapist when she expresses her clear preference to move to a different provider:

E: So, like I don't want to be rude or anything, but I'm not sure. I don't want to have to tell you all the crap that is in my head and then just have to say it all over again to someone new down the line.

Still early in her treatment process, and early in the development of a treatment relationship, it was more clinically attuned to provide Elyse with an opportunity to express her own needs and experience having them fulfilled than it would have been to explore her experiences of judgment and how those affected her sense of self. There would be time for that later, after she had developed some confidence about therapy and the therapist's ability to receive and contain what she expressed. By staying focused on Elyse's desires regarding the care she would receive, the above interaction was a small step in that direction.

In all likelihood, if the treatment had been able to progress over a longer period of time, the dyad would have experienced other examples of Elyse acting out an emotional ruthlessness in pursuit of receiving the therapeutic caregiving she needed to gain a more solid sense of herself. These instances might have been enacted through no-call/no-shows, or perhaps some deliberate statement or act in a therapy session. Not having experienced much reliable caregiving as a child, one might expect Elyse to "test" the relationship in ways that can feel quite ruthless or demanding in the moment. Her therapists' ability to withstand those tests while maintaining consistent boundaries would have been key moments of growth and healing for

Elyse. Examining their meaning with Elyse might provide an opportunity for her to take in new information about herself as worthy of care even in difficult moments.

Elyse's PTSD symptom experience interfered with her ability to relax and be alone with her thoughts. Her PCL-5 results were instructive: highest on the arousal and intrusion clusters, she experienced nightmares or flashbacks when she relaxed, such as at nighttime. With therapeutic guidance, Elyse also linked her symptom experience to at least a part of why she used opioids. In her words "well yeah, it's a sweet high, it mellows me, makes my head quiet down for a while. And makes every pain go away." The moment allowed her to explore the concept of symptoms as adaptations rather than defining the person, a very early statement recognizing Elyse's true self might be different from the person she had been presenting as she moved through her life (a false self-representation). In her words:

I want to not live like this, I don't want to do this anymore...I'm having night-mares, I don't want to use anymore...I want to be a mom for my kids. My kids will never experience what my mom did... but it's also like I don't want to think about any of this.

Interpreted through "theory language," Elyse might be understood as seeking her own identity as the person she wants to be but yet is not quite able to access because she has not developed an internal sense of herself independent of her use of drugs to escape her trauma symptom experience. Through the "high," drugs simultaneously rob her of a true sense of herself and act as facilitators of escape from the harsh, fragmented inner "self" she experiences. Over the years, in the face of repeated relational trauma and caregiving failures, Elyse adapted a protective false self-representation, culminating in severe opioid use disorder as a means of coping with her trauma symptom experience and under-developed, negative sense of self:

E: Yeah... [I'm realizing] ...I'm not just some piece of s*** druggie like peo-ple think.

Through her statement about the "sweet high," Elyse is likely indicating her lack of internal holding environment, the capacity to soothe herself in the face of need and desire (Applegate & Bonovitz, 1995). Optimal mature psychological develop-ment leads to an adult's ability to relax, delay gratification, and enjoy solitude and that feeling of flowing along in the present moment, which would have at its roots the sensations of un-integration in the presence of an attuned, reliable caregiver in infancy (Applegate & Bonovitz, 1995; St. Clair & Wigren, 2004; Winnicott 1945, 1960a). Winnicott suggests the ability to be alone later in life comes from the expe-rience of being alone in the presence of a caregiver in infancy. This allows the infant to discover her personal internal life in the presence of a non-demanding, reliable and reassuring presence; the culmination is an internalized representation of the caring other that eventually renders the actual physical presence of the caregiver unnecessary.

For Elyse, the only apparent means she had for experiencing a sense of uninte-grated relaxation was using drugs. A clinical indication of growth would be her ability to be able to sit in companionable self-reflective silence in the presence of her therapist, something she was not able to do much at all during this period of therapy. Throughout this therapeutic episode, the clinician sought to strengthen

Elyse's sense of dependence–independence and support her pursuit of her own treatment needs, an expression of "ruthlessness," as a means of facilitating later growth toward greater capacity to be alone at some point in the future. To accomplish this, she would need to develop healthy transitional objects, as opposed to relying on drugs.

In optimal developmental circumstances, as the infant becomes aware of me–not me self and otherness, she develops an intermediary stand-in object, a transitional object. The transitional object bridges between fantasy and reality as the infant attempts to hold onto inner subjective "good" feelings about the caregiver even when the caregiver is objectively in the moment "bad" by not meeting a need or not being present at all. This bridging—transitional—object could be a blanket, a stuffed animal, a pillow, or any other similar item, often though not always soft, that the infant invests with that representation as a defense against anxiety caused by the attuned caregiver's optimal failures (Applegate & Bonovitz, 1995; Flanagan, 2016; Goldstein, 2001; St. Clair & Wigren, 2004; Winnicott, 1953). Over time, the singular transitional object matures into an array of transitional phenomena encompassing the creative realm of not only art, religion, dreams, literature, play, and culture, but also lying, addiction, and obsessive behaviors (Applegate & Bonovitz, 1995; Winnicott, 1953).

Given the early and persistent caregiving failures, Elyse experienced throughout her childhood, her use of drugs as transitional objects to facilitate an escape from internal and external harsh reality makes sense. One might characterize her relationship with crack cocaine as a transitional object facilitating a period of unintegrated "holding" for Elyse: "it's the drug I can't say no to, I love the high." One might also view methadone as facilitating Elyse's ability to experience an unintegrated transitional phenomenon that allows her to experience herself as an entity separate from the highs and lows of heroin.

Interestingly, the timeline she created took on the role of a transitional object, though it was not necessarily intended that way initially. Elyse and her clinician worked through her history over several sessions, therapist writing down the story Elyse told, only minimally interrupting when clarification was necessary. Ultimately, the process resulted in a multi-page document neatly encapsulating Elyse's childhood in a degree of order. She kept a printed copy. In several subsequent sessions she produced it from her bag and referred to how she would read and re-read it during the week. When asked what it meant to her, Elyse shared that sometimes holding it would help her remember what it felt like to be in a therapy session, indicating that was a positive, helpful remembrance. Using supervision, her clinician realized the activity unintentionally provided a non-traditional but effective transitional object for Elyse.

In the last session, exploring Elyse's reactions to ending, Elyse voiced evidence suggesting her clinician's tacit goal had also been met through the interactions together; Elyse had developed a sense of being able to depend on the agency and on her clinician to meet her needs. Realizing she could allow herself dependence within therapy, thereby experiencing absolute to relative dependence at an appropriately adult level, Elyse could then move toward feeling more solidly "herself" (less anxious) when coming in for treatment, setting the stage for further growth from relative dependence toward mature independence:

Th: It sounds like this time in here has been important to you.

E: Well yeah. Yeah. I mean, you listen and you helped me get all that stuff written down, so maybe now when I have to work with other people, there's a little head start. And, like, you get it...I mean little things like you have crackers for me just in case my dose hits me.

Th: I'm glad if you felt like that was helpful. My hope was to help you start to feel comfortable coming in here.

E: Mmmm, yeah...you know, I appreciate that. I do feel good about coming in now, I'm not as anxious as I was at the beginning. You know, there's a group...that I really like. I've gone to it a few times. It's such a good thing, you know, it's just for women. And I wouldn't have found out about it if I wasn't coming in here. ...as I think about it, you really helped me start to feel comfortable coming here. Like there are actually people out there who can help me...who will help me.

Termination

The clinician's initial countertransference reactions—the strong maternal pull and the sense of Elyse's precarious solidity—suggested that Elyse's early treatment needs might be focused on gaining traction and confidence, both in herself and in the treatment environment. Since relationships, human and drug, had for the most part been damaging for Elyse, her clinician was aware that a key component of healing would be about Elyse experiencing herself in the context of an adaptive therapeutic relationship. Winnicottian object relations, positing developmental capacities formed in the context of relationships, provides a strong framework for assessing a client's underlying emotional and psychological development, the client's sense of true self. The treatment relationship becomes the vehicle for healing and growth.

The tangible products of the therapeutic time together—the timeline, the genogram, even the PCL-5 results—might meet Elyse's need to be fed, so to speak, to feel as though she was getting something out of therapy. The real "feeding" was in the relationship Elyse was establishing through weekly sessions. The shared tasks provided a means toward a desired end of establishing a holding environment Elyse felt she could trust, facilitating growth in ego relatedness, and developing Elyse's capacity to tolerate being alone in the presence of a non-demanding caregiver (therapist) rather than turning to drugs. In the process, one could theorize she would be creating or strengthening internal positive representations about herself and others. In the final session, she indicated a positive experience:

Th: Well, we are nearing time to wrap up. Thank you for sharing your thoughts with me about our time working together. It's been a privilege to help you start healing.

E: Thank you. I'm glad we got to talk through those things and write that all down. It helps me (she has copies of everything they did together in therapy).

Th: Before you go, I have this for you (it is a small slice of a polished rock, quite rough around the edges but a beautiful series of rings of different shades of green inside)...I liked this because I thought it was a lovely reminder that even when things seem pretty rough and ugly on the outside, there can be beauty on the inside.

E: Thank you. Oh, wow, thank you, that's beautiful. I...I...would it be ok, could I have the stuff it was wrapped in too? So, I can wrap it up again?

Th: Oh yes, of course, here...

E: Thank you. This is...thank you...I will...this is very meaningful, thank you.

Th: You are welcome. Thank you. It's been a great privilege to get to know you. I wish you well as you move forward.

E: Thank you.

The polished rock was intended as both a metaphor and as a representation of the therapeutic time together, a transitional object she could hold as a reminder of her treatment relationship. It might have helped her consolidate and retain the small steps she had accomplished in her early treatment. Winnicottian object relations theory suggests that might be the case, since the use of transitional objects as a representation of the caregiver when the caregiver is not present is a developmental achievement. The rock would serve as a stand-in for her first clinician as she moved forward into her next phase of treatment and healing with a new provider.

Cultural Considerations

The underlying assumptions of Winnicott's formulations, based in Western, white, male-oriented, two-parent heterosexual relationship-based child-raising norms (Flanagan, 2016) to some extent suit the family system into which Elyse was born and raised, and the societal context in which she existed, so the theory fits the client relatively well in this case. Winnicottian object relations can be applied in other sociocultural contexts as well, but the clinician must develop a nuanced, culturally relevant understanding of what dependence–independence means within the cultural norms of the presenting individual.

For Elyse, her childhood experiences, however, disrupted on multiple levels, fall well outside the assumptions of Winnicott's theory. The kind of caregiving Elyse received during the periods in which she lived with her grandparents would be an area for more complete exploration. If the treatment relationship was of longer duration, this area might have been able to be better understood, giving insight into one possible source of Elyse's internal strengths, seemingly developed despite persistent caregiving failures.

One of the strengths of object relations in general is the theory's ability to look beyond the individual by accounting for and incorporating environmental pressures when looking at an individual's developmental trajectory (Flanagan, 2016; St. Clair & Wigren, 2004). In addition to seeing Elyse situated within the influences of her family structure, object relations theory facilitates a perspective of Elyse within the influences of her broader societal context, developing her sense of self in response to messages received and perceived from broader society.

As a white, heterosexual, cisgender female, Elyse could enjoy a degree of social power and privilege. Because of her drug use and current unemployment, contributing to a position of lower economic status, she probably saw herself as lacking power or privilege. In a broader social context, her sexual, racial, and ethnic identities may mitigate her circumstances to a degree, but being female, drug-using, including methadone, which carries its own stigma, and dependent on public assistance could certainly contribute to real societally generated stresses (Altman, 2006; American Psychological Association [APA] 2007). Her perception of low social privilege and power within this societal context would be understandable.

Regarding the concept of power, Chambon (1999) suggests Foucault understood power as operating through social discourse, which then produces identities. Individuals develop a sense of self in reaction to perceived pressure to conform to societal norms, thus the disciplining of the self is internal (Chambon, 1999). This aligns with a Winnicottian view of the development of a self, if broadened to include societal influences. The social world becomes the corollary for the familial caregiving holding environment. Just as a true self/false self-balance would be attained in an attuned family environment responsive to a developing child's needs, a parallel process occurs as the child moves into the world and receives messages from her social interactions.

This aspect of Elyse's relationships was not explored during treatment, nor did the clinician address the power imbalances that lay between the dyad, both potentials for impasse had the treatment been able to continue longer (Perez Foster, 1998). That said, structuring the early treatment planning discussion to give Elyse the power to decide if she wanted to continue with her initial clinician or transition to a more permanent therapist was a conscious effort by Elyse's initial clinician to level the imbalance and counteract any potentially negative societal messages Elyse might have internalized. The ability to include this additional layer of understanding to Elyse's psychosocial development speaks to the strength and utility of object relations theory in framing human behavior. Though not without limitations, object relations theories facilitate developing a rich, nuanced understanding of a client, laying the groundwork for potential healing through relationships.

Discussion Questions

1. Object Relations Theory suggests that individual sense of self develops in a societal context as well as through interpersonal relationships. What does Elyse's comment about not being a "piece of s*** druggie" reveal about her interactions with the greater social world around her? How might Elyse's internalized expectations about societal interactions play out in a clinical setting?

2. How might one address those internalized impacts/expectations via the therapeutic relationship from an Object Relations perspective? Now apply a different theoretical perspective. How does your understanding change or stay the same?
3. Object Relations Theory suggests the transference and countertransference are rich ground for clues to unspoken, unrecognized needs the client is communicating. Consider your reaction (countertransference) to the client as you read through the case. What might your reactions suggest as possible clinical insights into the client?
4. What might your reactions suggest about your own role or beliefs in the treatment dyad? How might you use this awareness to advance the clinical work?
5. Compare an Object Relations formulation to another theoretical lens included in this book. How does your perception of the client's needs and thus your clinical approach change or remain the same based on the theoretical perspective you apply? Another way of thinking about this comparison is to identify areas of commonality and areas of divergence between object relations and the theory you choose in contrast.

References

Altman, N. (2006). Whiteness. *Psychoanalytic Quarterly, 75*, 45–72. https://doi.org/10.1002/j.2167-4086.2006.tb00032.x.

American Psychiatric Association [APA]. (2013). Diagnostic and statistical manual of mental disorders (5th ed.). doi:https://doi.org/10.1176/appi.books.9780890425596.

American Psychological Association [APA]. (2007). Guidelines for psychological practice with girls and women. *American Psychologist, 62*(9), 949–979. https://doi.org/10.1037/0003-066X.62.9.949.

Applegate, J. S., & Bonovitz, J. M. (1995). *The facilitating partnership: A Winnicottian approach for social workers and other helping professionals.* Lanham, MD: Rowman & Littlefield, Publishers.

Chambon, A. (1999). What was Foucault after? In A. Chambon, A. Irving, & L. Epstein (Eds.), *Reading foucault for social work* (pp. 52–81). New York, NY: Columbia University Press.

Flanagan, L. M. (2016). Object relations theory. In J. Berzoff, L. M. Flanagan, & P. Hertz (Eds.), *Inside out and outside in: Psychodynamic clinical theory and psychopathology in contemporary multicultural contexts* (4th ed., pp. 123–165). Lanham, MD: Rowman & Littlefield.

Goldstein, E. G. (2001). *Object relations theory and self psychology in social work practice.* New York, NY: The Free Press.

Greenberg, J. R. & Mitchell, S. A. (1983). Object relations in psychoanalytic theory. Harvard University Press.

Mitchell, A. (2019). Attached, addicted, & adrift: Understanding the rural opioid crisis. *Families in Society: The Journal of Contemporary Social Services, 100*(1), 80–92. https://doi.org/10.1177/1044389418812417.

Mitchell, S. A. (1984). Object relations theories and the developmental tilt. *Contemporary Psychoanalysis, 20*(4), 473–499. http://www.wawhite.org/uploads/PDF/SMitchell-Object_Relations_Theories.pdf.

Mitchell, S. A., & Black, M. J. (1995). *Freud and beyond.* New York, NY: Basic Books.

Perez Foster, R. (1998). The clinician's cultural countertransference: The psychodynamics of culturally competent practice. *Clinical Social Work Journal, 26*(3), 253–270. https://doi.org/10.1 023/A:1022867910329.

St. Clair, M., & Wigren, J. (2004). *Object relations and self psychology: An introduction* (4th ed.). Belmont, CA: Brooks/Cole Cengage Learning.

Weathers, F.W., Litz, B.T., Keane, T.M., Palmieri, P.A., Marx, B.P., & Schnurr, P.P. (2013). The PTSD Checklist for *DSM-5* (PCL-5). Scale available from the National Center for PTSD at www.ptsd.va.gov

Winnicott, D. W. (1945). Primitive emotional development. In *Through paediatrics to psychoanalysis: Collected papers* (1st ed., pp. 145–156). New York, NY: Brunner/Mazel, Publishers.

Winnicott, D. W. (1947). Hate in the countertransference. In D. Goldman (Ed.), *In one's bones: The clinical genius of Winnicott* (pp. 15–24). Northvale, NJ: Jason Aronson, Inc..

Winnicott, D. W. (1953). Transitional objects and transitional phenomena. In *Playing and reality* (pp. 1–25). New York, NY: Basic Books, Inc.

Winnicott, D. W. (1956a). The antisocial tendency. In *Through paediatrics to psycho-analysis: Collected papers* (pp. 306–316). London, England: The Hogarth Press.

Winnicott, D. W. (1956b). Primary maternal preoccupation. In *Through paediatrics to psychoanalysis: Collected papers* (pp. 300–305). London, England: The Hogarth Press.

Winnicott, D. W. (1960a). Ego distortion in terms of true and false self. In D. W. Winnicott (Ed.), *The maturational process and the facilitating environment* (pp. 139–152). Madison, CT: International Universities Press.

Winnicott, D. W. (1960b). The theory of the parent-infant relationship. *The International Journal of Psycho-Analysis, 41*, 585–595.

Chapter 4
Self Psychology: The Case of Evan

Rhonda Peterson Dealey

Introduction to Self-Psychology

Self-psychology, developed by Heinz Kohut (1971, 1977, 1984), is a comprehensive psychoanalytic theory which provides a developmental model as well as a therapeutic model. Kohut conceptualized the self as the psychological means of processing subjective experience in the development of the personality (Kohut, 1971). He suggested a healthier, normal psychological development in contrast to prior theoretical understandings of a development that occurs as a result of conflicts, drives, and repressions (Freud, 1933). Kohut was trained as a classical psychoanalyst who listened when clients suggested that his classic interpretations were not helping them. Considering the feedback of his clients that traditional psychoanalytic interpretation was insufficient and unsuccessful, Kohut (1971) presented a revolutionary theory in which normal psychological development was seen in the changing nature of the relationship between the self and its' selfobjects—objects being namely people—rather than in a process of change from dependence to independence and autonomy. He suggested that a line of healthy narcissistic development allows for development of a cohesive self which fosters adequate behavioral functioning and mental health. Kohut (1977) theorized that selfobject relationships are the essence of psychological life throughout the life span

Kohut (1984) proposed that everyone is born with a nuclear self, that is, a capacity to develop a healthy cohesive self. In order to develop a cohesive self, an individual must have specific selfobject needs met through an empathic caregiver. If throughout early life a child has an empathic caregiver who is attuned to the child's needs and who functions as a selfobject, a cohesive self will develop. Pathology develops—with the exception of instances of significant traumas, such as violence, which might fragment a self—as a result of a lack of empathic caregiving or

R. P. Dealey (✉)
Social Work, Washburn University, Topeka, KS, USA
e-mail: Rhonda.PetersonDealey@washburn.edu

© Springer Nature Switzerland AG 2021   43
R. P. Dealey, M. R. Evans (eds.), *Discovering Theory in Clinical Practice*,
https://doi.org/10.1007/978-3-030-57310-2_4

inconsistency in attunement and empathy whereby the selfobject needs are not met and the self-structure does not develop fully. Kohut suggested that individuals need selfobject interactions throughout life for the sustenance of a healthy self.

Selfobject Needs

Kohut's (1984) theory identifies three selfobject needs: needs of the grandiose self; needs for an idealized selfobject; and twinship needs. The grandiose self encompasses the need for affirmation, validation, praise, and reassurance. The grandiose self is marked by the need to feel omnipotence or competence. The nuclear, emerging self needs selfobjects to provide mirroring, guiding, and confirming functions which then help the self develop the ability to regulate self-esteem, to tolerate success and failure, and cultivate healthy ambition. These selfobject needs are often referred to as the mirroring needs, the need for an accurate reflection back of the self and one's emotions in relationship to experiences (Kohut, 1971, 1984). The mirroring needs include the need for assurance and guidance. Individuals whose early mirroring needs of the grandiose self were not sufficiently guided and supported or whose mirroring needs were neglected, mocked, or berated may exhibit self-effacing or self-deprecating language, fear of failure, fear of success and recognition, or over-achieving compulsions, for example. Individuals with unmet mirroring selfobject needs may display an exaggerated need to "be seen" or may be easily overlooked by others.

The second set of selfobject needs is the need for an idealized selfobject. This includes the need to merge with an omnipotent/omniscient other, the need for admiration of another, and the opportunity to glean wisdom, values, and ideals of an admired other. Successful merging selfobject relationships help the self to develop self-management, self-soothing, affect regulation, as well as the capacity to establish values and goals (Kohut, 1971, 1984). The absence of a role model or a selfobject worthy of trust and admiration inhibits the development of the self to find its own truth and sense of integrity and to develop adequate capacity to manage the stresses of life. Individuals with unmet idealizing/merging selfobject needs may display patterns of addiction or unhealthy use of substances, sex, or violence as means of coping.

The third set of selfobject needs, the twinship or alter-ego need, refers to the need for association or connectedness with others, the experience of a shared humanity, or a sense of likeness with others. This need emerges chronologically later than the previous needs, around the latency period of development, at the elementary school age. Successful fulfillment of this need throughout development allows an individual to tolerate differences and individuality (Kohut, 1984). Throughout life, individuals find fulfillment in connection with like-minded others who share the same interests, passions, and ideals. Individuals with unfulfilled twinship selfobject needs may express a lack of connectedness, severe loneliness, or an absence of a belonging and awareness of one's place in the world.

Optimal Frustration

Kohut (1982) identified the process by which a cohesive self is formed as transmuting internalization via optimal frustration, that is, necessary and inevitable "selfobject failures (e.g., responses based on faulty empathy) of a non-traumatic degree" (Kohut, 1984, p. 70). Later writings refer to this experience as optimal interactions or optimal responsiveness (Kitron, 1991). Kohut suggested that the cohesive self is formed through a series of gradual withdrawals of selfobject functions, through non-traumatic failures, and through minor mis-attunements by an empathic caregiver followed by empathic re-attunement. As a result, selfobject functions are transmuted into self functions; functions, such as self-esteem or self-regulation, which have been provided by an external selfobject are gradually internalized over time by a developing self which then becomes able to provide those functions independently (Kohut & Wolf, 1978). For example, presume that the hungry cries of an infant are typically met quickly by a responsive, consistent, empathic caregiver ready to supply nourishment. Occasionally, however, that empathic caregiver is briefly delayed in providing desired nourishment because of daily interruptions, such as driving the car, answering the phone, tending to a sibling, etc. During this brief ruptured attunement, the infant becomes stressed. Because the caregiver is able to reconnect quickly and provide an empathic, soothing response and the desired nourishment, the infant is reassured. Over time the infant learns that it will not be forgotten but that the caregiver may not be omnipotent and infallible. As a consequence of such optimal frustration and response encounters, the infant incrementally develops a greater capacity to self-soothe and sustain frustration for longer periods of time between demand and response.

An example of gradual withdrawal as optimal frustration might look like this: Baby is learning to walk. At first the caregiver provides physical assistance by holding on with two hands and provides protection by preventing injury when falling. Gradually the caregiver lessens physical assistance and eventually completely withdraws physical assistance all the while offering encouragement and praise. Baby's confidence builds and baby continues to try until successful at independent mobility. The gradual withdrawal of assistance allows for the increase of independence and confidence.

Kohut (1971) purported that an infant's ability to withstand the frustration is evidence of how much one has internalized the selfobject functions. Pathology (except in the case of severe trauma) occurs due to the lack of empathic caregivers or lack of consistency in early caregiving to fulfill the selfobject needs. When primary caregivers are unable or unwilling to provide empathic attunement and satisfy the child's selfobject needs, an unhealthy narcissism may appear resulting in a weak self, an underdeveloped self, or a fragmenting self. Personality of caregivers, Kohut (1978) hypothesized is more significant to infant development of self-cohesion and the transmuting internalization process than heredity or trauma, specifically the caregivers' own narcissistic fixations. It is the child's reaction to the caregivers and caregivers' capacity for response rather than the gross traumatic events themselves which account for narcissistic fixations and pathological defects in the development of the self. In other words, it is less about the events that happen during childhood that inform development of the self than it is about how the caregiving others are able to attune to the needs of the child to ensure a sense of safety, trust, and reassurance.

Empathy

A central tenet of Kohut's (1978) theory is his description of empathy as "vicarious introspection" (p. 205) and its role in the development of self. Kohut (1984) understood empathy to be "the capacity to think and feel oneself into the inner life of another person" (Kohut, 1984, p. 82), a capacity which can be used for good or harm. Empathy is the key to development of a cohesive self and the healing of the self in treatment.

Early in treatment empathy attempts to gain understanding and progresses along a developmental line from understanding and vicarious introspection (a lower form of empathy) to interpretation and explaining (a higher form of empathy). This is typically a long, slow process. Empathy in the therapeutic relationship follows the developmental line of empathic caregiving by attuned caregivers in the growing child—moving from the stage of holding and understanding to a level of interpreting with a look of pride and communicating, "Good job. I'm proud of you," as the child moves toward independent action (Kohut, 2010).

Empathy in Kohut's model is not a state of feeling or experiencing, but rather a means of listening and understanding the client's story, a methodology for the collection of the client's developmental data and modality for a reparative selfobject experience. Through the experience of receiving accurate empathy in the therapeutic setting, a client is "seen" and feels understood. By experiencing this feeling of being understood, a client may sense an awareness of aliveness and presence, a validation of one's capacity for communication with another, and a capacity to integrate and tolerate difficult thoughts and feelings. Ultimately this empathic responsiveness will serve to allow the self to develop to a point in which empathic failures can be tolerated (Geist, 2009).

Therapeutic Model

Kohut (1971) described the therapeutic process as an experience of transmuting internalization via optimal frustration. The therapist presents as a new selfobject. Through empathy and the experience of being understood in the present the client experiences archaic selfobject needs, repairs fractured or underdeveloped self cohesion, and develops the self-capacity to manage anxiety and self-esteem (Elson, 1987).

In his own therapeutic interactions, Kohut (1971, 1984) realized that his clients were experiencing selfobject transferences of their own mirroring, merging, and twinship needs. Kohut found that his adult clients continued to search for unmet selfobject needs from childhood. He believed that it was through this transference opportunity that reparation or development of cohesion of the self occurred. Kohut treated only adults who had a capacity for insight that children do not. However, Kohut did not consider insight as necessary for healing. Radically, Kohut suggested that healing did not occur as a result of interpretation. Rather it is the client's repetitive experience of self-selfobject relationship and the therapist's attuned responsiveness which provides restoration or sustenance to the cohesion of the self (Goldberg, 1978; Kohut, 1977, 1984). Subsequent theorists and clinicians have described how a self-psychology approach to assessment, diagnosis, and treatment with children and families is theoretically relevant and clinically advantageous (Elson, 1986; Leone, 2001; Ornstein, 1981, 2015; Pienaar & Molteno, 2010; Tolpin, 1986).

Introduction to the Case of Evan

All names and identifiers of this case have been changed to maintain the confidentiality of the client and family. Evan was a 9-year-old boy in third grade who had been meeting with the school social worker when school was in session once weekly since the third week of second grade. Evan lived with his biological parents and two teenage half-sisters in a lower middle-class neighborhood. Both parents were employed outside the home in blue-collar jobs. Evan's paternal grandmother came to the home in the morning to be with Evan and get him on the school bus. Evan's sisters were home in the afternoons when he arrived home after school, though they were mostly disinterested in interacting with him.

Evan reported his favorite activities as playing Legos and playing with his grandfather's model trains. He was quite artistic and enjoyed drawing. He performed adequately academically in school with moderate effort, earning A's and B's on his report cards. He received a specialized reading intervention daily and math intervention three times weekly. Evan and his father participated in Cub Scouts. His family attended church with his grandparents for Christian holidays. He enjoyed sports and his father frequently was a coach for his team.

Evan attended kindergarten and first grade at a different school. In spring of his first-grade year, at teacher request because of repeated disciplinary problems, Evan was placed on a restrictive behavior plan in which he had to earn the privilege of attending lunch, recess, and specials (i.e., music, art, P.E., assemblies). Records indicated that in the final 3 months of school, Evan earned all privileges only twice and lost them again within a day or two. Evan received social work support from the school social worker for the second half of kindergarten and second half of first grade for impulsivity, physical aggression, and disrespectful behaviors. The previous social worker's comment when transferring the case was, "Evan's problem is his parents don't care enough about him to punish him." Evan was identified by the previous school team when transitioning as, "He will be your biggest problem."

Prior to the beginning of his second-grade year, the school social worker shared the previous behavior plan with the classroom teacher. Together they agreed to allow Evan a fresh start to assess his current performance before selecting interventions. This classroom teacher was by nature strict and highly structured with a classroom-wide behavior management plan which included negative consequences and positive rewards for all students.

Evan was referred for school social work support the third week of second grade because, despite the classroom management plan, the teacher felt he was disruptive to the learning of others, frequently shouting out, talking at inappropriate times, and touching others inappropriately. The teacher's perception at that time was that he was "not mean," but rather was impulsive and "had his own agenda."

Based on information up to that point, the school social worker's preliminary suspicions were that Evan was likely experiencing executive functioning deficits which could explain his apparent impulsivity and need for frequent redirection. However, in the first session with the student, those impressions changed abruptly. Social worker introduced herself to Evan and invited him to draw a self-portrait. On a 9 × 12-in. piece of paper Evan drew a one-and-a-half-inch tall picture of himself wearing his favorite green shirt. When asked if he was finished or wished to add something to it, Evan indicated he would like to add more but was unsure of what to add. Social worker suggested he add something about his family or his favorite thing to do. Evan displayed a broad smile and filled the page with color. Oddly the picture was of the social worker's office with many details, including the social worker. Evan described it as his favorite place despite having only been there a few minutes.

In the early weeks Evan would express his aggravation with his parents, complaining that, when he brought home a bad report from school, he was ignored or not given a consequence. He reported hiding good notes from school from his parents. He expressed his upset—as though personally offended—when his mother sustained an injury that he perceived made her less available to him. He expressed no concern for her well-being. He related stories of lying about his sister and considered this justified because of some injustice she had caused him 2 years previously. His lies during his social work sessions were typically thinly veiled, and usually connected to his own abilities. For example, when given a sentence completion, "I am best at…," Evan reported "wrestling," a sport in which he had never participated and only seen on television. However, when invited to elaborate on this, Evan created an elaborate story about his father being his coach and having wrestling tournaments in the basement of his home. Evan's self-assessment of skills and talents was either grandiose or completely self-deprecating.

In the weeks prior to his second-grade parent–teacher conference Evan's negative behaviors and disciplinary consequences escalated. In social work sessions Evan would verbalize fear that his teacher would tell his parents about his behavior and his parents would be upset. He stated that after his first-grade conference he was grounded for 3 weeks, losing TV privileges and having to stay in his room after school. However, his actions and attitude suggested an excitement in anticipating this level of attention from his parents.

During the parent–teacher conference in late November, the school psychologist requested a functional behavioral analysis (FBA) because of difficulty maintaining behavioral expectations in less structured environments such as specials (music, art, PE), lunch, and recess. Parents consented. The FBA was completed by mid-January and parents did not attend the meeting to discuss it. At this point, the psychologist suggested that behavior had improved some again. However, Evan was monitored via a daily behavioral report card. Parents were invited to provide rewards at home in conjunction with this. Rewards were initially offered at home, but this did not sustain. Rewards continued at school throughout the school year.

During third grade, Evan required no individualized behavioral chart outside the classroom behavior management program which his third-grade teacher provided equally for all students. He had several bus referrals during third grade. Records (for both second and third grades) suggested that behaviors were more problematic prior to or following a break (long weekend, winter break, etc.) and/or when home factors changed (temporary parental separation). Evan had no fights or physical altercations in third grade. He received an in-school suspension for bringing his newly acquired Boy Scout pocket knife to school to prove to his peers that he had it. By the latter half of third grade, Evan was identified as "my friend" by many students, and several girls had indicated an interest in being his "girlfriend."

Theoretical Integration

Selfobject Needs

Evan did not present as the type of student who is typically referred to the school social worker. He did not present as having difficulty with theory of mind or executive functioning skills. His narcissistic, labile self-esteem combined with his social savvy suggested that his attention-seeking behaviors did not stem from a sensory integration need or affective dysregulation. Evan displayed selfobject needs in the areas of mirroring needs (grandiose self) and merging needs (idealized other) far beyond that of his peers. Examples of his mirroring needs included his attention-seeking behaviors, originally in misbehavior and then often in assistive behavior with adults, and in his frequent asking for approval of his work or actions. Evan was the child that everyone knew, not simply because he got into trouble, but because he made himself known. He would wave when any adult passed by and would interrupt adults just for the sake of being noticed. Evan's capacity to regulate his self-esteem was poor. He would either describe himself as infallible and greater than he really was or would be self-deprecating and believe himself to be totally and forever incapable of the task at hand. He seemed to struggle to regulate his behavior but did not demonstrate affective dysregulation or emotional lability. He did not typically act out of anger or emotionality.

Merging selfobject needs for an idealized other seemed to be the greatest area of concern for Evan early on. He seemed to be desperately seeking an omnipotent other whom he could admire. Examples of his merging selfobject needs could be observed in his relentless testing of certain adults but not others, as though he was convinced of the power and authority (idealized other) of some adults but doubted it in other adults he found to be inconsistent. He showed little to no remorse when being reprimanded by most adults.

Evan's selfobject needs in twinship emerged during the time when working with the social worker and will be discussed more fully below. Developmentally this was the appropriate time for development of peer connections and friendships. Evan demonstrated some success in this area.

Selfobject Transferences in Therapeutic Environment

Evan's mirroring selfobject needs were evident in the therapeutic situation and throughout the school experience. As in most environments within the school setting, during sessions with the school social worker, Evan sought praise and assurances of his actions and achievements. During the period in second grade when a daily behavior chart was utilized, Evan consistently selected attention, typically from the principal, as his reward. Over time, as teachers got to know him and were able to see his strengths and personality, his need to command attention lessened.

The merging needs for an idealized other were prevalent in the therapeutic environment from the first session. Evan's first self-portrait suggested a desire to merge with the social worker whom he had just met, describing her office as his "favorite place." Evan's thinly veiled lies were understood as part of his need to test the social worker's omniscience, whether she would see through his untruths and really know him. The social worker was very intentional to gently let Evan know that she did not believe his comments without judgment or accusation. Eventually the social worker and Evan could exchange a "look" without the social worker verbally challenging his remarks. When Evan was certain from the social worker's facial expression that his lie had been detected, Evan typically smiled broadly and changed the subject. A self-psychologically informed practitioner understands that a child's undetected lie can possibly serve as an optimal frustration in the growing awareness of the parents' lack of omniscience. In a therapeutic setting, the lie becomes a test of the clinician, not merely of the capacity to notice the lie, but also a test to see if the clinician will reject or judge negatively the client (Kohut, 1984).

Another example of Evan's merging need was observed in his differing reactions to various staff. The school psychologist frequently reported observing Evan being rude or disrespectful to teachers. The social worker, even with the same teachers, never observed inappropriate interpersonal interactions. It was hypothesized that Evan did not fear the social worker's power to punish or take away his rewards, but rather feared jeopardizing her willingness to stay merged with him. After social work sessions, Evan would always ask the social worker to walk him back to class and enjoyed being seen with the social worker by others. He would frequently ask to keep an object, such as a pencil or eraser, used during a session, and typically asked the social worker to keep and/or display artwork that he had made. One of Evan's favorite activities with the social worker was a variation of the squiggle game (Winnicott, 1971) which required the pair to "know what the other one is thinking." During building block play, Evan frequently wanted his dinosaur character to chase and capture the social worker's character, but always refused to "eat" her character despite having "eaten" multiple other characters that he controlled, stating, "You're too meaty. I only need a little meat." Much of Evan's artwork and play centered around the theme of "home," and he frequently insisted that the social worker either be "in" the home, work symmetrically with him in building/drawing it, or place the final piece to complete the building of the home. Near the end of the therapeutic relationship, as Evan was aware that he would be moving to another school for fourth grade, he persistently invited the social worker to one of his sporting events (of which his father was the coach). With caregiver permission, the social worker elected to attend one game, believing that symbolically this was an important merger event of Evan's two worlds of home and school.

Evan's interest in peers grew during the time he worked with the social worker. Early in the therapeutic relationship, during play-based activities Evan preferred the social worker to observe and comment on his activity. He progressed to inviting the social worker to play alongside him, and even invited her to take turns in choosing activities. On a few occasions near the middle of third grade, Evan's "homes" morphed into duplexes, identical and side-by-side, one each for Evan and the social worker. During third grade, Evan asked the social worker to assist him in facilitating twinship interactions with peers, and this became an important part of the work near the end.

Empathic Attunement and Optimal Frustrations

Early in the course of working with Evan, the social worker began to suspect that Evan's mother was "running on empty," physically and emotionally, and that his father was preoccupied with fractures in the relationship with his wife. The parents seemed to be well-intentioned, but did not seem to have enough of their own selves to give Evan what he needed. Parents individually and together were inconsistent in their interactions with the school, at times being very involved in the day-to-day experiences of Evan, and then suddenly and inexplicably becoming uninvolved and unresponsive. The social worker came to believe that the parents' own narcissistic frustrations were currently impeding—and had been for a long time—their availability to adequately provide empathic concern for their child or consistent modeling of self-organization. There was never evidence to suggest gross parental abuse or neglect nor trauma history of any sort. In child psychopathology, it is common to observe adequate parental physical caregiving and overt expressions of love yet an inability of parents to provide phase-appropriate empathic attunement to their children's selfobject needs (Ornstein, 2015). This appeared to be the case for Evan's family.

The goal of social work became to not only provide opportunity for the selfobject transferences to evolve in the therapeutic relationship, but to also attempt to create a selfobject milieu (Leone, 2001) within the day-to-day school environment. This was a daunting task indeed at times because the school personnel tended to be behaviorally oriented, addressing behaviors with rewards and consequences with limited recognition of the significance of empathic attunement. Fortunately, the school social worker had built the trust of staff, and in particular the principal, over years of working together and was requested and allowed to provide guidance and interpretation when disciplinary or puzzling situations arose. The social worker consulted with the principal and teachers, not just homeroom teachers, frequently to discuss their interactions or concerns about the student. Without using theoretical jargon, the social worker attempted to provide insight into the reasons and needs expressed by Evan's behavior and offered suggestions for ways to provide a selfobject milieu that provided assurance as well as predictable, authentic, supportive structure. Other students benefited from this milieu as well. Consultation with Evan's teachers decreased dramatically over time as self-esteem and behavior improved.

Empathy as vicarious introspection and attunement, "a value neutral mode of observation" (Kohut, 1982, p. 396)—not a sense of emotional connectedness—was always at the forefront of work with Evan. The social worker was very conscientious to be on time for weekly scheduled sessions and attempted to be aware of even the slightest behaviors or comments by Evan. Consistency of routines and expectations was prioritized. Evan's behavior was never judged, but rather was understood to the extent possible, and only interpreted for Evan when needed, such as in the event of disciplinary occurrences or to help Evan gain another's perspective. Empathy was "an informer of appropriate action" (Kohut, 2010, p. 126). Being able to understand Evan's need afforded the social worker the appropriate response to his need, such as allowing Evan to remake the rules to the squiggle game.

Working in the school setting rather than a private practice office afforded multiple unplanned disruptions to serve as potential optimal frustrations, e.g., interrupted sessions when the principal or a child in crisis needed something from the social worker. Empathic re-attunement immediately following such interruptions afforded Evan the assurance that his merger with the social worker was secure and he would not be abandoned, that the social worker was consistent and predictable, and that he was valued. Certainly, the social worker was not always able to discern the truthfulness of comments made by Evan, which served as another optimal frustration. However, because Evan's need was to be truly "seen" (mirroring) by the social worker, as well as for the social worker to serve as an idealized other (merging), Evan typically presented the untruths in ways that were easily discernable because of their grandiosity and/or implausibility. Social worker never criticized Evan's untruthfulness, but rather attempted to understand the need being communicated and to present authentic acceptance of the truthfulness of who Evan was. The instances of lying decreased steadily over time to the point of being virtually non-existent by the end of third grade. Whenever Evan was called into the office for a disciplinary referral, the social worker was invited to participate in the interview and consequence determination. Evan was never known to lie to the social worker when he was in trouble. His perception of the situation was often impacted by his fragile self-esteem, but he was honest in the details of what occurred.

Progress and Prognosis

Work with Evan revealed significant changes in his behavior and improvement in his capacity to manage injury to his self-esteem over time. By the middle of third grade an observer to his classroom would not identify Evan as a disruption to his teacher or a distraction to his peers. He worked hard at his school work, which was often academically challenging for him, and he sought to please his teacher by earning good grades. Rarely did he make grandiose proclamations of his abilities, and his disappointment presented in more typical ways. When he failed to pass his P.E. test (physical prowess was an actual talent and something in which he prided himself), he did not blame the teacher, nor did he resort to his former pattern of self-talk which would have declared, "I'll never be able to do it! I quit." Instead, he cried. And then he initiated ideas of ways to improve his skills in order to pass the skills test when he had the opportunity to retest later. His self-esteem was no longer so fragile that he could not tolerate disappointment or defeat.

The development of reciprocal peer relationships provided a great deal of hope for Evan's future. Kohut (1984) conceptualized a tripolar self, or the development of a cohesive, healthy self along the three poles of grandiosity/mirroring, idealization/merging, and twinship/alter-ego selfobject internalizations. Kohut suggested that a lack of sufficient development in one of the poles could result in pathology. However, he also suggested that adequate development along one or two poles accompanied by sufficient sustaining selfobject relationships could provide a level of functional compensation for insufficient development along another pole. This supposition provided the social worker with a great deal of hope for Evan as he appeared to be successfully developing along the twinship pole.

Evan and his family moved to a new school for fourth grade. The school social worker would have liked more time with Evan to ensure that his growth of self was supported and he had sufficient selfobject relationships to bolster the self-structure which he had developed. It would be naïve to think that Evan's self-cohesion will not be threatened as he moves into adolescence. But hope remains that Evan has the self-organization to seek selfobject relationships that meet his needs through healthy and safe avenues.

Cultural Considerations

Self-psychology was theorized by Heinz Kohut. Kohut was born to Jewish parents in Vienna, Austria in 1913. He was trained by tutors until finally being allowed to attend school in the fifth grade. Kohut completed medical school in Vienna, but left

Austria soon after the Nazi takeover of Austria. He eventually came to Chicago where he furthered his studies in neurology and psychiatry. He became a preeminent psychoanalyst and lecturer at the University of Chicago, and developed much of his theories based on his work with university students.

Evan was a White, English-speaking student from a nonsectarian, working-class family who was able to financially provide for his basic needs. The student population at this school was 80% White, and all of the adults mentioned in the case narrative were also White.

The school climate was supportive and inclusive of students but teachers were stressed by high expectations imposed by local, state, and federal standards of performance of students. School leaders valued positive and restorative forms of praise and discipline over punitive methods. Character education was an integral part of the learning experience.

How might this case look differently within another context or with a student from an ethnically different background? First, attention to relationship dynamics was key to this case. It is this author's contention based on experience that a competent, reflective mental health practitioner is often able to humbly seek to understand and bridge ethnic differences to form relationships with child clients and their families. Children from all backgrounds benefit from consistent opportunities for development of self-esteem, self-management, and connectedness. However, children from families with rigid boundaries who are very guarded and fearful of connection would pose a unique challenge for this type of intervention model.

Organizational culture was particularly significant in this case. A school environment which was highly punitive and/or not respectful of children's worth and individuality could result in undermining the small, incremental gains made. An environment in which collaboration between team members was non-existent or hostile would make this type of approach futile. A school setting in which all situations were approached from a behavior modification framework of rewards and punishments alone and did not make room for a milieu of nurturance and individualization would likely make it impossible for a school social worker to use a model such as this.

Discussion Questions

1. Are psychodynamic approaches to mental health such as self-psychology appropriate for working with children in school-based settings? Why or why not?
2. What are the potential pitfalls and/or plusses to integration of interventions from diverse theoretical lenses (such as self-psychology and behaviorism)?
3. Having read this case, what is your prognosis for Evan's future? What concerns do you anticipate? What skills or developmental acquisitions has Evan achieved that make you optimistic?
4. How would you gather practice-informed evidence in this case to justify your approach and outcomes?

5. If you were the receiving school social worker for Evan as he transitions to a new school, what would be your approach to this case? Where would you start? What would your intervention plan look like?
6. Utilization of self-psychology as a treatment approach is a commitment to change over an extended period of time. What do you see as potential challenges or benefits in that?

References

Elson, M. (1986). *Self psychology in clinical social work*. New York, NY: W.W. Norton & Co.

Elson, M. (Ed.). (1987). *The Kohut seminars on self psychology and psychotherapy with adolescents and young adults*. New York, NY: W.W. Norton & Co..

Freud, S. (1933). *New introductory lectures on psychoanalysis*. (W. J. H. Sprott, Trans.). New York, NY: W. W. Norton & Co.

Geist, R. A. (2009). Empathic understanding: The foundation of self-psychological psychoanalysis. *Self and Systems Explorations in Contemporary Self Psychology, 1159*, 63–74. https://doi.org/10.1111/j.1749-6632.2009.04353.x.

Goldberg, A. (Ed.). (1978). *The psychology of the self: A casebook*. New York, NY: International Universities Press.

Kitron, D. G. (1991). Narcissism and object love as separate but dependent developmental lines. *The Psychoanalytic Study of the Child, 46*(1), 325–336. https://doi.org/10.1080/00797308.1991.11822370.

Kohut, H. (1971). *The analysis of the self*. New York, NY: International Universities Press.

Kohut, H. (1977). *The restoration of the self*. New York, NY: International Universities Press.

Kohut, H. (1978). In P. H. Ornstein (Ed.), *The search for the self: Selected writings of Heinz Kohut, 1950–1978*. New York, NY: International Universities Press.

Kohut, H. (1982). Introspection, empathy, and the semi-circle of mental health. *The International Journal of Psycho-Analysis, 63*(Pt. 4), 395–407.

Kohut, H. (1984). *How does analysis cure?* Chicago, IL: University of Chicago Press.

Kohut, H. (2010). On empathy. *International Journal of Psychoanalytic Self Psychology, 5*, 122–131. https://doi.org/10.1080/155510210036610026.

Kohut, H., & Wolf, E. S. (1978). The disorders of the self and their treatment: An outline. *International Journal of Psychoanalysis, 59*, 413–425.

Leone, C. M. (2001). Toward a more optimal selfobject milieu: Family psychotherapy from the perspective of self psychology. *Clinical Social Work Journal, 29*(3), 269–289.

Ornstein, A. (1981). Self pathology in childhood: Clinical and developmental considerations. *Psychiatric Clinics of North America, 4*, 435–453.

Ornstein, A. (2015). Why Kohut's ideas will endure: The contributions of self psychology to the treatment of children and to the practice of psychotherapy. *International Journal of Psychoanalytic Self Psychology, 10*(2), 128–141. https://doi.org/10.1080/15551024.2015.1005798.

Pienaar, M., & Molteno, C. D. (2010). A self psychology on the formulation and treatment of psychopathology in children with fetal alcohol spectrum disorders. *Psycho-analytic Psychotherapy in South Africa, 18*(1), 58–79.

Tolpin, M. (1986). The self and its self objects. *Progress in Self Psychology, 2*, 115–126.

Winnicott, D. W. (1971). *Therapeutic consultations in child psychiatry*. London: Hogarth Press.

Chapter 5
Psychoanalytic Theory: The Case of Emma

Neil Gorman

Introduction to Psychoanalytic Theory

I've been continually immersed in psychoanalytic theory and practice since I first read Freud's Introductory Lectures to Psychoanalysis (1989) when I began my doctoral studies almost a decade ago. Early on, I was struck by the idea that the *unconscious* is a constant companion in our lives, for better or for worse, and that through psychoanalytic practice, the unconscious can transform from an undermining presence into, perhaps, a friend that reveals hard but important truths. Today, I'm deeply committed to furthering the psychoanalytic cause by introducing it to people who can use it. The goal of this chapter is to present the essential conceptual components of psychoanalytic praxis (the merging of theory and practice) as I understand them, making them accessible to the student who is beginning his or her journey as a mental health professional. No matter how well-crafted my rendition of these concepts is, the constraints of space will require me to leave deeper exploration on the cutting room floor. What follows here is a collection of starting points and signposts one can use as they move deeper into a psychoanalytic worldview.

The Psychoanalytic Cause

On January 15, 1964, the psychoanalyst Jacques Lacan conducted the first session of his annual series of lectures in Paris, which he called his seminar. The title of that year's teaching was *The Four Fundamental Concepts of Psychoanalysis* (1981). According to Lacan, these concepts were the *unconscious, repetition, drives,* and *transference*. Lacan focused his teaching on these cornerstones of psychoanalytic

N. Gorman (✉)
Social Work, Aurora University, Aurora, IL, USA

© Springer Nature Switzerland AG 2021 57
R. P. Dealey, M. R. Evans (eds.), *Discovering Theory in Clinical Practice*,
https://doi.org/10.1007/978-3-030-57310-2_5

thought because he believed, as Freud had, that the magic of psychoanalysis lay in helping the suffering individual transform his extremely painful misery into a sort of normal unhappiness by attempting to understand his unconscious desires (Freud & Breuer, 2004).

A state of "normal unhappiness" might strike you as a rather low bar and an unuseful clinical project. Like most of us, you've likely been taught by culture to view whatever falls short of perfection—in other words, *failure*—as a stain to avoid. Psychoanalysis, on the other hand, has us believe that by failing, we learn how we might do better the next time around (Svolos, 2018). We become miserable because our attempts to fully achieve and sustain satisfaction are inevitably frustrated. However, we might become satisfied with, and perhaps even interested in, the ongoing project of attempting—and failing—to find what *might* satisfy. Or, as McGowan (2016) puts it, "the crucial insight of psychoanalysis is that the subject's satisfaction is located in how it desires and not what it obtains" (p. 35). The concepts that Lacan spoke about in 1964 illuminate how and why people fail to find the mythical satisfaction they believe they want, and how they might come to enjoy the act of seeking something better, however elusive it may be.

The Unconscious and Repression

The unconscious, a core aspect of psychoanalytic theory, has become a colloquial term and despite its long history, the unconscious is often misrepresented (Fink, 2017). To approach an understanding of the unconscious, a return to Freud's early work is instructive (Phillips, 2014). The psychoanalyst Jonathan Lear (2005) points out, "Freud was not a magician; nor did he have supernatural power. He looked carefully at strange phenomena of everyday life, and he thought hard about how to make sense of them. [Freud did this by asking] What is the unconscious and how does it work? (p. 23)." In short: Freud witnessed people living lives made difficult by symptoms without any obvious common sense or physical explanation. When Freud tried to identify the cause, he discovered and conceptualized what we now call the unconscious.

The unconscious is a repository of desires we're unaware of because they have been *repressed*. Therefore, to understand the unconscious, we must also understand what repression is and how it operates. Put simply, there are two types of desires: approved and problematic. Approved desires are likely to be looked at positively by the world around us, and we are typically conscious of these desires. As an example, a student's desire to study for an exam and achieve a good grade will generally be met with approval. Other desires, the problematic variety, are unlikely to meet with the approval of others. They might *get us in trouble* or *make us look bad* if we try to realize them. These desires, the problematic, become part of the unconscious.

The "others" doing this approving and disapproving are both the larger society we exist within, and the significant individuals in our lives (often, our parents or other authority figures), who enact their own interpretations of societal norms. As we become children, then adults, society's approving and disapproving postures toward desire become internalized, and, over time, we begin to police ourselves according to these norms. In effect, the disapproval of others becomes our own, self-judgment of what we want. When faced with non-approved desire, the mind hides it away, someplace inaccessible by consciousness. The process of hiding desires is repression, and the place where the hidden desires reside when repressed is the unconscious.

Importantly, when a desire is repressed, it is not destroyed and it continues to exert an influence on how we live. The student who consciously wants to study for an exam might also want to avoid graduating to remain within the comfortable life of a student, free from adult responsibilities. Wanting to avoid the adult world is, for most, not an acceptable desire, and is the sort of desire likely to be repressed. However, even when a desire is repressed, its symptoms tend to manifest in problematic ways. Our hypothetical student who consciously wants to study but unconsciously wants to avoid the adult world might find himself binge-watching Netflix rather than studying. Our unconscious desires can and will undermine us, even as we consciously attempt to accomplish that which society approves of.

Repetition

When desire is repressed, it tries to escape the repression. One of the ways it does so is through the creation of what Freud called a repetition compulsion, a pattern of repeated, problematic behavior (Freud, 1990a). Patients commonly enter therapy saying, "I don't want to keep making the same mistake but can't seem to help myself." The goal of therapy, then, is to help the patient's unconscious desires rise above the barrier of repression (Fink, 2017; Freud, 1990b). If unconscious desires are elucidated, the patient becomes more consciously aware of his repressed desire, and awareness can create an insight. The insight changes how the patient understands both *how* and *why* he unconsciously desires. Psychoanalysts may attempt to spark this sort of insight using the techniques of psychoanalytic interpretation and construction (illustrated in this chapter's case study). Using these techniques, the therapist offers descriptions of the patient's unconscious desires that may include a *potential* explanation of how the unconscious desires undermine the patient's conscious desires and *potential* rationale as to why the patient keeps failing in the same way over and over.

The Drives, Jouissance, and Re-description

Freud identified two powerful desires present in the lives of the human animal and called them drives. The first is the sex-drive but I like to think of it more broadly, as a desire for bodily pleasure of any sort; it is the drive to feel good (Laplanche, 2011;

Zupančič, 2017). The second is the drive to be aggressive. Think of this as the desire to force ourselves, others, and our environment to do what we want them to do; it is a drive to enjoy domination and mastery over the building blocks of our lives. Our drives pull us toward experiences that make our bodies feel good and increase our capacity for mastery.

Thinking of the drives in this way shows that while they can be problematic, they are not evil. They're a longing, nearly universally shared, for comfort, satisfaction, and enjoyment. However, anything enjoyable holds the potential to become addictive and destructive. What feels good can have disastrous effects if we overindulge, and mastery involves a degree of domination. Lacan used the French term *Jouissance,* which has no direct English equivalent, to describe the addictive and oftentimes self-destructive quality of short-term drive satisfaction which undermines longer-term stability and security (Fink, 2011; Lacan, 1964/1998). Anyone who has ever hurt a loved one by saying something unkind in a moment of anger can understand the effect of jouissance. It *felt so good* to say it, but regret sets in and if one could take the words back, they would.

Freud identified that when drives are repressed, they operate in the shadows of the mind where they create havoc in the lives of patients. Psychoanalysis can be seen as a drawing out process, whereby the drives are coaxed from the shadows of repression to a place where the patient can better see the drives at work. When the process of psychoanalysis is done in a good-enough way for a long-enough time, the therapist may re-describe the patient's drive forces and heretofore unconscious motives, allowing the patient to digest his behavior and ask himself new questions (Phillips, 2009). Effective re-description allows patients to better understand how drives and jouissance operate in their day-to-day lives. They take one step closer to solving the mystery of why their conscious desires are repeatedly undermined.

Transference and the One Who Knows

For psychoanalytic re-description of unconscious drives and desires to be effective, the patient must develop what psychoanalysts call a transference to the therapist (Freud, 1912; Lacan, 1953/2013). When a transference develops, the patient transfers something from other relationships, usually significant ones, into the therapeutic relationship (Freud & Breuer, 2004). The question is, *what is transferred?* Because psychoanalysis is concerned with one's past relationships to parental figures, to answer this question we have to examine the sort of relationships formed to one's primary caregivers and other more powerful authority figures, as compared to the relationship formed to the therapist (Fink, 2017).

The process begins when children realize they are incapable of accessing all the things and experiences that produce satisfaction, which is to say that children become aware of how powerless they are—a fact that, when confronted head-on, is terrifying at any age. Children see adults, often their parents, as ones who have the power to satisfy desires (their own and those of the child) with ease. The child copes with their powerlessness by entering a fantasy where the parent uses her adult-powers to grant whatever the child desires. The child then seeks the most effective methods—obedience, tantrums, etc.—for convincing the powerful adult to use her adult-powers in the service of the child's desires, ultimately keeping the child satisfied, safe, and secure. Over time, as children mature and create relationships with other powerful figures (e.g., doctors, teachers, coaches, therapists, etc.), the fantasy expands to include them. Rather than confronting our powerlessness, we continue to engage the fantasy that powerful "others" can keep us safe. We rally to the coach's motivating speech, comply with the teacher's instructions, and seek the doctor's diagnosis. The perceived, safety-giving power of these individuals, however, is part of the fantasy. Following the teacher's instructions does not guarantee a successful life. Our doctors can't prevent death.

People often operate with the mistaken belief (i.e., fantasy) that others in positions of privilege and authority are powerful because they have access to certain knowledge. The young child believes his parents to be all-knowing; the player believes the coach knows how to win; students believe professors wiser and learned. Lacan describes transference as the patient casting the therapist as "the one who knows" (Lacan, 1964/1998). A transference occurs when the patient believes the therapist has the knowledge, skills, and answers to satisfy or "cure" their suffering. The patient comes to therapy with the fantasy that if they do or say the right thing, they can convince the therapist to use their therapist-powers to grant curative knowledge. To call this a complete fantasy would be inaccurate; the therapist does, of course, have training and specialized knowledge. Regardless, the patient's fantasy that the therapist can cure him is an exaggeration of the therapist's capacities.

Over the course of therapy, the patient divests from the fantasy that the therapist can cure. The patient tentatively claims his own power, and ultimately, his powerlessness to understand and cure himself, and begins to create something better (Lacan, 1959/1997; Ruti, 2013). The "something better" is a deeper, less fantastical, and more realistic relationship with mastery. Our absolute obsession with the impossibility of mastery permeates the psychoanalytic worldview, from the drive to develop mastery in our lives to our willingness to assign power and mastery to others when our sense of safety is threatened. When the patient realizes he cannot *fully* master his drives or unconscious, he establishes a new kind of mastery, a pseudo-mastery where he comes to believe he can "get over" the fantasy of being able to "get over" anything at all (McGowan, 2016; Ruti, 2012). The patient of successful psychoanalysis thus divests from the fantasy of living a life he has mastered and becomes more interested in the beauty of a life that will not accept any master. At this point, his misery can be transformed into a tolerable, and perhaps even interesting and motivating, dissatisfaction.

Introduction to the Case of Emma

As I come down the hall, enter the waiting room of my practice and see my patient, I note the stark contrast she offers to the other typically suburban people (one of whom is her mother) sitting in the chairs around her. Emma's iconoclast appearance might put these buttoned-up people on edge. Half her head is shaved, while the hair that remains has been dyed bright purple. She wears the sort of garb common among teenagers who see themselves as outsiders forced to live inside a society they believe will never understand them: a black leather jacket a few sizes too big for her small frame and boots with metal spikes protruding from the toes. For Emma, a teenager who hides razor blades in places where her parents don't think to search for them, this armor covers both her metaphorical and literal scars. (All names and identifiers of this case have been changed to protect the confidentiality of the client.)

History.

As I filled out forms with her and her mother, and occasionally asked a question, Emma tried to make herself as small as possible on the large couch. She spent most of the time looking down at her hands, chipping off nail polish. Emma was a rather shy freshman, who occupied a place at the bottom of a social class system that pervades American high schools. She was returning to school after discharge from an inpatient behavioral health program. The return to school was a shock after Emma had grown accustomed to the highly structured life at a hospital. Emma's feelings of anxiety and inadequacy, and the associated self-injury, had recently intensified.

In the early stages of treatment, I occasionally met directly with Emma's parents, two people who worked hard to give their children the best lives they possibly could. The strain of supporting Emma's recovery, and setting appropriate limits on her emerging adolescent self, was no easy task. After all, adolescence can be a troubling time in which teenage children engage in a sort of guerrilla warfare against the adults in their life. Even under ideal circumstances, no family emerges from this war without some damage. In Emma's case, the damage included scars, monuments built with blood to inspire guilt in the perceived enemy of the family. The pain of Emma's scars was at times more visible on the faces of her parents, who were full of questions that are impossible to answer. How supportive should (and could) they be? How much of her behavior was just "normal teenage stuff"? The most difficult dilemma that Emma's parents faced: they wanted to be as supportive as possible, but were haunted by the possibility they were enabling their daughter. They were baffled by the cutting and feared for her safety.

Development within the Context of the Family

If you were to look at a photograph of Emma's family, you would notice the two oldest of the three children, one of which is Emma, look remarkably similar. Emma and her sister Siobhan had been born just over 12 months apart. Early in treatment,

I learned that Emma was a remarkably healthy baby, while Siobhan was plagued with a variety of health complications. Siobhan remained in the hospital for many months following her birth, enduring a slew of complicated and risky surgical interventions that had trailing effects for many years.

Throughout her infancy and childhood, Emma's parents were, by necessity, more interested in seeing to the health of her sister. By the time Emma and Siobhan were four, their parents had a third child, this time a son. Out of the three children, one was an infant in a state of complete dependence and one of the sisters was frequently recovering from ongoing medical intervention, requiring more attention than most 4-year-old children. This left Emma as the "strong one," who required much less of her parents than her sister and brother. As this dynamic perpetuated, Emma's experience became bittersweet. She was indeed the strongest of three, praised for how strong and capable she was. At the same time, she received the smallest share of her parents' limited attention. Emma's childhood was far from Dickensian, but it was filled with the loneliness born from being strong in the presence of those who are weak. This dynamic continued as Emma and her siblings sailed from the tranquil bay of childhood into the turbulent seas of adolescence.

As we got to know one another in therapy, Emma started to speak with less difficulty. She described a very lonely childhood and early adolescence as a chronic outsider, longing to be a part of some sort of group, a desire typical of most young adolescents. However, when her peers sensed Emma's desperation to belong, they took joy in actively excluding her. Emma described frequent attempts to tell significant others in her life (her parents, her teachers, the school social worker, and her sister) about her loneliness, and the pain it caused. She wanted to tell them how hard it was for her to be "the good kid," strong enough that people didn't need to worry about her. During these attempts, which took place over approximately 2 years, Emma couldn't seem to find the words to communicate her feelings of isolation. When she tried, she was offered platitudes: "It's not that bad. You're a good kid. You've got a good head on your shoulders. You'll be alright!"

Emma's normally good grades started to slip and she began to spend time with a group of unpopular kids, often labeled as "freaks." She felt more accepted by this group, and began performing non-normative dress, makeup, speech, and visible non-compliance with the demands of authority figures. However, despite a refrain of "I don't care what *they* think," the lack of acceptance continued to cause Emma a great deal of pain. Sometimes the pain would overwhelm Emma's ability to contain it, and she began cutting, leaving visible marks on her wrists. The cutting grew in frequency and severity. One day she "accidentally" cut too deep, and the injury could no longer be ignored. An ambulance was called, and shortly after that Emma became a resident of an inpatient unit in a hospital. She was eventually discharged and encouraged to begin regular therapy.

Theoretical Integration

The Repressed Unconscious Desire

When we first spoke, Emma insisted she wanted to stop self-injuring. I believed this was her conscious desire speaking; the important people in her life (e.g., her parents, siblings, etc.) approved of and supported her attempts to become "well." I could have taken Emma at her word in our early sessions—"I want to stop cutting"—but her history told another story. Emma's cutting was not an isolated instance but rather a repetitive compulsion that had increased in frequency over time. As our exploration of drives shows, when someone is unconsciously driven to repeat a behavior, they'll repeat it. It also follows that if one's unconscious desire is to stop a behavior, they will. During the early phase of our sessions together, I asked myself *what unconscious satisfaction drove Emma to engage in self-injury?*

I believed it was important to create a space where it would be easier for Emma's unconscious to have a voice in our sessions. If I immediately allied myself with Emma's stated goal to stop cutting, I risked further repression of her unconscious desire and so I decided to share with Emma that I imagined she cut because it provided her something she wanted. Emma appeared somewhat surprised by what I had said, but she did not recoil, nor did she insist that she wanted to stop cutting. I moved forward with a question: Did Emma *really* want to stop cutting? She produced a wry smile and told me that while part of her did, part of her didn't. I asked Emma to say more about the part that didn't, and she described a part of herself that wanted to be able to cut into her skin without prompting a strong, negative reaction in the people whose lives were intertwined with hers. She said, "I just want people to see it as something I do to cope and see that it's not this big deal they need to freak out about." However, Emma's cuts were positioned such that they were certain to be seen by people unlikely to ignore what they saw, and who Emma had every reason to believe would indeed become "freaked out." The placement of the cuts signaled Emma's unconscious desire, unlikely to be approved of and therefore repressed: a desire to provoke a concerned response in others at the sight of her self-injury.

Freud (1925) postulated that clinicians can begin to discern the repressed desires of their patients by listening for what he called *negations*. Negations are verbal enactments where people give voice to their unconscious desires by making an overt claim about the "sort of person" they are or aren't, or what they feel. On the surface, these claims are very conscious descriptions of the version of one's self that have been met with approval. However, they are often an attempt to hide—or negate—a real but unsettling unconscious truth about one's self. Negations are extremely common, and the careful listener will begin to identify them in daily life. A relative who insists, "I'm not the sort of person that holds a grudge" may be the aunt that derives a huge amount of enjoyment from holding onto and enacting her resentments. Or, listen the next time a colleague begins a sentence with "With all due respect ..." What follows is almost guaranteed to be disrespectful.

For the psychoanalytic practitioner, the unconscious is like a wild animal. When glimpsed, the observer wants a closer look. However, like a wild animal, when one moves closer it's likely to bolt, disappearing deeper into the woods. Emma's negations were the first glimpses of her unconscious. She described how other people judged her and assumed she was cutting herself for attention, followed by statements like, "I'm not an attention whore, and I don't care what *they* think about me." In this instance, *they* were the people whose thoughts and opinions Emma cared a great deal about. Spontaneous and unprompted utterances often signal negations, and during our sessions, I never suggested that Emma's actions were done for attention, nor did I suggest she cared a great deal about other's assessments of her. In fact, in an effort to maintain a safe space for Emma's unconscious, I was deliberate in my effort not to align myself with what *they* thought. Emma's often-repeated, unprompted sentiment that she "did not care what *they* think" smelled of defensive negation. Emma had repressed a desire for others to care about and express concern for her, and this unconscious desire gave birth to her negations. The negations pointed the way to her desire for attention and regard, which she insisted she did not want throughout our early sessions together.

The Drives

As I got to know Emma, I began to understand her cutting as a manifestation of jouissance, the addictive and self-destructive quality of short-term drive satisfaction. When self-destructive behaviors present themselves in therapy, it is tempting to coach the person to stop, or to provide a set of coping mechanisms when the urge to cut surfaces. However, doing so would discount the buried desires and powerful but repressed drives that formed the deep root system of Emma's self-injury, and would likely result in the continuation of the behavior. When a desire is repressed, it is not destroyed, but pushed into the shadows of the mind. Paradoxically, the more a desire is repressed, the greater its capacity for destruction becomes. Psychoanalysis tends to view the concept of "coping" as repression by another name, and when the mental health system helped Emma "cope" with her behaviors, it inadvertently created yet another layer of repression. I believed the best way to help Emma was to encourage her to give voice to that which she had worked to silence.

As our sessions with one another added up and I gained a deeper understanding of the significant relationships in her life, it became apparent that Emma hated any display of aggression. Whenever she described expressions of anger or yelling, Emma had an almost emotional-allergic reaction, her cheeks flushing and her eyes welling with tears. When Emma talked about emotionally charged interactions with others, usually her parents or siblings, the same physical response appeared as she struggled to silence and control her own feelings of aggression.

I began to form a picture of Emma as a child, one where her inevitable expressions of childhood aggression were met with extreme disapproval. Her exhausted parents, caring for two other needy children, relied on Emma to behave in a more emotionally regulated way than she would have been able as a young girl. As the young girl grew into an adolescent, her aggression saturated the ground of her unconscious and threatened to overflow. To let aggression flow toward others was simply too anxiety-producing, and so Emma directed the flow toward her own body. This expression of aggression directed toward the self was remarkably effective at giving Emma what she unconsciously desired. At the most basic level, Emma's self-injury allowed her to express built-up aggression, but the cutting was working much harder on behalf of her unconscious. Specifically, when her parents, siblings, and teachers saw Emma's self-inflected injuries, they reacted in two ways: first, they lavished her with the attention she craved. Additionally, afraid for her safety, they stopped directing frustration (i.e., aggression) toward Emma, treating her gingerly instead. Emma had unconsciously discovered her Swiss army knife in cutting, a single tool that met multiple, powerful unconscious needs.

Transference

When Emma and I started our work together, she transferred the disapproving responses others exhibited in reaction to her self-injury into the therapeutic relationship we were forming. Before we met, Emma had experienced numerous mental health professionals, all of whom had attempted to fix, cure, and coach her to behave differently. Since these other professionals had been agents of the social normativity that Emma rebelled against, Emma suspected that I, too, would "look down" on her self-injurious behavior and the desires that animated it.

Given that Emma initially viewed me, along with the larger mental health apparatus, as agents of oppression, she did not enter therapy seeing me as someone useful to her. Early in the treatment, she parroted phrases she had been taught during several stays in inpatient and outpatient behavioral health units, such as "I used my coping skills today." When Emma used language such as this, I typically responded with one-word questions: "Coping?" Without communicating my own judgments about these terms, my one-word responses were an invitation to Emma to say more about what the words meant to her (Fink, 1999).

Other times, Emma made provocative statements like, "I'm a stupid piece of shit who should just die." When presented with bold statements like this, the clinician is tempted to provide the reassurance and placation the patient appears to be seeking: *You're not! You have so much to live for. Just look at your wonderful life.* However, based on our work together, I knew that in addition to reassurance, Emma desperately wanted (and simultaneously feared) to be understood and to understand her own intense emotions. Before responding, I decided to invite Emma to take a small step toward deepening her own understanding of her self. Emma had spent her life, as we all do, subject to the approval and disapproval of society, her parents, and other authority figures in her life. Over time, she internalized these attitudes, gave birth to her own internal authority figure and began to police herself according to them.

Instead of telling her what I thought, I created a space for Emma to project. In other words, I invited her to apply a problematic part of herself (in this case, an unreconciled authority figure) to me, thereby allowing her to more comfortably reveal a belief she didn't know she held: "Emma, I'm curious what you think *I'm* thinking, having heard what you just said?"

Using this technique revealed that Emma assumed I was judging her, thought she was overreacting, or that she should find "better" ways of dealing with her emotional turmoil—all attitudes she had internalized as a child growing up in a household where she was expected to regulate her emotions beyond her capacity.

As Emma began to experience our therapeutic work together as different from her previous interactions with mental health professionals, I sensed the beginning of a transference, the development of a belief—a fantasy—that the therapist has the knowledge, skills, and answers to cure. It's important to remember how anxiety-producing good therapy can be, to sit in an office and display the parts of one's self believed to be flawed and ugly, to speak openly about one's seemingly unforgivable desires. The transference fantasy allows the patient to keep anxiety at a manageable distance. Through the psychoanalytic process, the patient realizes that while the fantasy that a therapist (or parent, romantic partner, etc.) can provide what's missing (e.g., a cure, unconditional approval, etc.), affords him a sense of safety and comfort, that comfort, like the fantasy, is not real. In other words, he recognizes that the safety of the cure provided by the fantasy is unattainable. Eventually, the patient accepts that no amount of fortification will create a truly safe life, and neither can he fully protect himself from that which he fears most: his desires. Ultimately, I would look for signs that Emma was ready to divest from the fantasy that I wielded the power to cure, and would come to view curative power as an illusion.

One day, after I felt I had a firmer grasp on the transference, Emma told me she had hidden multiple razors at home and school. I responded by saying, "Of course you did. That makes sense." Emma asked if I was going to make her tell me where the razors were. "I don't really see how that would be useful," I replied. This answer surprised Emma, and she asked me if I was violating some sort of ethical injunction by not demanding she reveals the hiding places. I thought for a moment and then said, "Emma, you're smart. You have a car, you have a credit card, and there's a Walgreens about 5 min away. Even if you tell me where your razors are, or your mom finds them, you can always get more. If I followed you around all the time, I might be able to 'keep you safe' but I'm not going to do that...no one is." Emma was silent. I continued, "I don't know if you like hearing this or not, Emma. I'm not going to keep you safe from your desire to cut yourself. I can't do that. No one can do that. Except maybe you." After this interaction, our real work together started.

The Re-description

One day, after more than a year of sessions, usually two times per week, Emma was crying in my office. "I don't understand why *I want to cut,*" she said. This marked a change from previous statements: "I don't want to cut anymore, but I can't stop." Or, "I don't know why I keep cutting." The fact she said *I want* struck me as significant.

Although a small difference in Emma's normal speech, it showed that she had begun to recognize the presence of her own desire in her actions. With this signal, I could see Emma balanced on the *very edge of knowing*. Emma's repressed desires were just below the surface and with the right verbal intervention, she might be able to realize something significant. I decided to offer re-description, the technique whereby the therapist describes the patient's drives and unconscious motives in a way that allows the patient to consume the information and see his behavior through a new lens. Over the course of treatment, Emma and I had unearthed a variety of bones in the form of her negations, projections and a variety of other interactions, and I felt I now possessed enough bones to construct and offer her a skeleton of her repressed desires and the repetition they manifested in her life.

I began to re-describe what Emma had told me many times, in many ways: "It makes sense that you would want to cut yourself. You tried to tell your parents, the teachers, the social worker, how much pain you were in. They said they understood, but they clearly didn't. If they had understood, they would have said something other than 'You're our strong one, Em!' They failed to see. You needed them to really see something you didn't know how to tell them, and when you showed them cuts, they *almost* understood. You don't want to cut yourself. You want all of us to convince you that we know *how much* you need what you can't find, and how needing what you can't find hurts you."

After I said this, we were both silent. Emma cried, but did not speak. At the end of the session, she thanked me and I told her I would see her again later that week. Shortly after this point, the cutting diminished and eventually came to a complete stop. Several months later, Emma told her that she had cut herself again, and showed me a scratch on her upper shoulder. The other cuts had been deeper and performed on her wrists.

Cultural Considerations

When I consider the culture that Emma was most immersed within the usually suspects of race, socioeconomic class, gender, politics, and religion do not seem as important as another cultural group—the culture of adolescent misfits and outcasts, what Fisher (2017) called the weird and the eerie. Writing about this culture, Fisher states, "What the weird and the eerie have in common is a preoccupation with the strange. The strange—not the horrific. The allure that the weird and the eerie possess [has] to do with a fascination for the outside, for that which lies beyond standard perception, cognition and experience (p. 8)." When I read the description that Fisher wrote it seemed to be a good fit for Emma, a teenaged girl who had discovered an anti-culture of the outside that was dramatically different from the culture of the inside.

To belong in this anti-culture, Emma had to render herself strange in comparison to the people she believed to be inside the protective walls of normativity. Being part of this culture accounts for Emma's overt displays of non-conformity through style choices, such as making her hair purple and wearing "punk-rock" leather jackets and boots with metal spikes pointed out toward the world she believed had rejected her attempts to join it. Emma's most powerful way of rendering herself strange was through her self-injury. Consciously, Emma desired to scare the "normies," which was Emma's word for people who did not belong to her anti-culture, by being weird and eerie. However, as Fisher points out, Emma's unconscious desire might best be described as a desire to be outside. Why would her unconscious desire be to be on the outside? Could it be that Emma secretly desired to be on the inside? I believe that Winnicott's idea that it is a joy to be hidden, and a disaster not to be found provide an explanation; when we are hidden outside, maybe someone will come looking for us (Phillips, 1989). Emma desired, more than anything, to be important enough to get someone to enter the weird and the eerie outside and find her there.

Conclusion

The application of psychoanalytic principles has often been described as more of an art than a science. My hope is that through this chapter, I've presented psychoanalytic ideas as a series of potential starting points and signposts that clinicians might make use of as they begin their own journey deeper into the landscape of psychoanalytic theory. Some readers will have found the free-range style of applying psychoanalytic ideas to be invigorating and possibly inspirational, while others may have found the lack of a clear map to be frustrating. If concepts in this chapter resonated with you, I hope you'll further explore and experiment with the brushstrokes and rich colors of this practice. However, if your imagination *wasn't* sparked by the contents of this chapter, I encourage you to look to other bodies of theory that are more to your liking. Far too often when clinicians invest their time and energy into a theory that isn't a fit for them, they attempt to foist the theory upon others—often, students and even patients—regardless of how well it fits. Nothing could be further from the psychoanalytic cause than to attempt to force or manipulate those who do not desire it to take it up.

Discussion Questions

1. How does the way psychoanalytic idea are presented here compare with your prior exposure to these concepts?
2. In this chapter, the idea of the drives is re-described. Rather than being simply about sex and aggression, it is suggested that drives can be understood as a desire for pleasure and a desire to master our self, others, and our environment. What do you make of this re-description?
3. When people are first exposed to psychoanalytic ideas, they can be somewhat taken aback by the idea that we are strangers to ourselves, that our carefully

constructed identities cover over a deeper unconscious that we can't ever completely know. What is your reaction to the psychoanalytic claim that we will always be mysteries to ourselves?

4. What did you notice the most about the therapeutic technique, as it was described in this chapter?
5. Often times, clinicians believe it is their responsibility to keep a patient safe from themselves. This chapter states that this is not possible. Do you agree or disagree with this claim? Why do you agree or disagree?
6. The idea of negations is used in the application section of this chapter. When you try to listen to yourself and others use negations what do you hear?
7. Would you refer a patient to someone who practices in the way described in this chapter? Why or why not?

Acknowledgments I would like to thank the editors of this volume for providing me with an opportunity to write about something that matters to me, and my wonderful partner, Tracy, who provided me with generous feedback on the words I wrote. And, of course, I would also like to thank Emma, who taught me so much.

References

Fink, B. (1999). *A clinical introduction to Lacanian psychoanalysis: Theory and technique.* Cambridge, MA: Harvard University Press.

Fink, B. (2011). *Fundamentals of psychoanalytic technique: A Lacanian approach for practitioners.* New York, NY: Norton.

Fink, B. (2017). *A clinical introduction to Freud: Techniques for everyday practice.* New York: Norton.

Fisher, M. (2017). *The weird and the eerie.* London, UK: Repeater Books.

Freud, S. (1912). The dynamics of transference. Strachey, J. (1958). *The Standard Edition of the Complete Psychological Works of Sigmund Freud, Volume XII (1911–1913): The Case of Schreber, Papers on Technique and Other Works.* [Electronic version]. Retrieved from PEP Archive database. http://search.ebscohost.com/login.aspx?direct=true&AuthType=ip,shib,cookie,url&db=pph&AN=SE.012.0097A&site=ehost-live

Freud, S. (1925). Negation. The standard edition of the complete psychological works of sigmund freud, Volume XIX (1923–1925): The ego and the id and other works, pp. 233–240.

Freud, S. (1989). *Introductory lectures on psycho-analysis.* New York, NY: Norton.

Freud, S. (1990a). *Beyond the pleasure principle.* New York, NY: W.W. Norton & Co.

Freud, S. (1990b). *Five lectures on psycho-analysis.* New York, NY: Norton.

Freud, S., & Breuer, J. (2004). *Studies on hysteria.* New York NY: Penguin.

Lacan, J. (1953/2013). *The Seminar, Book I: Freud's papers on technique, 1953–1954.* (Trans: J. Forrester). New York: Norton.

Lacan, J. (1959/1997). *The Seminar, Book VII: The ethics of psychoanalysis, 1959–1960.* (Trans: D. Porter). New York: Norton.

Lacan, J. (1964/1998). *The Seminar, Book XI: The four fundamental concepts of psychoanalysis, 1964–1965.* (Trans: A. Sheridan). New York: Norton.

Laplanche, J. (2011). *Freud and the sexual.* New York, NY: The Unconscious in Translation.

Lear, J. (2005). *Freud.* New York, NY: Routledge.

McGowan, T. (2016). *Capitalism and desire: The psychic cost of free markets.* New York: Columbia University Press.

Phillips, A. (1989). *Winnicott*. Cambridge, MA: Harvard University Press.

Phillips, A. (2009). *Promises promises: Essays on psychoanalysis and literature*. New York: Basic Books.

Phillips, A. (2014). *Becoming Freud: The making of a psychoanalyst*. New Haven CT: Yale University Press.

Ruti, M. (2012). *The singularity of being: Lacan and the immortal within*. Fordham: Fordham University Press.

Ruti, M. (2013). *The call of character: Living a life worth living*. New York: Columbia University Press.

Svolos, T. (2018). *Twenty-first century psychoanalysis*. New York, NY: Routledge.

Zupančič, A. (2017). *What is sex? (Short circuits)*. Cambridge, MA: MIT Press.

Chapter 6
Person-Centered Therapy: The Case of Tommy

Ann F. Trettin

Introduction to the Person-Centered Approach

History and Theory Development

Grounded in humanistic psychology, person-centered therapy was developed during the 1940s and 1950s as an alternative to the behavioral and psychodynamic forms of treatment that dominated the field at the time. Carl Rogers, Abraham Maslow, and Rollo May were motivated by their concern about the devaluing of the person in therapies where the clinician was positioned in the role of expert. Although the client set treatment goals and had the ultimate responsibility to achieve behavioral change, it was also true that the client was encouraged to follow the lead of the clinician in these existing therapies (Bankart, 1997; Merrill, 2013).

In the early 1940s, Rogers credited others for their work in developing a new approach to psychotherapy, but he was really the first to clearly articulate a hypothesis about human growth and personality change that was radically different from the other commonly used approaches of the time (Kirschenbaum, 2004). Rogers theorized that clients have within themselves important capabilities including the capacity to understand the aspects of life that are causing distress and the ability to reorganize the self in the direction of self-actualization in such a way as to increase internal comfort. Therefore, the function of the clinician is to create a space where these strengths become apparent to clients, leading to the effective use of these strengths (Clay, 2002; Maslow, 1968; Rogers, 1950). He described this clinical work as *nondirective counseling.*

Distinctly different from the directive and interpretive approaches of the time, Rogers chose to minimize the power of the therapist and instead reinforce the inherent power of the client. He saw the clinician's role as helping the client clarify

A. F. Trettin (✉)
Trettin Play Therapy Center, Toledo, OH, USA

© Springer Nature Switzerland AG 2021
R. P. Dealey, M. R. Evans (eds.), *Discovering Theory in Clinical Practice*,
https://doi.org/10.1007/978-3-030-57310-2_6

feelings with the goal of improving self-concept (Bozarth, Zimring, & Tausch, 2002). This nondirective therapeutic relationship included two experts, the clinician as expert of the theories and techniques of therapy, and the client as the expert of self (Ackerman, 2020).

Rogers created this nondirective therapeutic space by totally avoiding the use of questions, persuasion, diagnosis, interpretation, suggestions, advice-giving, or other directive techniques. In addition, he noted that diagnostic concepts and procedures were often inadequate, reflected prejudice, and were sometimes misused by clinicians. Instead, Rogers' techniques were mainly the use of reflection and clarification of the clients' verbal and nonverbal communication. This acceptance and reflection of feelings created the safe space for deeper exploration by mirroring the client's own experience, leading to increased insight and positive action (Corey, 2009; Kirschenbaum, 2004).

During the 1950s, Rogers renamed his approach *client-centered therapy*. He did so to emphasize the lived experience of the client rather than the nondirective methods used by the therapist. During this time period, Rogers shifted from the clarification of the client's feelings to a focus on the client's internal frame of reference. Rogers recognized that the essential motivator that facilitates change occurs within the client and is mobilized by the warmth and acceptance of the person-centered therapist (Bohart & Watson, 2020; Seligman, 2006). During this time, he also conducted extensive research that provided strong evidence for the value of the therapeutic relationship and the client's resourcefulness as the foundation for successful therapy (Bozarth et al., 2002; Corey, 2009).

The third stage of development, which began in the late 1950s addressed the necessary and sufficient conditions for therapy. Rogers described the process of "becoming one's experience" as an openness to and trust in one's experience, an internal locus of evaluation, and the willingness to be in the process (Rogers, 1961). His research focused on the core conditions that he found necessary for successful therapy. The therapist's attitude and empathic understanding of the client and the therapist's genuineness and nonjudgmental stance were all found to be essential to a positive therapeutic outcome (Bozarth et al., 2002).

Key Terms and Concepts

The person-centered therapeutic process incorporates the concepts of meaning, values, freedom, tragedy, personal responsibility, human potential, spirituality, and self-actualization into its holistic approach to human existence (Aanstoos, Serlin, & Greening, 2000). Recognizing the applicability of the client-centered approach, Rogers and his colleagues began using a broader term, *person-centered,* to describe their work. This term refers to a theoretical view of the nature of human beings and their interactions, and to a philosophy of how to relate to human beings in growth-producing ways, both inside and outside of psychotherapy (Bohart & Watson, 2020; Kirschenbaum, 2004).

Person-Centered Process

During his many years of professional practice, Rogers noticed commonalities in the process of person-centered therapeutic relationships. These common elements include two persons coming into psychological contact, the client, in a state of incongruence who is vulnerable and anxious, and the clinician who is congruent, meaning real and genuine. The clinician then demonstrates unconditional positive regard for the client and experiences an empathic understanding of the client's internal frame of reference. The clinician then works to communicate this experience to the client (Cain, 2010).

Clinical Goals

Although the specific goals of person-centered therapy depend on the client, there are a few common overarching goals for person-centered work that are broad in nature and include the following:

- To facilitate the client's trust and ability to be in the present moment; this allows the client to be honest in the process without feeling judged by the clinician.
- To promote the client's self-awareness and self-esteem.
- To empower the client to change.
- To encourage congruence in the client's behavior and feelings.
- To help clients gain the ability to manage their lives and become self-actualized (Seligman, 2006).

Qualities of the Clinician

Rogers identified three crucial therapist qualities. *Unconditional positive regard* is the clinician's acceptance of the client for who they are. The clinician provides care, refrains from judging the client, and is a source of complete acceptance and support. This does not mean that the clinician agrees with everything that the client says or does. Rather, the client is seen as doing their best. The clinician expresses concern rather than disagreement. This quality facilitates the change process by demonstrating acceptance. *Genuineness* refers to the therapist's ability to feel comfortable sharing his or her own feelings with the client. This quality contributes to an open therapeutic relationship, demonstrates a model of good communication, and gives permission for the client to be vulnerable in the therapeutic space. *Empathic understanding* is experienced by the client when the therapist acts as a mirror of the client's thoughts and feelings by reflecting them back through the use of tracking and reflective statements. This provides the therapeutic interaction that helps the client increase self-awareness and understanding (Ackerman, 2020; Seligman, 2006).

Link Between Person-centered Approach and Child-Centered Play Therapy

Although Carl Rogers is mostly credited for his work with adults, he began his career, from 1928 through 1940, at the Child Study Department of the Society for the Prevention of Cruelty to Children. During this time, he wrote his book, *The Clinical Treatment of the Problem Child,* one of his first writings related to nondirective techniques intended to be used with children.

Virginia Axline, widely recognized as the originator of nondirective play therapy, was strongly influenced by the work of Carl Rogers. Axline adapted his approach to honor play rather than speech as the child's natural medium of expression (Goicoecha & Fitzpatrick, 2019). In turn, Garry Landreth applied Axline's basic principles of play therapy to his child-centered work in the playroom. Landreth (2012) defined client-centered play therapy (CCPT) as a comprehensive therapeutic system grounded in the belief that children are resilient and have an innate tendency to grow and develop in a self-directed manner. CCPT is developmentally appropriate for children from 3 to 10 years of age, as children communicate best through play (Axline, 1947; Landreth, 2012). In CCPT, the therapist does not direct the therapy or aim to change the child. The therapist avoids imposing the adult's agenda on the child. Instead, the therapist attempts to understand the child and accept the child exactly as he or she is (Goicoecha & Fitzpatrick, 2019).

Child-centered play therapists ground their limit-setting responsibilities in Roger's conditions for personality change. Congruence, unconditional positive regard, and empathic understanding are attitudinal expressions that promote a nonthreatening environment. Limits allow the therapist to maintain psychological contact while setting a limit on the behavior that is not safe in the playroom. At the same time, these limits allow the therapist to acknowledge the child's anxiety or vulnerability (incongruences) and promote the child's perception of empathy and acceptance in the relationship (Ray, 2011). Axline (1947) states that limits in the playroom contribute to a sense of physical and emotional security and she emphasized maintaining empathy and unconditional positive regard when setting these limits.

Cultural Considerations of Child-Centered Play Therapy

Because CCPT is a relationship-based intervention, it is ideal when working with children who have experienced adverse childhood experiences. Post, Phipps, Camp, and Grybush (2019) conducted a review of the literature that examined the impact of CCPT conducted with marginalized children. This review of the meta-analyses revealed that nondirective approaches had larger effect sizes than directive approaches (Bratton, Ray, Rhine, & Jones, 2005) and that non-Caucasian children demonstrated greater benefit from nondirective therapy than Caucasian children (Lin & Bratton, 2015).

Introduction to the Case of Tommy

Tommy is an 8-year-old Caucasian male, short and stocky in stature, who appears physically strong and intellectually advanced for a child of his chronological age. (All names and identifiers have been changed to protect the client's confidentiality.) I began working with Tommy in child-centered play therapy when he was 7 years old. He was referred to the community mental health center for treatment to address his history of sexual abuse, neglect, and loss. Tommy was not only grieving for his biological family and the loss of his powerful role within that family system, but also for his first pre-adoptive family, a placement that abruptly ended after several months. Together with his younger sisters, Tommy had successfully transitioned to his new home and begun to build meaningful relationships there with family, friends, classmates, and his clinician when this placement fell through because of extended family complications unrelated to the children. Tommy's new placement, a significant distance from his previous home, necessitated a change in both his school and community mental health settings. As a result, Tommy experienced more loss, that of his friends, classmates, and the therapeutic connection that he had established with his clinician.

Tommy and his younger sisters were removed from his birth parents' home when he was 6 years old, after significant and ongoing abuse and neglect were substantiated by the child welfare system. Both of Tommy's birth parents had a history of developmental delays and substance use problems. They were unable to meet the care and nurturance needs of the children or provide safety and protection. As a result, from a very early age Tommy assumed a leadership role as a parent and caregiver within his birth family system. Tommy described feeling responsible for not only the care of his younger sisters, but also of his parents. Upon his placement in a second pre-adoptive home, Tommy's need to care for his younger sisters in a parental manner seemed to intensify. Although his new pre-adoptive parents understood the birth family dynamic, they often framed Tommy's parentified behaviors as willful disobedience and therefore responded with a behavioral consequence. The pre-adoptive parents had a long history of providing excellent care for foster children. They successfully completed extensive training about family systems, attachment issues, and the child's need for power and control, but the degree to which they understood Tommy's behavior appeared to be more at an intellectual rather than insightful level. The structure and predictability of the home environment that the parents provided for the children was essential, meaningful and loving and yet it was difficult for them to see Tommy's need to take care of his sisters as a manifestation of the loss of his previous family role, one reminiscent of his birth family, and therefore difficult to relinquish. Although the parents' goal was to help Tommy successfully transition to his new family as quickly as possible, the parent–child interaction was sometimes experienced by the child as minimizing his loss and the depth of his grief. Instead of facilitating growth and healing, it appeared that their somewhat authoritarian parenting style actually exacerbated Tommy's sense of loss and complicated the attachment process.

Other family members living in this new placement included the parents' two biological children, both in high school, an adopted son, also 7 years old, and a foster child infant. Tommy appeared to revere his older siblings, but was most often distant, withdrawn, and irritable with his parents. His relationship with his younger brother was described as competitive, often adversarial, and with significant sibling conflict.

Theoretical Integration

To illustrate the impact of a nondirective stance when working with hurt children and then to compare this approach with more direct interventions, examples from Tommy's therapy sessions are organized here by approach style.

Use of Person-Centered Creative Arts Therapy

Tommy often chose creative expression to reach for insights and work through his loss. Early in his therapy with me (session 4), Tommy used the process of making a necklace to openly discuss his mixed loyalties. As he created the jewelry, he spoke of his birth mother, and how much he missed her and wanted to give her the jewelry. With a confused facial expression, he then said that he would give the necklace to Mary, his adoptive mother, but then later decided to leave the item in the playroom. Reflective statements were used throughout this creative process and were focused on Tommy's ambivalent feelings and reluctance to let go of his hope for reunification. He responded to these reflections with an increase in verbal interaction. He continued with creative options in the playroom by drawing a picture while providing his own verbal narrative. He began by stating that the characters in the drawing were in danger but were hopeful to be rescued. Later, there were elements of playfulness and nurturing in his story, followed by a sense of freedom. Tommy chose to take this artwork home. However, he sealed the art in an envelope and slid it into his coat pocket before leaving the room.

I believe that this art piece and narrative depicted some acknowledgment of Tommy and his sisters' abusive history as well as his understanding and experience that they are all now free from exposure to harm. On the other hand, that Tommy chose to seal his artwork in an envelope and hide it in his coat pocket before leaving the playroom, as well as leaving the necklace behind, indicated a reluctance to share these insights with anyone else at this time. Rather than share these interpretations, which would reflect a psychodynamic approach, I instead mirrored the behaviors and feelings back to Tommy for his consideration, a child-centered response.

Use of Child-Centered Play Therapy (CCPT)

Throughout Tommy's CCPT sessions, he chose a large, rather gruff looking playroom character who represented the judge that made decisions regarding his placement and adoption. Tommy would often verbally express his strong feelings to this character. Although Tommy rarely had the opportunity to talk directly to the judge overseeing his case in real life, he could "talk" to him every week in the playroom, if that is what he needed to do. There were no limits regarding the use of language or decibel level in the playroom. Tommy would yell, "you stole me from somebody" and "my heart is hurt forever" and, in the child-centered playroom, that was all right.

As a prelude to expressing himself through play, Tommy began one particular play therapy (session 10) by summarizing a session with his previous clinician. He described aggressively engaging in intrusive play that appeared to be a powerful therapeutic experience and reflective of past abuse. He looked for my reaction to this graphic description. The content, emotions, and level of intensity were reflected back to him, Rogers' mirroring technique, and Tommy then began to add to his story with an in-depth play narrative in the moment. He used the playroom lighting and a flashlight in a way that projected a large and powerful image of himself against the wall. He then set up a very small space in the corner of the playroom and instructed that I join him there. At this time, my reflections focused on Tommy's need to feel in control, the value of a safe space to tell his story, and on the strength and safety of our therapeutic relationship. In silence, Tommy appeared to be intently thinking for a few seconds and then stated that the space where we sat together is his mother's grave, a place where he can think about her and it is all right. I then mirrored the importance of a safe place to think about and mourn the loss of his birth mother. Tommy nodded his head in agreement and continued to sit in contemplation for a while. He then used the flashlight to focus in on two drawings from one of his earlier sessions that were hanging on the wall across the room. The first, a picture of a broken heart, and the other, a picture of a family, hung side-by-side. He spoke of his birth mother as he began slowly, but then gradually escalating to a rapid pace, moving the flashlight's beam from one picture to the other. He verbalized both his sorrow related to the loss of his mother and some gratefulness for the support of his adoptive family. As he continued to verbally share his complex feelings and mixed loyalties, the beam of the flashlight became a blur between the two images on the wall. Tommy then began to cry aloud that, as he becomes more and more a member of his new family, he is very afraid that he will forget his birth mother. His fears were again mirrored back to him. Through the use of these reflective statements, Tommy experienced validation, felt understood, and this seemed to have a soothing effect. We continued to sit at his "mother's grave" while Tommy shared some good memories of his early childhood, such as going fishing. He shared regretting that he does not know where his fishing pole is right now. I provided active listening and reflective statements about his positive recollections. To include that not knowing where his fishing pole is now might mean that he has no more access to good times with his birth family would have been an interpretation, again more aligned with a psychodynamic rather than a child-centered approach. Instead, I reflected back Tommy's statement for his own consideration and interpretation.

Tommy then returned to the play narrative and moved to the center of the room. Although not verbalized as such, he seemed to be moving on to another chapter of his story. I used a tracking statement at this point, "now you are moving to the center of your playroom." Tommy continued to use the control of the lighting, but this time it seemed to depict an ominous rather than sorrowful tone. He placed a character often used by children to depict a person in power, a large stuffed "monster," in the center of the room. He then aggressively took out his anger on this "bad guy" while listing losses and sharing pain. He verbalized his grief for the loss of his parents and an uncle who committed suicide, blaming these losses on whomever the playroom character represented. He then continued to punch at the character while he explicitly described an incident of sexual abuse. He expressed feeling like he will "never be able to get over it." Again, rather than interpret the meaning of his play, these powerful images and strong feelings were validated and reflected back to Tommy. As this session ended, he walked from the room, expressing through his posture, body language, and facial expression a sense of feeling understood, in control and empowered. This is an example of a child taking the lead to work through his grief and loss, in the manner of his own choosing, in the safety of his playroom. He did not require an interpretation of his play to move toward healing. He experienced it at his own direction. His resilience and strength were mirrored back to him through tracking and reflective statements. That is all he needed from the therapist.

Direct Techniques

I believe that Tommy engaged best in his therapy when Rogers' nondirective techniques were used. However, as time passed, other approaches were integrated into his care, often to address behavioral reports from the home or school environment. For example, at one point (session 28), some of Glasser's reality therapy concepts were incorporated into our discussion, that of Tommy's unfulfilled needs for power, love, and belonging (Glasser, 1998). Although not confrontational, this was a very direct conversation shared between Tommy and myself. In hindsight, this discussion was clearly too direct, as Tommy's behavioral response was to cover his face and crawl under a chair. His reaction reinforced the value of child-centered interaction. I quickly returned to a nondirective style with the use of tracking statements to describe Tommy's behavior and allowed him the space to verbalize his thoughts and feelings in the moment. He then came out from under the chair, but rather than share his distress through a nondirective play narrative, he maintained a direct approach and verbally described some parent/child interaction that he witnessed in the waiting area that triggered his memory of when he was removed from his parents' home. He described in detail how another family member used force to attempt to "rescue" Tommy and his sisters from the police officer and child welfare worker. Tommy then framed his family member's behavior as a loving act with the intention of protecting the children rather than aggressive behavior or breaking of the rules. After his feelings were validated, we continued in direct discussion about how this memory influences Tommy's current level of aggressiveness and behavioral choices when he is feeling threatened. This session provides an example of integrating both direct and nondirective responses.

Cultural Considerations of Developmental Stage

Childhood has its own distinct culture. If childhood is a subculture, then the dominant culture is that of adulthood. The child-centered play therapist represents the culture of adulthood to the child and often serves as the translator between these two cultures when interacting with parents (Mullen & Rickli, 2014). I often found this to be the case as I served as Tommy's voice with his adoptive mother. Informed by the vivid narratives Tommy shared in the safe space of the playroom, I was able to offer Mary alternative explanations for Tommy's behavioral choices beyond that of willful disobedience. Linked to his history and framed as working through the grieving process, Mary gradually increased her understanding of Tommy. Likewise, within the nondirective relationship that Tommy and I shared with each other, I could translate Mary's reasonable behavioral expectations to him in a manner that increased his understanding of the value of the healthy family dynamics present in his new home.

Termination

After nearly 2 years of outpatient care, Tommy's parents felt that he had gained as much as he could from the process. Tommy shared a differing perspective, expressing anger over ending another meaningful relationship in his life. We used our last few sessions together to celebrate Tommy's increased ability to better cope with loss. He was involved and receptive to the therapeutic growth that was reflected back to him.

Cultural Considerations

In general, being present in the moment and respecting the client's values, hallmarks of Rogers' person-centered approach, are essential in therapy with culturally diverse clients (Corey, 2009). However, there are shortcomings from a diversity perspective. For example, some clients who seek services at community mental health centers may expect more structure than the person-centered approach provides. In addition, it may be difficult to translate Rogers' core therapeutic conditions into practice with specific cultures. For some clients, the most culturally sensitive way to express empathy would require a respect for the need for distance (Bohart & Greenberg, 1997). In other cultures that stress the common good, the focus on the development of personal growth may be viewed as selfishness (Cain, 2010). But because the clinician works with the client in an interested, accepting, and open manner, the person-centered philosophy is particularly useful when working with clients who have been marginalized (Bohart & Watson, 2020).

In his essay, *Social Implications,* Rogers shared his vision of applying person-centered approaches to influence larger systems, such as education and medicine. He saw the potential for his methods to facilitate communication between opposing groups involved in political and international conflicts. During the last decade of his life, he facilitated cross-cultural conferences. He saw that acceptance of the whole person in conflicting groups led to "constructive awareness and positive, tension-reducing action" (Kirschenbaum & Land Henderson, 1989. p. 434) and applied his person-centered approach to training policymakers. His efforts were directed toward the reduction of interracial tension (Corey, 2009), and provided a meaningful contribution to exposing white privilege and addressing racial and ethnic disparities in access to resources.

Strengths and Weaknesses

Research findings validate several strengths of the person-centered approach. This therapy offers an optimistic perspective and provides a positive experience when the focus is on clients and their problems. Clients feel that they can express themselves more fully when they are heard by the clinician without judgment and they feel empowered as they are responsible to make decisions for themselves within the therapeutic process (Seligman, 2006). Some weaknesses of this approach include the possibility that clinicians might provide support but without challenging the client to make behavioral change. The clinician's nondirective language may be experienced by the client as passive, weakening the clinical process. In addition, the person-centered approach is not appropriate for those who are not motivated to change and may not be useful when working with clients with significant psychopathology. This approach may also lack the specific techniques that help clients solve their own problems (Corey, 2009; Seligman, 2006).

Discussion Questions

1. What are some ways that a person-centered clinician who is working with children and families can provide parenting support and guidance in a manner that reflects the acceptance of the client as expert?

2. Some clinicians hold that the first priority of therapy for a client who has been sexually abused is to begin by working to resolve the trauma of abuse. In the case of Tommy, the child chose to work through complicated grief prior to processing his feelings related to past abuse. Using your understanding of person-centered concepts, how would you explain Tommy's priorities to the clinician who prioritizes addressing trauma issues?

3. When working with a child, consider how you will respectfully verbalize your informed consent process with the parents that includes your child-centered approach to avoid imposing the adult's agenda on the child's therapeutic process. What will this informed consent sound like?

4. How will you respond to a child who refuses to join you in the playroom with a statement that reflects your unconditional positive regard, acceptance, and respect?

5. How will you maintain a nondirective approach with a caregiver who asks you directly for some guidance and direction with parenting techniques?

References

Aanstoos, C., Serlin, I., & Greening, T. (2000). A history of division 32 (humanistic psychology) of the American Psychological Association. In D. Dewsbury (Ed.), *Unification through division: Histories of the divisions of the American Psychological Association* (Vol. V). Washington, DC: American Psychological Association.

Ackerman, C. E. (2020). *Client-centered therapy.* Retrieved from: https://positivepsychology.com/client-centered-therapy/.

Axline, V. (1947). *Play therapy.* New York, NY: Ballantine.

Bankart, C. P. (1997). *Talking cures: A history of Western and Eastern psychotherapies.* Pacific Grove, VA: Brooks/Cole.

Bohart, A. C., & Greenberg, L. S. (1997). Empathy and psychotherapy: An introductory overview. In A. C. Bohart & L. S. Greenberg (Eds.), *Empathy reconsidered: New directions in psychotherapy* (pp. 3–32). Washington, DC: American Psychological Association Press.

Bohart, A. C., & Watson, J. C. (2020). Chapter 7: Person-centered and emotion-focused psychotherapies. In S. B. Messer & N. J. Kaslow (Eds.), *Essential psychotherapies: Theory and practice* (4th ed., pp. 221–256). New York, NY: Guilford Press.

Bozarth, J. D., Zimring, F. M., & Tausch, R. (2002). Client-centered therapy: The evolution of a revolution. In D. J. Cain & J. Seeman (Eds.), *Humanistic psychotherapies: Handbook of research and practice* (pp. 147–188). Washington, DC: American Psychological Association.

Bratton, S., Ray, D., Rhine, T., & Jones, L. (2005). The efficacy of play therapy with children: A meta-analytic review of treatment outcomes. *Professional Psychology: Research and Practice, 36,* 376–390. https://doi.org/10.1037/0735-7028.36.4.376.

Cain, D. J. (2010). Defining characteristics, history, and evolution of humanistic psychotherapies. In D. J. Cain & J. Seeman (Eds.), *Humanistic psychotherapies: Handbook of research and practice* (pp. 3–54). Washington, DC: American Psychological Association.

Clay, R. A. (2002). A renaissance for humanistic psychology: The field explores new niches while building on its past. *American Psychological Association Monitor, 33*(8), 42.

Corey, C. (2009). *Theory and practice of counseling & psychotherapy* (7th ed.). Belmont, CA: Thomson Learning.

Goicoecha, J., & Fitzpatrick, T. (2019). To know or not to know: Empathic use of client background information in child-centered play therapy. *International Journal of Play Therapy, 28*(1), 22–33. https://doi.org/10.1037/pla0000087.

Glasser, W. (1998). Choice theory: A new psychology of personal freedom. New York, NY: Harper.

Kirschenbaum, H. (2004). Carl Rogers's life and work: An assessment on the 100th anniversary of his birth. *Journal of Counseling and Development, 82*, 116–124.

Kirschenbaum, H., & Land Henderson, V. (1989). *The Carl Rogers reader: Selections from the lifetime work of America's preeminent psychologist*. New York, NY: Houghton Mifflin Company.

Landreth, G. L. (2012). *Play therapy: The art of the relationship* (3rd ed.). New York, NY: Routledge.

Lin, D., & Bratton, S. (2015). A meta-analytic review of child centered play therapy approaches. *Journal of Counseling & Development, 93*, 45–58. https://doi.org/10.1002/j.1556-6676.2015.00180.x.

Maslow, A. H. (1968). *Toward a psychology of being*. New York, NY: Van Nostrand Reinhold.

Merrill, C. (2013). Reflections on humanistic psychology and the person-centered approach. *The Person-Centered Journal, 20*(1–2), 69–79.

Mullen, J. A., & Rickli, J. M. (2014). *Child-centered play therapy workbook: A self-directed guide for professionals*. Champaign, IL: Research Press Publishers.

Post, P. B., Phipps, C. B., Camp, A. C., & Grybush, A. L. (2019). Effectiveness of child-centered play therapy among marginalized children. *International Journal of Play Therapy, 28*(2), 88–97. https://doi.org/10.1037/pla0000096.

Ray, D. C. (2011). *Advanced play therapy: Essential conditions, knowledge, and skills for child practice*. New York, NY: Routledge.

Rogers, C. (1950). A current formulation of client-centered therapy. *Social Service Review, 24*, 442–450.

Rogers, C. (1961). *On becoming a person*. Boston, MA: Houghton Mifflin.

Seligman, L. (2006). *Theories of counseling and psychotherapy: Systems, strategies, and skills* (2nd ed.). Upper Saddle River, NJ: Pearson Education, Ltd..

Chapter 7
Cognitive Behavioral Therapy: The Case of Wally

Jessica D. Cless

Introduction to Cognitive Behavioral Therapy

Cognitive behavioral therapy (CBT) has long been argued to be the "gold standard" of psychotherapy models. It is the most researched therapy model (David, Cristea, & Hofmann, 2018), and has been shown to be an effective intervention for common problems such as anxiety, depression, and attention deficit hyperactivity disorder (Hans & Hiller, 2013; Hofmann et al. 2012; Manicavasgar, Parker, & Perich, 2011; Weiss et al., 2012). This model of therapy has been widely used to treat mental health concerns in adults as well as adolescents and children (Chiu et al., 2013; Spirito, Esposito-Smythers, Wolff, & Uhl, 2011). In its most simplified form, CBT is concerned with the relationship between a person's thoughts, feelings, and behaviors. This model of therapy is often credited to the work of Aaron Beck (Folsom et al. 2016), but stems from both behavioral and cognitive psychological theories.

The history of behavioral therapies can be traced back to the famous works of Ivan Pavlov, B. F. Skinner, and John Watson. The focus of this branch of therapy is to eliminate problematic behaviors and elicit desired behavioral outcomes using techniques born out of research on classical and operant conditioning. For example, operant conditioning systematically uses positive and negative reinforcements in order to promote changes in behavior. Early cognitive therapies were developed by influential psychologists such as Alfred Adler and Albert Ellis. Specifically, Ellis's Rational Emotive Behavior Therapy (REBT) is credited as an early form of CBT (David, Cotet, Matu, Mogoase, & Stefan, 2018). Cognitive therapies were founded on the premise that problems existed and were maintained in the realm of thought, but could be challenged and shifted.

Cognitive behavioral therapy is the result of a convergence between the previously described branches of cognitive and behavioral therapies. Aaron Beck, an

J. D. Cless (✉)
Family and Human Services, Washburn University, Topeka, KS, USA
e-mail: Jessica.Cless@washburn.edu

American psychiatrist originally trained in psychoanalysis, developed the practice of CBT in the 1960s.

Basics of CBT

Several key psychological concepts form the foundation of this therapeutic model.

Problem Maintenance

According to CBT, mental health problems occur due to the presence of maladaptive thoughts. These unhelpful thoughts, often termed to be "automatic thoughts," are believed to produce emotional distress and dysfunction in individuals (Beck, 1970). A person's automatic thoughts are seen as representative of their schemas, or core beliefs about themselves, others, and the world around them (Beck, Rush, Shaw, & Emery, 1979). At times, a person's schema, their perception of the world, may be distorted or irrational. The individual then experiences distress, as their perception of their surroundings often produces negative emotions and/or dysfunctional behaviors. Just as a person's attitude, thoughts, beliefs, and attributions are seen as crucial influences of problematic behavior, they are equally seen as influential tools that can be challenged and shifted in order to bring about healthy and preferred behaviors.

Change Mechanisms

The interconnectedness of thoughts, emotions, and behaviors lends itself nicely to the understanding of change according to CBT. When patterns of automatic thoughts and cognitive distortions are disrupted, more positive ways of thinking, interactional patterns, and behaviors can emerge. This is most often achieved through intentional and direct challenging of automatic or irrational thoughts and schemas in an effort to realign these with "reality" or replace them with more positive, preferred, and healthy alternatives (Beck, 1970; DeRubeis, Tang, & Beck, 2001). The goal of challenging these thoughts and schemas is to ultimately build an individual's capacity to have power over their own cognitions and effectively manage them in order to experience more positive emotions and behaviors. The therapy process often involves actively identifying the relationships between thoughts, emotions, and behaviors in order to bring awareness to problematic patterns and introduce new, more functional ways of being. Change is said to occur when a person successfully experiences new ways of thinking and new interactions.

Method and Interventions

Cognitive Restructuring

As a primary goal of CBT is to alter one's unhelpful thoughts, cognitive restructuring is a main method of intervention in which the therapist assists the client in learning to identify and challenge irrational or maladaptive thought patterns. By first gaining insight into one's schemas and automatic thoughts, these cognitive patterns are exposed and can be challenged using rational thoughts. For example, a client may find it distressing that they were not selected for a promotion at work. When thinking about their scenario, they may have the thought, "I didn't get the promotion because my boss doesn't think I do a good job." They may have feelings of inferiority or sadness as a result of this automatic thought and their appraisal of the situation as negative. Cognitive restructuring can occur as the therapist and client work together to rationalize this thought and belief about oneself by examining evidence that supports and doesn't support the thought. Assisting the client in actively challenging their automatic thoughts may decrease their feelings of distress surrounding the situation.

Downward Arrow Technique

While uncovering a person's underlying thoughts and beliefs about themselves and others is a necessary task in CBT, these are not always apparent to the client and/or the therapist. The downward arrow technique is a means of identifying a person's core beliefs by systematically identifying negative automatic thoughts (NATs) in a given situation. The therapist and client begin by examining a distressing situation and the associated cognitions that the client experiences. The therapist helps to elicit subsequent NATs by asking the client what it would mean if their thought was true and why it would be bothersome. This process continues until a core belief about oneself or the world is identified (Leahy, 2003). It should be noted that the identification of these beliefs is meant to be a first step in understanding a person's schema, and is a precursor to challenging unhelpful thoughts in order to promote the experience of more positive emotions.

Skill Building

As clients and therapists work together to understand how thoughts, emotions, and behaviors are interconnected, therapists often challenge clients to engage in new behaviors to disrupt problematic cycles. Skill building refers to a broad range of cognitive behavioral therapy interventions in which the client is assigned homework in order to practice new ways of being. This portion of therapy can be highly individualized and aimed toward problem solving to find relief for clients in especially distressing situations. A common goal in skill building in counseling is to assist the client in developing healthy coping strategies.

Thought Records

Examining a client's thoughts and emotions often occurs while they are in a therapy session, but there are also ways to prompt clients to reflect on these while outside of treatment. Therapists may ask clients to complete "thought records" outside of sessions. These are lists which often appear in table form in which clients record their thoughts that occur after a distressing situation, associated feelings, and evidence for and against negative or automatic thoughts. The purpose of these thought records is to assist the client in gaining an awareness of their thought patterns as well as prompt them to examine and shift their thoughts by introducing rationalization. Thought records have been shown to be helpful in assisting clients in shifting negative beliefs (McManus, Van Doorn, & Yiend, 2012).

Behavioral Experiments

As negative thoughts and emotions begin to shift as they are challenged, therapists may encourage their clients to engage in "behavioral experiments," defined as activities designed as "a means of checking the validity of thoughts, perceptions, and beliefs, and/or constructing new operating principles and beliefs" (Bennett-Levy et al., 2004, p. 11). Once again, the interconnectedness of thoughts, emotions, and behaviors is used in order to create positive change in the client. Encouraging clients to engage in behaviors that will result in more positive interactions to build and/or support healthy beliefs and schemas is meant to positively alter negative thoughts and emotions. Behavioral experiences have been shown to be effective for clients, specifically as it relates to shifting negative emotions (Bennett-Levy, 2003).

Introduction to the Case of Wally

All names and identifiers have been changed to protect the confidentiality of the client. Wally is a 62-year-old retired African American male. He has been living alone in his home since the death of his wife, Sondra, to whom he was married for 40 years. Recently, Wally's life has gone through several major transitions. Two years ago, he retired from his job, and Sondra, who had been terminally ill, passed away last year. Together, Wally and Sondra had two children: Sammy (age 39), who lives in another state, and Natasha (age 35), who lives locally. Since the passing of his wife, both of his children have encouraged him to consider moving to a retirement community as they say he needs to "get out more" and "see people," but Wally assures them each time that he could never be happy living anywhere other than his home.

Wally began receiving mental health counseling after his children expressed growing concerns about him being alone at home and its effect on his mental health. An in-home therapist began visiting him every 2 weeks in his home in order to discuss what his children referred to as "how to feel better and move on." Wally was reluctant to begin counseling but agreed that this would be better than having to move out of his family home.

Work History

Wally spent his working years as a warehouse laborer for a tire manufacturing plant. He secured this job after completing his high school diploma, and enjoyed working with his hands. He often worked long hours at the plant, and his job served as his main source of social engagement. His colleagues became his second family, and he had many men there whom he called his brothers. When he was 35 years old, he sustained an injury in the workplace that rendered him unable to continue performing physical labor at the plant. He was modestly compensated by the company due to this injury and was given the opportunity to continuing working as a supervisor instead. Wally describes this injury as a "major blow" to his self-worth, as he had always enjoyed feeling useful and strong. Nevertheless, he was grateful to be able to continue to work at a place where he felt valued and had a sense of community. Though he never attained a formal education beyond high school, he was a loyal and dedicated worker who moved up in the company and went on to manage the warehouse, which became a point of pride for him and gave him a sense of achievement that he reports people in his family had never had before. While he was working, Sondra worked in the home and took the primary role in raising the children, as Wally often worked long hours overseeing the warehouse and attending to the needs of his employees.

Family of Origin and Marital History

Wally grew up in what he calls a "traditional home" which instilled in him the value of family and hard work. He had a close relationship with his mother and had four brothers and sisters with whom he has little contact with at the present. Wally's father was drafted to serve in the Vietnam War, a prospect that the family saw as an opportunity to advance despite the dangers of serving in combat. His father worked as a mechanic prior to deployment, and upon returning home from the war, was "changed." Wally remembers that his father struggled with alcohol and seemed to turn to drinking to avoid distressing memories from the war. Even amidst the changing landscape of African American life amidst the Civil Rights movement, Wally's family struggled to find a sense of economic stability and family harmony.

Wally and Sondra were married in 1958, and had known each other from childhood. Growing up in the same neighborhood community, they shared many social connections, and even attended the same church. Having both been socioeconomically disadvantaged, they found comfort in spending time with friends and family. When they married, they had a shared vision of creating a stable life for their children that was free from the financial stress their own families faced. Their marriage definitely experienced rough patches over the years. At times, Wally believed that Sondra tended to be "too controlling" and demanded too much from him in the home despite his hard work at the warehouse. Despite these minor issues, they generally lived a peaceful life together. His family never went on expensive vacations or had the nicest things, but they were happy together and grateful for what they had.

Family Context

Both of Wally's children seemed to have a typical childhood. Though Wally was often away at work, he made an effort to have a positive relationship with his children and show them a good example of what a father should be. When Sammy reached his teenage years, he began to drink with his friends and sometimes skipped school. Wally, whose own father had a history of alcohol abuse, tended to be very strict with Sammy by requiring him to do extra labor around their home and attempting to restrict the amount of time he spent with his friends who he saw as bad influences on his son. Sondra tended to take a gentler approach, and expressed worries that Sammy was struggling to fit-in and just wanted to belong. Sammy was able to finish high school, but continued to struggle with alcohol on and off throughout his adulthood. He is currently out of state in a sober living facility following a recent stay at an inpatient rehabilitation center. Though Wally and Sammy do not often talk, Wally feels concern for his son and is sad that he can't do more to help him with his problems. In the past, Sammy has expressed feeling guilty that he hasn't lived up to his parents' expectations for him, and feels as though he needs to work on his own life before he can fully reengage with his family.

As an adolescent, Natasha never had any overt struggles in school or in her social life, instead playing the role of pleasing her parents with a desire to maintain a sense of peace in their household. She made plans to go to college and went on to successfully complete a business degree, the first in her family to do this. Currently, Natasha and her wife Annie own and manage a real estate firm and live on the opposite side of town but make time to visit Wally often. He is happy to see them when they visit, especially when they bring their 5-year-old son Camden, but he dreads when his daughter suggests that he needs to move. Natasha often expresses feeling responsible for her father, especially given that her mother has passed away and her brother is not able to help at this time. Wally feels loved by his daughter and appreciates her care and concern for his wellbeing; however, he also worries that he will become a burden to her.

Current Symptoms

Since he has been living alone, Wally often feels as though he has no motivation to do the things he used to enjoy. Having retired only 2 years ago at age 60, and experiencing the death of his wife the year later, he has experienced a lot of change in his life in a short amount of time. He used to make time to read the daily newspaper, go for a walk in his neighborhood, and make a trip to the grocery store each week. In the past few months, he finds himself lacking energy to do these things. Instead, he has developed a habit of sitting alone at home, occasionally turning on the television, and sometimes goes a few days without bathing or leaving the house. He is experiencing thoughts such as "Nothing I do matters anymore" and "Life is pointless." He does not feel a need to begin therapy and the thought of talking to someone else about his problems seems fairly daunting, but he is eager to appease his children and dreads that they will eventually see him as a burden.

Theoretical Integration

During the initial stage of therapy, the therapist gathered information about Wally including his personal and family history, his history of mental health treatment, and his perspective of why he was beginning treatment. The client reported no history of mental health treatment, and that he grew up with the idea that therapy was only for "crazy people" who "couldn't deal with life." In the initial session, Wally indicated that he had lived a "mostly happy life" until the recent passing of his wife combined with adjusting to retirement. The therapist spent a significant amount of time building a rapport with Wally and listening to his life story. Particular attention was paid to understanding the role of Wally's social and family relationships as well as the sense of identity that he found in doing his work at the tire plant. The therapist was careful to ask about and keep track of the various thoughts and emotions Wally shared about his life. Wally described that he was incredibly proud of the work that he had done to "pave a way to succeed" for himself and his family, contrasting his own experience with his perceived economic and social failures of his own home life.

When asked about how he was currently doing, Wally shared that "work was his life" and he felt "lost and unsure" of what to do in this next phase of his life without his job and without his wife by his side. The therapist normalized these feelings as understandable for a person who was grieving the losses of both a romantic partner and a career. Discussing grief as a normal process seemed to allow the client to talk more openly about his experiences. Though at first Wally shared that he was only participating in therapy to appease his children, he later admitted that he was feeling "not like myself anymore" and "very lonely." The therapist again validated these concerns and discussed Wally's daily routine as well as his goals and desires for his future. The client shared that his days seemed to blend together, and he had yet to find a routine without his wife or his job that felt normal to him. He described that he spent his days thinking about how things used to be, worrying about his future and the future of his children, and sometimes trying to distract himself by watching television. In his own words, "everything reminds me of how different my life has become." Though Wally initially struggled to articulate a specific goal, the therapist and client broadly determined that his overarching goal for therapy would be to develop a new sense of normalcy.

The therapist provided Wally with some direct psychoeducation in order to empower him to identify his own unhelpful patterns. Together, the therapist and Wally discussed how a person's thoughts can affect their feelings and behaviors. Using examples of thoughts that Wally had shared thus far in the therapy process, the therapist prompted Wally to explore how these thoughts have affected him in the past few years. Wally identified that these thoughts that he doesn't matter often produce feelings of loneliness and listlessness, which has led to behaviors of skipping meals, not engaging in grooming, and choosing to stay at home instead of taking the initiative to socialize with others. This collaborative psychoeducational process in therapy allowed Wally to gain insight into the underlying mechanism of his own experience. Wally acknowledged his understanding of this process, and an overt discussion of the connection between thoughts, emotions, and behaviors allowed the therapist and the client to directly target problematic parts of the process.

Over the course of therapy, the clinician worked together with Wally to identify maladaptive and automatic thoughts that seemed to cause him distress. Often, the therapist directly asked Wally how he was feeling and what thoughts were going through his head as they recalled times when he was experiencing a negative emotion. Wally shared that when he was home alone, he would often talk himself out of doing daily activities because "it never matters" anyway. The therapist challenged this notion that "nothing matters" in Wally's life by encouraging the client to discuss what matters to him. In this discussion, Wally mentioned that his children are very important in his life, even though he doesn't see them as often as he would like. Together, the therapist and client engaged in cognitive restructuring to challenge the idea that what Wally does doesn't matter and were collaboratively able to identify rational and more positive thoughts to replace this idea. Wally shared in this process that he and his wife always wanted to provide their family with a legacy that they could be proud of even though they came from humble beginnings. The therapist and client talked about how Wally can continue his legacy and engage as an important part of his family, even in this stage of his life. Wally described that it would be nice to feel as though he could still contribute, even if that wasn't through working his job or living with his wife.

As the therapeutic relationship deepened with the client, the therapist employed the downward arrow technique to assist Wally in identifying a maladaptive core belief about himself that he was "useless." The therapist and Wally discussed how this belief about himself came to be and how it tends to affect other areas of his life.

Wally shared that his early life family experiences taught him that hard work was "the only way for a Black man to have a chance to make it in the world." This theme of hard work to overcome adversity and create a life of safety, stability, and pride for himself and his family was processed in therapy. The therapist and Wally were able to identify that Wally found both comfort and identity in his work with the ultimate goal of providing for his family, which served as main elements of motivation for him throughout his life. This was contrasted with the client's present situation, in which Wally indicated that he often doesn't see the point of getting up to do the things he used to do because at the end of the day, "it won't matter to anyone." The thought that he is "useless" and the emotions of loneliness and depression were explored. As the therapist and Wally had previously challenged the idea that "nothing matters," they began to similarly challenge the core belief that he was "useless." As Wally became more familiar with challenging his automatic thoughts about himself and his situation, the therapist encouraged him to track his thoughts throughout each day by keeping a thought record. Initially, the therapist asked Wally to fill in as much information as possible about situations, thoughts, and emotions that he experienced during the day. As he became accustomed to this tracking, the therapist asked him to begin to evaluate these thoughts by providing evidence for and against them as a part of his tracking. Wally found this practice to be helpful and reports that "at least it gives him something to do," and over time began to add more of his thoughts which developed into a personal journal. During sessions with the therapist, Wally was able to discuss how he began to see patterns and drew connections between his thoughts, feelings, and how these affected his behavior.

Wally and the therapist continued to work together. The therapist encouraged Wally to engage in behavioral experiments by trying something new in his routine to support his new shifts in thoughts and emotions. To provide more structure and a sense of purpose in his daily routine, the therapist encouraged the client to begin to develop behavioral habits that promoted his overall health. They worked together to create a schedule for Wally that included times to wake up and go to sleep, mealtimes, and activities throughout the day that he could rely upon such as reading the paper, going for a walk in his neighborhood, and calling his children. These behaviors provided Wally with a sense of a schedule that he found comforting from his days of working and living with Sondra, and resulted in some improvements in his mood as evidenced by the client's reports in therapy.

In order to promote a greater sense of social engagement and connection that he lost from work and from his spouse, the therapist and client discussed behavioral changes that could help this area of his life. Wally identified that he and his late wife used to attend a church group together with other same-aged couples, and that he missed the social interaction he gained from those meetings, but felt too sad to go without her. The therapist and Wally engaged in problem solving in order to identify community groups that the client could engage with in order to cope with and address feelings of loneliness. After some discussion, Wally decided to reach out to old friends from church to meet them for weekly lunches.

Finding ways to engage with his family was an important task for Wally, as it provided him with much-needed social connection and also solidified his shifted view of contributing to the world through his family and continuing his legacy. Wally began to call his son every week to check-in with him. In therapy he shared that these phone conversations helped him feel "not only more connected to my son, but also to my wife" as he knows that even in the end of her life, Sondra was deeply concerned for his wellbeing and hoped that he would be able to find his way. Additionally, Wally volunteered to babysit his grandchild Camden every other week in order to build a relationship with the future generation of his family and to feel like an active and useful part of the family, instead of feeling like a burden to his daughter. At first, Wally felt somewhat uncomfortable engaging in these activities and talked about his reservations in therapy by examining his thoughts and emotions. He reported that he sometimes "feels like a burden" and "doesn't think things will ever be the same without my wife or my job." The clinician worked with Wally to challenge these thoughts, which became easier over time as this was a familiar process in the therapy relationship. Near the end of the therapy process, Wally began to catch himself in faulty ways of thinking and often challenged his own thoughts without needing to be prompted by the therapist to do so.

As Wally continuously challenged his thoughts and engaged in small behavioral changes, over time he reported feeling better about his situation and even said that "he knows he will be okay." He reported that even his children noticed the change in him, saying he "seems to be in better spirits." Even though he continued to report feelings of grief and sadness, he said he felt like he could better manage these emotions in order to keep them at bay and "keep living my life." When Wally shared these revelations, the therapist and client collaboratively reflected on how these changes came about in order to clarify what worked in the therapy process and to solidify change.

Cultural Considerations

When working with any client, it is crucial to consider how several aspects of the person's cultural context may influence the problem, its maintenance, the treatment process, the therapist–client relationship, and more. In Wally's case, there are several cultural factors that should be considered and are described below.

Race and Sex

As an African American, it is likely that Wally has experienced issues related to discrimination in various ways throughout his life. It is also likely that Wally may experience a heightened stigma around seeking mental health treatment as an African American male. Wally was likely influenced by traditional male gender norms which present several obstacles for men receiving treatment (Wester & Vogel, 2012). Additionally, perceived stigma and cultural mistrust may inhibit African American clients' willingness to seek out mental health care (Charles & Witherspoon, 2019). Therapists working with male African American clients should be considerate of these potential challenges and attend to them intentionally. Cognitive behavioral therapy may be advantageous to use with these clients due to its emphasis on empowerment, collaborative problem solving, skill building, and building on existing strengths and supports (Kelly, 2006).

Age

Older adults may experience both social stigma and internalized stigma which can be barriers to seeking mental health treatment. These stigmas may uniquely overlap with stigmas associated with race, as older African Americans may be more likely to internalize stigma (Conner et al., 2010). Because Wally is both an older adult and an African American, addressing stigmas associated with seeking treatment would be an important part of the therapy process in order to moderate potential negative thoughts about self as well as increase the likelihood of continued engagement in treatment services. The therapist can help to facilitate this process by highlighting Wally's strengths, discussing his beliefs and values, and creating a supportive and encouraging environment.

Sociohistorical Influences

As a 62-year-old man, Wally was born in the late 1950s. As a child, Wally grew up as the United States was experiencing both social and political changes amidst the Civil Rights movement and the Vietnam War. Seeing his father's involvement in the army and the subsequent development of his substance use disorder as a veteran in the context of his African American heritage likely had a profound influence on his development. In Wally's case, it seems as though his identity and values emerged in a way that made him feel driven to prove himself and succeed with hard work, even as a man that witnessed and experienced inequality. It is likely that Wally would have had to work harder to provide for his family in the same way that his non-minority peers. Additionally, his subsequent retirement and losses associated with working may be more keenly felt for Wally, as this seemed to be a large part of his identity and self-worth as an African American male who worked his entire life to overcome personal and family discrimination, as well as avoid the problems of alcoholism in his own family history.

Discussion Questions

1. How can CBT practices be used by therapists to specifically attend to Wally's unique cultural contexts?
2. Which CBT intervention do you think had the greatest impact on Wally? Which could have been utilized more?
3. How might this case have been different if Wally didn't live alone? How can family members be engaged in the therapy process in order to support clients experiencing individual symptoms?
4. Which seemed to be most effective for Wally: shifting thoughts, emotions, or behaviors?
5. Wally experienced several developmentally normal stressors and losses. How can CBT be used to assist in other stages of development?

References

Beck, A. T. (1970). Cognitive therapy: Nature and relation to behavior therapy. *Behavior Therapy, 1*, 184–200.

Beck, A. T., Rush, A. J., Shaw, B. F., & Emery, G. (1979). *Cognitive therapy of depression.* New York, NY: Guilford Press.

Bennett-Levy, J. (2003). Mechanisms of change in cognitive therapy: The case of automatic thought records and behavioral experiments. *Behavioural and Cognitive Psychotherapy, 31*, 261–277.

Bennett-Levy, J., Westbrook, D., Fennell, M., Cooper, M., Rouf, K., & Hackmann, A. (2004). Behavioural experiments: Historical and conceptual underpinnings. In J. Bennett-Levy, G. Butler, M. Fennell, A. Hackmann, M. Mueller, & D. Westbrook (Eds.), *Oxford guide to behavioural experiments in cognitive therapy* (pp. 1–20). Oxford: Oxford University Press.

Charles, S. M., & Witherspoon, K. M. (2019). Factors influencing help seeking relationships of heterosexual African American males. *Journal of Black Sexuality and Relationships, 5*(4), 43–67.

Chiu, A. W., Langer, D. A., McLeod, B. D., Har, K., Drahota, A., Galla, B. M., Jacobs, J., Ifekwunigwe, M., & Wood, J. J. (2013). Effectiveness of modular CBT for child anxiety in elementary schools. *School Psychology Quarterly, 28*(2), 141–153.

Conner, K. O., Copeland, V. C., Grote, N. K., Rosen, D., Albert, S., McMurray, M. L., Reynolds, C. F., Brown, C., & Koeske, G. (2010). Barriers to treatment and culturally endorsed coping strategies among depressed African-American older adults. *Aging & Mental Health, 14*(8), 971–983.

David, D., Cotet, C., Matu, S., Mogoase, C., & Stefan, S. (2018). 50 years of rational-emotive and cognitive-behavioral therapy: A systematic review and meta-analysis. *Journal of Clinical Psychology, 74*(3), 304–318.

David, D., Cristea, I., & Hofmann, S. G. (2018). Why cognitive behavioral therapy is the current gold standard of psychotherapy. *Frontiers in Psychiatry, 9*, 4. https://doi.org/10.3389/fpsyt.2018.00004.

DeRubeis, R. J., Tang, T. Z., & Beck, A. T. (2001). Cognitive therapy. In K. S. Dobson (Ed.), *Handbook of cognitive behavioral therapies* (pp. 349–392). New York: Guilford Press.

Folsom, T. D., Merz, A., Grant, J. E., Fatemi, N., Fatemi, S. A., & Fatemi, H. (2016). Profiles in history of neuroscience and psychiatry. Book chapter in The Medical Basis of Psychiatry.

Hans, E., & Hiller, W. (2013). A meta-analysis of nonrandomized effectiveness studies on out-patient cognitive behavioral therapy for adult anxiety disorders. *Clinical Psychology Review, 33*(8), 954–964.

Hofmann, S. G., Asnaani, A., Vonk, I. J. J., Sawyer, A. T., & Fang, A. (2012). The efficacy of cognitive behavioral therapy: A review of meta-analyses. *Cognitive Therapy and Research, 36*, 427–440.

Kelly, S. (2006). Cognitive behavioral therapy with African Americans. In P. A. Hays & G. Y. Iwamasa (Eds.), *Culturally responsive cognitive-behavioral therapy: Assessment, practice, and supervision* (pp. 97–116). Washington, DC: American Psychological Association.

Leahy, R. L. (2003). *Cognitive therapy techniques: A practitioner's guide*. New York: Guilford Press.

Manicavasgar, V., Parker, G., & Perich, T. (2011). Mindfulness-based cognitive therapy vs cognitive behaviour therapy as a treatment for non-melancholic depression. *Journal of Affective Disorders, 130*, 138–144.

McManus, F., Van Doorn, K., & Yiend, J. (2012). Examining the effects of thought records and behavioral experiments in instigating belief change. *Journal of Behavior Therapy and Experimental Psychiatry, 43*(1), 540–547.

Spirito, A., Esposito-Smythers, C., Wolff, J., & Uhl, K. (2011). Cognitive-behavioral therapy for adolescent depression and suicidality. *Child & Adolescent Psychiatric Clinics, 20*(2), 191–204.

Weiss, M., Murray, C., Wasdell, M., Greenfield, B., Giles, L., & Hechtman, L. (2012). A randomized controlled trial of CBT therapy for adults with ADHD with and without medication. *BMC Psychiatry, 12*, 30.

Wester, S. R., & Vogel, D. L. (2012). The psychology of men: Historical developments and future research directions. In N. A. Fouad, J. Carter, & L. Subich (Eds.), *Handbook of Counseling Psychology*. Washington, DC: American Psychological Association.

Chapter 8
Dialectical Behavioral Therapy: The Case of Moses

Rachel M. Bailey

Introduction to the Dialectical Behavioral Therapy Framework

Dialectical behavioral therapy (DBT) has long been established as one of the most effective treatments for clients exhibiting life-threatening behaviors. The protocol was developed by Dr. Marsha Linehan in 1993 to treat clients with chronic suicidal behaviors. DBT has since been determined effective with a number of additional issues including substance use disorders, eating disorders, and depression (Koerner, 2011). Countless research studies have deemed DBT advantageous for the treatment of suicidal clients, and those with borderline personality disorder (BPD) (Lynch, Trost, Salsman, & Linehan, 2007). While it is common for clients engaged in DBT treatment to exhibit symptoms of, or meet full criteria for BPD, it is not required. Additional diagnoses associated with DBT include posttraumatic stress disorder, major depressive disorder, bipolar disorder, and eating disorders. This chapter will focus on the application of DBT for clients primarily diagnosed with BPD and presenting with life-threatening behaviors. For the purpose of clarity, the term life-threatening behaviors can include attempted suicide, preparatory behaviors, suicide planning, suicide ideation, self-injury, self-injury ideation, and morbid ruminations (O'Caroll et al., 1998).

R. M. Bailey (✉)
School of Social Work, University of Missouri Columbia, Columbia, MO, USA
e-mail: BaileyRM@missouri.edu

© Springer Nature Switzerland AG 2021
R. P. Dealey, M. R. Evans (eds.), *Discovering Theory in Clinical Practice*,
https://doi.org/10.1007/978-3-030-57310-2_8

The Biosocial Model

Clients exhibiting extreme emotional dysregulation are frequently met with judgment by society, their friends, family, and even clinicians. It is difficult to be in a relationship with a person who demonstrates marked uncertainty regarding their sense of identity and hypersensitivity to environmental feedback. This manifests behaviorally as attempts to gain validation from stakeholders in the client's life. When the attempts are unsuccessful, clients engage in desperate behaviors which appear as chaotic, unsafe, and emotionally driven.

Stakeholders in the client's life are confused and frustrated by these attempts. However, it is the DBT client who is especially exhausted by their internal state. The biosocial model explicates where this severe emotional and behavioral dysfunction originates. The biological component represents the client's predisposition to emotional dysregulation related to a family history of mental illness. It also helps to explain and validate for clients why they are more sensitive and display "bigger" emotions comparatively speaking. It is known that BPD clients are more reactive, are quicker to high states of emotionality, and take longer to reach baseline. The social component represents the manner in which the client's historical and current environments have shaped their experiences with emotions and self-image. When the BPD client does experience hypersensitivity to emotion, they receive feedback from the environment that their response is wrong, unfitting to the scale of the situation, and should be changed. This is what is deemed an invalidating environment in DBT. The client is informed by their environment both implicitly and explicitly that the way they feel and how they show emotions are in error. The result is confusion in the DBT client, as well as a persistent state of uncertainty about their internal experience.

Secondary Targets

An additional framework used to understand the experience and behaviors of the Borderline client is secondary targets, or frequently referred to as patterns of dysregulation. Secondary targets are patterns of behavior which both sustain and interfere with effective and skillful means in the client's quest for equilibrium. There are three distinct "sets" of secondary targets discussed below, each representing a polarization of emotional and behavioral experiences of which clients vacillate back and forth. The goal in DBT is to help clients recognize these patterns of behavior and engage in increased dialectical thinking.

> Dialectical thinking requires the ability to transcend polarities and, instead, to see reality as complex and multifaceted; to entertain contradictory thoughts and points of view, and to unite and integrate them; to be comfortable with flux and inconsistency; and to recognize that any all-encompassing point of view contains its own contradictions (Linehan, 1993, p. 121)

Emotional Vulnerability and Self-Invalidation

Clients experiencing emotional vulnerability endure high sensitivity to environmental cues, where the slightest emotion becomes excruciating and insufferable. They think they are the only people who experience this intensity of emotion and judge themselves for their inability to cope according to societal standards. As such, they receive messages from their environment that their internal experience should not be trusted and move to self-invalidation. During self-invalidation, clients view environmental feedback as much more trustworthy and diminish their actual experience. Clients frequently tell themselves "I should not be this way," and "I am not this way." It is important to note that self-invalidation is the result of chronic emotional reactivity being negatively reinforced by the client's environment. Moreover, the rejection of the client's true emotional experience is viewed as synonymous with the potential for actual rejection from others, which is the Borderline's greatest fear.

Apparent Competence and Active Passivity

Clients presenting with apparent competence send the message to the world that they are doing okay and do not need assistance regulating emotions or solving problems. They behave in a capable manner, denying feelings of vulnerability and expending copious amounts of energy trying to anticipate future events that may lead to emotional vulnerability. This state is short-lived. When the Borderline client fails to communicate emotional suffering and difficulties accomplishing tasks, stakeholders in their life are unaware of their internal state. This serves to invalidate the client even further. In an attempt to communicate the amount of suffering and uncertainty they are enduring, clients then drastically move to active passivity. Clients in active passivity engage in desperate behaviors to both communicate their level of distress and get their needs met. Actively passive behaviors include suicide attempts, self-injury, quitting jobs, avoidance, substance use, violence toward others, and attempts to be hospitalized (Linehan, 1993). Because these behaviors typically garner responsiveness, ineffective displays of emotion are viewed as the best way to get needs met and are therefore reinforced.

Unrelenting Crisis and Inhibited Grieving

Unrelenting crisis is the proverbial never-ending, no good, bad day. Borderline clients frequently awake with intense feelings and thoughts of suicide. When they are unable to engage in skillful means to decrease these intense feelings, they proceed to engage in life from emotion mind. Any happenstance feels intolerable, and the dysregulation builds. The client becomes overwhelmed with the inability to solve problems and manage emotions effectively and moves to deny their feelings. Unable to distinguish justifiable emotions from overreaction, the client pushes down all feelings. The result is failure to get what they actually need.

The Comprehensive Model

DBT is a comprehensive model that includes four primary components. The first component of DBT is individual therapy, which occurs weekly. In individual sessions, therapists use a combination of change and acceptance strategies to aid the client in identifying problematic behaviors which are impacting their quality of life, and apply DBT skills to what is called target behaviors. The second component is Group Skills Training. This occurs once per week, for 2 h. The focus of this group is on psychoeducation and acquisition of DBT skills. The third component is coaching, which allows clients' access to their therapist outside of regular treatment so they can receive assistance applying and generalizing skills to their natural environments. The final component is the Consultation Team. Providers of DBT treatment are required to meet weekly to identify and address issues and barriers related to the delivery of effective and adherent DBT treatment. The focus of the consultation team meeting is not on the clients, but the therapists.

Stages of Treatment

DBT has four primary stages of treatment. Each stage of treatment has specific goals, known as targets, which are identified and treated in hierarchical order. The rationale for this lies in the assumption that clients must gain mastery over life-threatening behaviors prior to changing other target behaviors and/or symptoms. The stage, targets involved, and primary strategies associated with the four stages are represented in Table 8.1. Pre-treatment and Stage 1 will be discussed in depth. Stage 2 and 3 DBT treatment both utilize alternative evidence-based strategies, and occur only after life-threatening behaviors have subsided or decreased significantly. The relationship between trauma and BPD has been well established. As such, DBT prioritizes reduction of post-traumatic stress symptoms (hyperarousal, cognitive and mood disruption, etc.) during Stage 2 treatment. The rationale being that clients learn coping skills needed during Stage 1 treatment to work to fully resolve their trauma (Linehan, 1993). Stage 3 treatment focuses on further mastery and generalization of DBT skills in order to fully meet quality of life goals.

Pre-treatment

After being assessed as appropriate for DBT, the client and therapist engage in what is called "Orientation and Commitment." Once this commences, the client is in pre-treatment. For the next 4–6 weeks, the therapist and client engage in meaningful and direct dialogue about what treatment will entail. DBT is a robust and arduous process for the already emotionally vulnerable client. It is important the client is an

Table 8.1 The hierarchy of primary targets in DBT

Stage of treatment	Targets addressed	Strategies
Pre-treatment	1. Orientation to treatment and agreement upon goals	1. Psychoeducation on: (a) DBT model, history, and research. (b) Biosocial model. (c) Stage 1 targets of behavior. (d) Patterns of dysregulation (secondary targets). (e) Behavior chain analysis. (f) Expectations for treatment. 2. Commitment strategies. 3. Gaining commitment from client to treatment and taking suicide and/or self-injury off the table for 1 year.
Stage 1	1. Decreasing suicidal behaviors. 2. Decreasing therapy interfering behaviors. 3. Decreasing quality of life interfering behaviors. 4. Increasing behavioral skills. (a) Core mindfulness skills. (b) Interpersonal effectiveness. (c) Emotion regulation. (d) Distress tolerance. (e) Self-management.	1. Behavioral chain analysis. 2. Diary card. 3. Validation. 4. Problem solving. 5. Location perspective. 6. Coaching.
Stage 2	1. Decreasing posttraumatic stress.	1. Deployment of additional evidence-based treatments and strategies related to client's remaining symptoms .
Stage 3	1. Increasing respect for self. 2. Achieving individual goals.	1. Deployment of additional evidence-based treatments and strategies related to client's remaining symptoms.

Adapted from Linehan (1993)

informed consumer of services, develop a shared language with their therapist, and be fully aware of the commitment they are asked to make. Once this process is complete, both the client and the therapist make a verbal and written agreement to embark on a yearlong journey together.

Stage 1

Once the client has made the commitment, they are officially in Stage 1 DBT treatment. At this point they begin coaching between sessions, completing their diary card, attending skills group, and engaging in individual treatment according to the target hierarchy. The primary goal of Stage 1 treatment is the elimination or reduction of life-threatening behaviors. Many DBT clients have experienced years of chronic suicidality, so it is common for them to continue to have occasional suicide and self-injury ideation and morbid ruminations post treatment.

The goals of the therapist are to help their client adopt a more dialectic worldview, to replace maladaptive behaviors with skillful means, and to help their client create a life worth living. The practice of DBT is an art, and the therapist is required to have many different tools. Of most importance is the unrelenting capacity to balance acceptance and change (Koerner & Linehan, 2007). DBT clients have been characterized as the quintessential "black and white thinkers and doers." This refers to their inability to see things, experience emotions, and respond to cues in a synthesized manner. This polarization is due in part to responses and reinforcement received in their natural environment. When a client exhibits a desperate behavior (a suicide attempt for example), the people in their lives act in polarized ways. They either provide immediate and unrelenting support and soothing, or they distance themselves from the client entirely. The job of the therapist is to face desperate behaviors and emotional dysregulation with unconditional regard and validation, while continuously pushing for change. This chapter will discuss just some of the core strategies of DBT practice: targets, skills, validation, behavioral chain analysis, and commitment strategies.

Targets

Targets is a term used to denote the behaviors that are being targeted for change. In DBT practice, there are three primary targets, and they are treated in hierarchical order. Target 1 behaviors include anything that can interfere with the client being alive and are called life-threatening behaviors. This may include attempted suicide, preparatory behaviors, suicide planning, suicide ideation, self-injury, self-injury ideation, and morbid ruminations. For some clients, eating disordered behaviors like restriction, binging, and purging fall into Target 1 behaviors if the motivation for the behavior is to cause injury to the body. These behaviors must be treated first in an effort to keep the client alive (Linehan, 1993). This is often stated to the client as the improbability of reaching their quality of life if they are dead. Target 2 behaviors include anything that interferes with the therapeutic relationship or treatment itself. There are a multitude of behaviors that fall into this category including not completing diary cards, arriving late to session or group, not attending session or group, and willfulness. It is important to note that therapists identify and reconcile their own Target 2 behaviors within the therapeutic relationship as well, such as, cancelling sessions, being late for session, being judgmental toward the client, rigidity, and not explaining limits. These behaviors are addressed openly in session due to the profound impact and reliance on the relationship between the client and the DBT therapist, the rationale being that lack of authenticity and unaddressed conflict will interfere with the work. Target 3 behaviors are those which interfere with the client's acquisition of their quality of life. The term "quality of life" is frequently used in DBT, and denotes the life the client is striving for, and in many cases, hopes to have once their suicidality has subsided and they gain skills for emotional regulation. Target 3 behaviors vary by client, but may include use of substances, lack of social connections, and other depressive behaviors.

Diary Cards

The client diagnosed with borderline personality disorder experiences an array of painful emotions, unhelpful thoughts, and engages in ineffective behaviors on a daily basis. When a client arrives to session, it is the therapist's job to help bring order to a likely chaotic week. This is done by assessing and treating problematic target behaviors according to the hierarchy discussed above. The client is responsible for tracking target behaviors, and corresponding emotions, thoughts, urges, and environmental changes with a diary card. This serves three primary purposes. First, it brings order to the session and aids in the treatment hierarchy. Second, it fosters the use of mindfulness skills, as the client must engage in a reflective process where they note tracked targets on a daily basis. Third, it serves as exposure work. The Borderline client lives a chaotic and painful life and is habituated to avoiding thinking about their emotions and behaviors. The diary card requires them to engage in opposite action, and to sit in the emotions rather than avoid them.

DBT Skills Training

Clients receive psychoeducation on DBT skills in the group setting. The therapist works to reinforce use of these skills during sessions, as a means of solution analysis to problematic behaviors. The term skill "is used in the sense of using skillful means, as well as in the sense of responding to situations adaptively or effectively" (Linehan, 1993, p. 329). Clients typically go through each of the modules twice in order to gain a deeper level of insight and generalize skills more fully to their environment. During skills group, individual targets are not discussed. Skills group follows a predictable and purposeful routine. Group begins with mindfulness intended to bring clients into the space, as well as allow them the essential opportunity to practice the skills of observing and describing their emotional state and environment. The first hour of skills group is dedicated to diary card review, where clients identify skills used during the week, barriers to skill usage, and discuss questions and/or insights related to their own mastery of DBT skills. The second half of skills group is dedicated to psychoeducation, where the leaders provide group members with concrete information and examples for new skills. Group members are assigned homework related to the new skills, and close with observations. The skills taught in DBT can be conceptualized as behaviors to increase. The general goal of skills training is actively learn and gain mastery in skills that will reduce suffering (Linehan, 1993). The four primary sets of skills are discussed below.

Core Mindfulness Skills teach clients how to be in control of their emotions, versus their emotions being in control of them. Clients learn skills that allow them to be a participant in an experience without necessarily reacting. They gain valuable knowledge and skills for seeking what is known in DBT as "wise mind" and finding the synthesis. It is a unique experience for the DBT client to sit with an emotion, notice it, and describe it, versus acting on the emotion immediately.

Distress Tolerance Skills help clients survive moments of extreme emotional dysregulation without making the situation worse or engaging in destructive behaviors. These skills do not solve long-term problems, but help clients endure painful experiences and stay alive. It is common for the DBT therapist to inform their clients that although the emotions and urges they experience in any given moment are real and excruciating, they are temporary. Suicide, however, is permanent. This set of skills help clients survive their temporary emotional state so they can make decisions from a more regulated place.

Emotion Regulation Skills teach clients how to identify, decrease, accept, or change a number of intensely painful emotions including fear, hopelessness, despair, confusion, and impulsivity. These emotions are frequently attached to intense urges like suicide and other behaviors that sustain or create long-term problems.

Interpersonal Effectiveness Skills teach clients how to more effectively interact in their social worlds. Borderline clients have frequent conflicts and display ineffective resolution skills in relationships with family, friends, and employers. These skills teach clients how to both ask for what they need, and say no to unwanted requests effectively and without causing further disruption.

Validation

The significance of validation in DBT treatment cannot be overstated. The Borderline client has received messages for a very long time that the way the feel, what they think, and what they do is irrational, overly emotional, and nonsensical. Therapists use validation not just as a strategy for helping, but truly believe that the client has inherent wisdom and makes effective choices in the moment the best way they can. This is a new message for the client, one that serves to normalize their internal experience and fosters self-acceptance. Target 1 behaviors are frequently viewed as extreme and attention-seeking. In DBT, the therapist does not promote life-threatening behaviors, but validates that they occur in the context of the client's experience. Koerner (2011) tells us that "It is the therapist's job to search for and find the validity in the client's behavior, not to create it" (p. 121).

Behavioral Chain Analysis

The behavioral chain analysis (BCA) is an active process where the therapist and client examine target behaviors closely, collaboratively identify environmental, affective, and cognitive influences, and posit solution analysis. The BCA is a primary strategy for change, used in most individual sessions. The DBT session begins with a review of the client's diary card, and the BCA is applied to targets according to the treatment hierarchy. The BCA begins with the therapist and client agreeing on the problem behavior. An example of a Target 1 problem behavior is writing a suicide note. It is important for the client, and not just the therapist, to demonstrate the capacity to articulate why the behavior is problematic. The therapist prompts the client to describe in excruciating detail each moment, or "links in the chain," that led to the problem behavior. For each "link," the therapist prompts the client to identify feelings, thoughts, and behaviors. The next step in a BCA is to identify the prompting event. This is the moment in time during the chain of events leading up to the problem behavior, which was the precipitating factor. In other words, without the prompting event the problem behavior would not have occurred. Throughout the process of a BCA, vulnerability factors are identified. These are both chronic and acute factors that made the client increasingly vulnerable to engaging in the problematic behavior. Examples include using substances, not getting enough sleep, not eating enough, intense emotions, and environmental factors. Outcomes are identified, and highlight both positive and negative consequences of the behavior. Examples include feeling relief, hospitalization, having needs met by others, and scarring. The final step in the BCA is solution analysis. The therapist and client work to identify where in the chain of events the client could have used skillful means. The BCA is a perfect example of the need for unrelenting balance of acceptance and change. During the process, the therapist unequivocally validates the client's feelings, thoughts, and choice in behavior; while simultaneously pushing for change by highlighting missed opportunities for use of skills.

Commitment Strategies

DBT treatment requires a lot of willingness from the client. They are asked to engage in a rigorous program for 1 year, to sustain from life-threatening behaviors, and to be willing to change how they feel and act. This is a big ask. It is common for client's commitment to treatment to diminish intermittently throughout treatment. This is expected and addressed in the treatment model via commitment strategies. It is the therapist's job to accept decreased motivation and willfulness as a part of the process, and deploy these strategies as needed. The following seven unique strategies are used to increase client commitment to treatment during initiation of therapy and throughout.

Pros and Cons identifies advantages and disadvantages for engaging in problem behaviors. Examples include suicide, self-injury, completion of diary card, giving up lethal means, etc. The therapist acknowledges fully during this process that there are in both pros and cons to problematic behaviors. During this strategy, the therapist may even posit advantages to problematic behaviors. This serves to validate the client and present a dialectical stance. For example, an advantage of suicide is the fact that the client would no longer have to suffer, while a disadvantage may be the fact that they would not get to graduate college.

Foot in the Door, Door in the Face aims to increase willingness to engage in effective behaviors by making an initial request for change that is either small and sensical, or big and radical. If a client presents with willfulness toward completing a diary card, the therapist can ask a question that almost any client would agree to and then ask for slightly more (foot in the door). As an example, a therapist might ask "Don't you want to feel better?" and connect this with the act of completing the diary card. Conversely, the therapist could ask for a radical commitment to complete the diary card every day for 1 year (door in the face) and then settle on a commitment for 1 week of completion.

Devil's Advocate can be used when clients have made a seemingly quick commitment to a difficult task. Therapists list all the reasons they should not engage in the effective behavior in an effort to increase the client's insight into the commitment as well as strengthen their sense of choice. As an example, a client may state a strong commitment to take suicide off the table for the year of treatment. To solidify and enlighten, the therapist can then name all the challenges the client would face (giving up means of problem solving, managing urges, etc.).

Connecting Present Commitments to Prior Commitments is deployed as a negotiation tactic, wherein the therapist highlights how the client's ineffective behavior is in contrast to previous statements. A client who suddenly presents with willfulness and a desire to quit DBT may find their therapist reminding them of their desired quality of life and/or previous statement that they will complete the full year. The therapist may also remind the client of previous accomplishments, denoting their actual capacity to endure difficult challenges.

Freedom to Choose in the Absence of Alternatives is the ultimate strategy to increase willingness and commitment. The deployment of this strategy includes highlighting how the client's ineffective behaviors will not lead to their idealized quality of life, that they will have to ultimately face the outcomes of chosen behavior regardless, and that the choice is theirs. The therapist presents the client with the option of continuing with the ineffective behavior, such as self-injury or planning for suicide, while highlighting how the ineffective behaviors will not meet their goals. The therapist may also review all the ways the client has attempted to reach their goals unsuccessfully, and that DBT is the remaining option available.

Shaping is used to help clients make change. For many clients their desired quality of life seems extremely distinct from the life they are currently living. In an effort to provide the client opportunities to gain mastery, the DBT therapist helps the client set small and attainable goals. As an example, a client who believes a life without self-injury is improbable is prompted to self-injure one less time in a weeks' time.

Cheerleading is used to posit hope for the DBT client. The therapist deploys positive and affirmative statements in order to reinforce use of skillful means and the client's internal capacity to be successful. A client who is unable to meet a goal (i.e., go a week without self-injuring) is presented with a statement that they tried everything within their power to accomplish the goal, that they have been successful in past attempts of goal attainment, and that the therapist believes unequivocally that they have the wherewithal to be successful.

Introduction to the Case of Moses

Moses is a 35-year-old white male who successfully completed one full year of DBT. All names and identifiers have been changed to maintain the confidentiality of the client. He was referred to DBT by a local behavioral health center after receiving a provisional diagnosis of borderline personality disorder. He received a variety of therapeutic interventions prior to DBT. He was born in a rural community to a middle-class family with strong religious values. His family of origin consisted of him, an older sister, and his mother and father. At the onset of puberty, he was subjected to hour-long interrogations by a member of the church after he was found masturbating. He described these events as extremely shameful and traumatizing. His upbringing also consisted of physical discipline, a lack of privacy, and emotional and verbal abuse. Moses graduated high school and left his community and the church. His parents continued to support him financially throughout his education, which was a great source of shame for him.

Moses had limited social support. He lived alone in a rented apartment, and was employed part-time at the local university. His adult relationships included colleagues from work and patrons at bars. He experienced multiple intimate relationships since early adulthood which were intense and volatile. He reported that he enters into relationships quickly, sometimes against his better judgment, because he prefers not to be alone. Moses frequently sought intimacy at strip clubs, bars, and via social media. The length of these relationships varied from one night to a few weeks, and was wrought with dysfunction. Moses found himself going to their homes unannounced, would provide them with money he did not have, and would engage in ineffective communication with them online.

Moses is of above-average intelligence and works in the STEM field. He completed his Doctoral Degree near the end of DBT. He thrived during intellectual conversations and in the academic world. The positive feedback he received was reinforced and was converse to feedback he received in other social settings. Moses found himself feeling awkward and undesirable in intimate settings, while feeling pride and confidence in professional ones. His communication was frequently littered with data, which blocked his true desire of connection with others. Moses had extreme difficulty with activities of daily living. At the start of treatment, he had not checked his mail or email for over 30 days. He struggled to maintain basic hygiene and cleanliness of his apartment. He was chronically late to most obligations including work, church, and treatment. He experienced alcohol use, misuse, and abuse (to varying degrees) since early adulthood. He had two DWIs on his record, which caused significant issues in his personal, familial, and academic life. In the year leading up to DBT, he became involved in a bar fight that led to a car chase, pulled a knife on someone, and was subsequently arrested for a DWI. His criminal record served as a significant barrier to obtaining employment in his field.

Moses reported experiencing the desire to die as early as Kindergarten. He would hit himself in the head and other body parts. At age 16, he would burn himself in the shower with scalding water when feeling shameful about sexual abuse. He reported experiencing morbid ruminations his entire life. At age 19, he developed and acted on his first suicide plan. After his parents threatened to cut off funding for his education, he drove to a bridge intending to jump. He received a call, which he said saved his life. At age 25, he attempted to die by drowning himself in the river after a fight with his girlfriend. Through his early to late twenties, Moses reported that he engaged in reckless driving while intoxicated. This included "hill jumping," in hopes that he would die. He began shopping for a firearm about 6 months prior to initiation of treatment. He had done this two or three times at various locations, but did not purchase one. He reported a suicidal plan that included purchasing a firearm and a nice bottle of scotch, driving to the morgue, and shooting himself in the head on Christmas Eve. His reasons for living at the time of assessment included his faith, finishing his Doctoral degree, vengeance, and his will to hate.

Moses's target behaviors, desired quality of life, and secondary targets were assessed and identified early in treatment according to DBT protocol. The Linehan Risk Assessment and Management Protocol (Linehan, 2009) was used to assess risk for suicide. He scored in the clinically significant range on the BSL, PCL, PHQ-9, and GAD-7. He was subsequently diagnosed with major depressive disorder, recurrent, severe; and presented with multiple characteristics of borderline personality disorder.

Theoretical Integration

Moses was an ideal candidate for DBT. The comprehensive model was applied to him, with as much fidelity as a person is capable.

Pre-treatment/Orientation and Commitment

At the initiation of treatment, Moses presented with life-threatening behaviors including daily morbid ruminations, suicide plan, and suicide ideation. It was important to develop a crisis plan and gain commitment to stay alive during the pretreatment phase of DBT. Moses made weekly commitments to stay alive during this phase of treatment. Orientation and commitment lasted approximately 4 weeks for

Moses. During this time, he was educated on DBT including the comprehensive model, the biosocial model, targets and target hierarchy, and patterns of dysregulation/secondary targets. The following is a synthesis of Moses's behaviors and symptoms in the context of DBT targets and secondary targets, which he was educated on during the pre-treatment stage.

Target 1

Moses's Target 1 behaviors in order of severity and treatment included preparatory behavior, suicide ideation, and morbid ruminations, and were assessed at mild risk for suicide during intake (Rudd, 2006) as he denied intent. His risk factors for suicidal behavior included lack of social support, previous suicide attempt/behaviors, anger, being a middle-aged male, and severity of depression symptoms. His protective factors included commitment to stay alive, attachment to therapy, desire to attain quality of life goals, and history of coping.

Target 2

Moses's Target 2 behaviors included instability of finances, chronic tardiness, depressive symptoms, and intellectualization, and were assessed as potential therapy interfering behaviors. During the first few sessions, Moses presented with research studies and used intellectualization. This Target 2 behavior was addressed by gaining a commitment from him to refrain from outside research. He was amenable to this agreement.

Target 3

Moses's desired quality of life included completion of his doctoral degree, elimination of suicidal ideation, capacity to support himself financially, increase in activities of daily living, and to create meaningful relationships. It should be noted his history of complex trauma served as a precursor to dysfunction in quality of life behaviors.

Secondary Targets

Moses exhibited all three of the secondary targets (patterns of behavior). Of most significance was his behavioral pattern of active passivity and apparent competence. Initially Moses frequently presented diary cards littered with Target 1 urges and behaviors, which are by nature representative of active passivity. His chronic suicidality was invalidated by family and co-workers. When interpersonal conflict arose, he would manage the overwhelming emotions with desperate behaviors including rumination of death, binge drinking, and avoiding. When these attempts were unsuccessful, he would become polarized and begin acting as if everything was okay (apparent competence). Moses also experienced the pattern of unrelenting crisis and inhibited grieving. His inability to respond effectively to environmental stressors frequently led to days of dysregulation and suicidality. After which, he would avoid his emotional experience all together by denying justified emotions and/or pushing them down. Moses also experienced the pattern of emotional vulnerability and self-invalidation. Due to his historical trauma and family history, he was hypersensitive to rejection, fear of failure, and interpersonal conflict. This resulted in Moses being quick to emotion mind and engaging in reactive behaviors unfitting to the scale of the situation. When he received feedback that his reactions were dramatic and/or unreasonable, he would tell himself that the way he felt was nonsensical, therefore invalidating his emotional state.

Stage 1 Treatment

Once the commitment was made, Moses began attending skills group and completing a diary card daily. Because suicidal behaviors are targeted as primary, his first few months of tracking and treatment focused on the reduction of Target 1 behaviors. After approximately 4 months, Moses's Target 1 behaviors decreased significantly and he began tracking Target 3 behaviors on his diary card. Target 2 behaviors were tracked throughout therapy. By month 6, Moses's treatment focused primarily on Target 3 behaviors.

Stage 1 Treatment: Decreasing suicidal behaviors. After Moses committed to taking suicide off the table, he presented primarily with suicide ideations and morbid ruminations. During treatment, BCAs were used each session to dissect and identify factors sustaining his suicidality. He frequently had thoughts including "I would be better off dead," "I should kill myself," and "Life is not worth living." His urge to engage in suicidal behaviors and intensity of these thoughts during the early part of treatment was frequently 4 out of 5, with 5 being the highest. Prompting events for these thoughts and urges usually included interpersonal conflict, financial distress, and perceived or actual rejection. Vulnerabilities often included his past history of trauma, alcohol use, chronic loneliness, and stress. To manage impulsive suicidal thoughts and behaviors, Moses commonly used distress tolerance skills while he worked to learn other skills during group. As a very cognitive person, the skills of fact finding, pros and cons, and radical acceptance were deployed often. Figure 8.1 shows a BCA completed with Moses early in treatment, focused on the Target 1 behavior of suicide ideation with an intensity rating of 3 out of 5.

Moses self-identified how experiencing suicide ideation is problematic. This is an essential component of the BCA, as it is much more important for the client to verbalize how suicidal behaviors are problematic for them versus the therapist verbalizing it for the client. Moses verbalized that experiencing suicide ideation was a

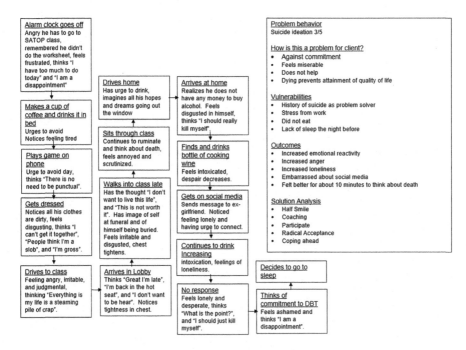

Fig. 8.1 Behavior chain analysis focused on Target 1 behavior

problem for him because it went against his commitment to take suicide off the table, did not solve long-term problems, that dying would prevent him from reaching his qualify of life, and that thinking that way made him feel generally miserable. Each link in this chain was explicitly identified, as well as corresponding thoughts, emotions, and bodily sensations. The prompting event for this problem behavior was identified by Moses as getting dressed and realizing he did not have clean clothes to wear. That moment is when he first became emotionally dysregulated, and led to continued and increasing distress throughout the day noted.

This particular BCA is exemplary of the pattern of behavior known as unrelenting crisis. Though completely understandable in light of vulnerabilities and previous experiences, Moses was unable to engage in skills to halt and manage the crisis. This lack of skillfulness prevented him from problem solving the moment the precipitant occurred, and therefore decreasing suicide ideation throughout his day. Instead, he continued to engage in unhelpful thinking and ineffective behaviors resulting in continued dysregulation.

This pattern of behavior was discussed during the chain, and missed opportunities for skillful means (both in that moment and in the future) were identified. Moses awoke feeling dysregulated, and it was agreed he could have engaged in the learned skill of half smile while he laid in bed. He might have also used coaching to garner therapeutic assistance for managing his overwhelming emotions and thoughts throughout the day. Upon noticing he did not have clean clothes to wear, the skill of radical acceptance, an emotional regulation skill that posits full acceptance (not necessarily agreement) of the situation to reduce emotional reactivity, could have been used. It was noted how helpful it would have been for Moses to accept his clothes were dirty, and that he would be late for his class. Looking to the future, it was decided that Moses could engage in the skill of coping ahead to prevent the precipitant from occurring all together. In this situation, Moses could use coping ahead by laying out his outfit the day prior to big obligations.

Validation was used throughout the BCA to send the message to Moses that it was completely understandable that he experienced emotions like despair, self-disgust, irritability, and anger, and moreover, that he thought of death as a solution to such a difficult and overwhelming problem. In the moment, this sounded like, "Of course you felt despair and had the urge to avoid. Just the act of getting up each day is so difficult for you. And when you noticed the dirty laundry it felt like an insurmountable obstacle." The use of validation was essential for Moses, as he experienced such chronic invalidation growing up and had difficulty seeing any validity in his emotional experience. Like most clients, he became more engaged in problem solving when his internal experience was noted as having inherent wisdom.

Stage 1 Treatment: Decreasing therapy interfering behaviors. Moses was notably committed to treatment, and only missed one skills group throughout the entire year. This level of commitment is quite extraordinary and may be attributed to the effectiveness of Orientation and Commitment, the client–therapist relationship, as well as his strong desire to attain quality of life.

Despite his commitment, Moses still presented with Target 2 behaviors. Of most significance was his chronic tardiness. This behavior extended beyond treatment to his work, church, and other commitments. Many things sustained this behavior. Because Moses was viewed by others as emotionally unstable, his tardiness frequently went unaddressed. In this way, he was fragilized by his environment. Moses also experienced great anxiety related to social situations, which prompted him to avoid activities associated with readiness including waking up, showering, and getting dressed. It was agreed early on in treatment that lateness in excess of 5 min to either group or individual therapy would be chained. Like many clients, the process of behavioral chaining can be excruciating at times. Moses experienced great shame, and at times anger, over BCAs related to tardiness. This, in and of itself, reduced the instances. In his words "I'd rather be on time than chain being late."

Moses experienced financial distress that often prohibited him from paying treatment co-pays. He relied on his parents for financial support, so it was especially difficult for him to chain this therapy interfering behavior. He felt shame and anger when the topic was addressed openly. He would say, "What do you want me to do about it?" and stated the therapist was, "Just one more person with their hand out." The behavior was consistently chained in an effort to avoid fragilizing Moses, and to send the message that difficult subjects can be discussed effectively. This was a novel concept for him, and he gained quite a bit of mastery in communication about this difficult topic.

On occasion, Moses would use coaching while he was intoxicated. This was addressed as a therapy interfering behavior, as clients are asked not to use substances during active treatment times. The commitment strategy of shaping was used, and Moses was able to commit to not coaching after he had more than two drinks. It was essential for all of his Target 2 behaviors to be validated. Stating the unsaid was frequently used to hypothesize his feelings of shame associated with inability to pay, tardiness, and coaching after intoxication. The relevance of this strategy lies as a converse to his normed experience. Typically, those in Moses's life would express irritability, frustration, and shock and awe over these behaviors. In therapy, he was validated for doing the best he could, while constantly being asked to do better.

Stage 1 Treatment: Decreasing quality of life interfering behaviors. In order to determine Target 3 behaviors, Moses identified specific behaviors, emotions, and experiences he would like to have by the end of treatment. These were then transformed into specific behaviors to decrease. Due to Moses's depression, he struggled to find motivation to complete normal activities of daily living. He hypothesized a life where hygiene and cleanliness were not issues. He also expressed hopelessness that he would be able to attain such a transformation. The skill and commitment strategy of shaping was deployed. Moses made small, incremental commitments to engage in behaviors that would lead to change. He began by tracking showering and soon he was able to shower seven times which led to feelings of mastery. Moses then began to track housekeeping. To keep this ideal behavior measurable and attainable, he agreed to set a 15-min timer each evening and clean up until the timer went off. He continued this for a month and found his house was to his preferred standards. It was around this time in treatment, that Moses began to arrive with a more hygienic appearance.

Moses's idealized quality of life also included feelings of connectedness and healthy relationships. Moses was asked to identify ineffective relationship behaviors to decrease and noted showing up to partner's houses unannounced, texting while intoxicated, and seeking assurance excessively. He began tracking these behaviors, and noted substantial decrease within 6 weeks. Moses also wanted to feel more connected to his family, whom he typically avoided. He began tracking the ideal behavior of reaching out to family, and was able to do so approximately one time per week. An essential skill used was mindfulness, wherein Moses took care to observe feelings of loneliness prior to making contact with partners. If he did in fact note this feeling, he agreed to refrain from making contact. These changes in behavior led to decreased shame and loneliness.

He strongly desired a more meaningful work life, one that would use his education and skills. Moses assumed this was not possible due to his mental health and criminal record. "What if" thoughts frequently littered his mind and blurred his worldview. He would become very dysregulated if he received an email from his boss, had a job interview, or thought about his future. In response to this tremendous pain, Moses would avoid. This pattern was explicated to him, and the skill of shaping was used once again. Moses worked to develop a timeline of his ideal career, and then partialized out incremental steps to take. These included things like completing his resume, getting feedback from his mentor, and applying for jobs. He skillfully set one goal per week, and slowly made progress.

His financial distress was a result of years of avoidance. Moses had outstanding credit card debt and was facing wage garnishment. This felt unsurmountable to him, and he frequently had the thought "I will never get out of this." The fear he experienced related to finances was compounded by the shame felt when asking his parents for money. He would time travel to the future, and said multiple times "I would rather be dead than have to live at home again." Moses began tracking small steps toward mastery over finances. He agreed and followed through on one task per week, which eventually led to payment plans with all debtors.

It should be noted that Moses did not want to stop drinking entirely, so becoming sober was not identified on his quality of life goals. However, the harm reduction model and shaping were used to reduce vulnerabilities prompted by alcohol use for all target behaviors.

Stage 1 Treatment: Increasing behavioral skills. To manage Target 1 behaviors early and throughout treatment, Moses was effective in using Distress Tolerance skills including STOP, Pros and Cons, TIP, and Radical Acceptance. STOP is an acronym for Stop, Take a Step Back, Observe, and Proceed Mindfully (Linehan, 2015). As is common for DBT clients, Moses would experience life-threatening urges and act somewhat impulsively. It was essential for him to begin with STOP in an effort to recognize that ineffective and desperate behaviors were not compulsory, and that he could experience suffering without the certainty of ineffectiveness. Moses frequently used Pros and Cons, developing a comprehensive list of reasons to both engage and not engage in problematic behaviors. During one session early in treatment, this list was established and he carried it with him. To combat intense and extreme emotions and urges, Moses would engage in TIP. TIP is an acronym for Temperature, Extreme Exercise, Paced Breathing, and Paired Muscle Relaxation (Linehan, 2015). This was often a first line of defense for Moses, and he responded best to the T, holding ice cubes and taking a cold shower. He understood that the use of Distress Tolerance skills was not a long-term solution to problems. Instead, they were effective in managing intensely painful emotions and urges to prevent him from acting upon them further and increasing his suffering.

To manage Target 2 behaviors, Moses focused on Emotional Regulation skills including Opposite Action, Checking the Facts, and Building Mastery and Coping Ahead. Moses experienced intense urges to avoid discussions surrounding tardiness and finances. He became quite skillful at identifying the shame and guilt associated with these urges, and acting in an opposite fashion to generate a converse emotion. As an example, he was asked to report out on his inability to pay therapy co-pays during the session. As a result, he noted decrease in shame and acceptance. To remediate tardiness, Moses would cope ahead the evenings before obligations by completing all tasks before bed, setting out his outfits, and not taking his sleeping medication to prevent oversleeping. He began to build confidence and mastery over timeliness. He also received positive praise, which served to strengthen his sense of mastery. On one occasion, Moses presented as extremely dysregulated due to the inability to pay for the third week in a row. He began to have thoughts that he would be kicked out of treatment and that the therapist would no longer care for him. These unhelpful thoughts were addressed directly and with compassion by identifying the facts of the situation versus his inaccurate affective perception.

To manage Target 3 behaviors, Moses focused on Emotion Regulation skills including Opposite Action, Checking the Facts, Building Mastery, and Coping Ahead. He also deployed Core Mindfulness Skills of Observe, Describe, and Participate. It was essential that Moses use Interpersonal Effectiveness skills including DEARMAN, and Dialectics in the attainment of his quality of life goals. Moses's truest desire was meaningful and connective relationships. As a result of his severe loneliness, he would drink in excess and/or communicate his feelings via social media to partners. This, of course, was wrought with dysfunction and inhibited the attainment of his goal. He used mindfulness to increase his awareness of emotional vulnerability, and was able to refrain from acting on impulses to seek comfort and companionship. During events where connection was appropriate, Moses used the skill of Participate by throwing himself into the moment fully to enhance his sense of belonging and capacity to connect to others. At the start of treatment, Moses would angrily and ineffectively communicate with co-workers during conflict. He would also avoid criticism and problem solving with his employer. The skills of Opposite Action, Checking the Facts, and DEARMAN were used. DEARMAN is an acronym for Describe, Express, Assert, Reinforce, stay Mindfully, Appear confident, and Negotiate (Linehan, 2015). Many sessions consisted of Moses and therapist working to identify his goal in the situation, and writing out a DEARMAN to effectively communicate his desires and needs. By the end of treatment, he had gained a good deal of mastery in interpersonal communication.

Cultural Considerations

DBT falls into the category of mindfulness and acceptance-based treatments, and research on such modalities with individuals from nondominant, traditionally underserved backgrounds is in its infancy (Fuchs, Lee, Roemer, & Orsillo, 2013). There are a multitude of cultural issues that impact the delivery of DBT. Of most significance may be religious beliefs around death and dying. The presence of high religiosity/spirituality, and/or belief that suicide is immoral is a protective factor (Linehan, Comtois, & Ward-Ciesielski, 2012), meaning it can serve as a reason *not* to complete suicide. Treating strongly held religious beliefs about taking one's life is quite complex. In many religions there is a strong opposition to hasten death, and interfere with God's plan for the soul (Traina, 1998). Many clients feel immense shame about the mere presence of suicidality, seeing it as a direct contradiction to their own beliefs. This is of course excruciating for the suicidal client. In DBT, these clients are asked to practice dialectics by accepting the part of them that wants to be dead, while continuously striving to strengthen the part of themselves that wants to be alive. The DBT therapist may struggle asking a client to accept something that does not align with the client's spiritual beliefs.

Another issue of relevance is client-held beliefs about mental illness. DBT treats mental health disorders as symptomatic of biological predispositions and events from their social world. In this way, DBT serves to justify and explain mental health as a sensical reaction to biology and childhood experiences. This rationalization may contradict strongly held beliefs about what it means to live with a mental illness, as well as messages received from society and family.

In both instances, the therapist uses the concept of dialectics which asserts that two strongly opposed ideas can be true at the same time (Linehan, 1993). So, for example, it is possible to simultaneously think "I want to die" and "I want to live." It is important to remember that clients with chronic suicidality and/or mental health diagnoses have endured years of shame and self-blame. An additional strategy is to link belief related emotional vacillation to the secondary target of emotional vulnerability and self-invalidation. It can be helpful to deploy level 4 validation, wherein the therapist describes how the client's beliefs are "probable," given their history of invalidation, conflict, and/or biological predisposition to emotional dysregulation (Koerner, 2011).

Areas for future consideration include translation of skills manuals into various languages and cultural contexts (McFarr et al., 2014), the availability of DBT services for marginalized populations, and strategic deployment of skills that minimize power inequities (Fuchs et al., 2013).

Discussion Questions

1. Discuss what you perceive to be the primary characteristics of a client who may benefit from DBT.
2. Consider a previous client and explicate their behaviors from the biosocial perspective.
3. The ideal DBT therapist has the capacity to balance change and acceptance consistently. Identify and discuss client behaviors that may test your ability to do this.
4. Every person has behaviors that are problematic and do not align with their desired quality of life. Identify a problematic behavior you have engaged in the last 30 days, and conduct a behavior chain analysis.
5. What values are fundamental to DBT? Discuss both the discrepancy and alignment between social work values and ethics and DBT.
6. Describe a minimum of two behaviors that represent willfulness or lack of commitment in clients. Discuss how you could use the strategies of commitment to intervene.

References

Fuchs, C., Lee, J. K., Roemer, L., & Orsillo, S. M. (2013). Using mindfulness- and acceptance-based treatments with clients from nondominant cultural and/or marginalized backgrounds: Clinical considerations, meta-analysis findings, and introduction to the special series. *Cognitive and Behavioral Practice, 20*(1), 1–12.

Koerner, K. (2011). *Doing dialectical behavior therapy: A practical guide.* New York, NY: The Guilford Press.

Koerner, K., & Linehan, M. M. (2007). *Handbook of psychotherapy case formulation.* New York, NY: Guilford Press, Chapter 11.

Linehan, M. (2015). *DBT skills training manual* (2nd ed.). New York, NY: The Guilford Press.

Linehan, M. M. (1993). *Cognitive-behavioral treatment of borderline personality disorder.* New York, NY: The Guilford Press.

Linehan, M. M. (2009). *University of Washington risk assessment action protocol: UWRAMP.* Unpublished Work: University of WA.

Linehan, M. M., Comtois, K. A., & Ward-Ciesielski, E. F. (2012). Assessing and managing risk with suicidal individuals. *Cognitive and Behavioral Practice, 19*(2), 218–232.

Lynch, T. R., Trost, W. T., Salsman, N., & Linehan, M. M. (2007). Dialectical behavior therapy for borderline personality disorder. *Annual Review of Clinical Psychology, 3*(1), 181–205.

McFarr, L., Gaona, L., Barr, N., Ramirez, U., Henriquez, S., Farias, A., & Flores, D. (2014). Cultural considerations in dialectical behavior therapy. In A. Masuda (Ed.), *The Context Press mindfulness and acceptance practica series. Mindfulness and acceptance in multicultural competency: A contextual approach to sociocultural diversity in theory and practice* (pp. 75–92). Oakland: Context Press/New Harbinger Publications.

O'Caroll, P. W., Berman, A. L., Maris, R., Moscicki, E., Tanney, B., & Silverman, M. (1998). Beyond the tower of Babel; A nomenclature for suicidology.

Rudd, M. D. (2006). *The assessment and management of suicidality.* Sarasota, FL: Professional Resource Press/Professional Resource Exchange.

Traina, C. K. H. (1998). Religious perspectives on assisted suicide. *The Journal of Criminal Law and Criminology, 88*(3), 1147–1154.

Chapter 9
Solution-Focused Brief Therapy: The Case of Jim

Philip Miller

Introduction to Solution-Focused Brief Therapy

Two frameworks are used in this case. The first framework is the solution-focused brief therapy (SFBT) clinical approach, and the second framework is the behavioral health in primary care model. The SFBT framework is a therapeutic approach that emphasizes client strengths, construction of solutions rather than solving problems, and the development of personalized goals to produce change as quickly as possible (Gingerich & Eisengart, 2000; O'Hanlon & Weiner-Davis, 1989; Rothwell, 2005). The behavioral health in primary care framework provides guidance integrating behavioral health services into the primary care setting (Robinson & Strosahl, 2009). To comprehend the intricacies of this case, the SFBT clinical approach must be examined in the context of the primary care model.

Solution-Focused Brief Therapy Framework

Development of the solution-focused brief therapy approach originated from clinical practice within the Brief Family Therapy Center in Milwaukee, Wisconsin in 1980 and, a short time later in 1982, this new therapeutic approach was officially named solution-focused brief therapy (de Shazer & Berg, 1997; Gingerich & Eisengart, 2000). The SFBT approach quickly became popular because of its applicability in a variety of settings with a diverse clientele. SFBT is now used worldwide (Franklin, 2015). Professionals from diverse disciplines and work settings have broadly applied SFBT to include physicians and nurses in health care settings, teachers to creatively engage with students and families, mental health providers to

P. Miller (✉)
Social Work, Keuka College, Keuka Park, NY, USA
e-mail: PMiller@keuka.edu

facilitate individual, group, and family therapy, and businesses to better equip management by integrating SFBT into coaching strategies (Franklin, 2015; Redpath & Harker, 1999; Shilts & Thomas, 2005; Stevenson, Jackson, & Barker, 2003). Ongoing research on SFBT has further reinforced its popularity by favoring SFBT as an effective approach to quickly produce sustainable behavior changes (Corcoran, 2016; Franklin, Zhang, Froerer, & Johnson, 2016; Gingerich & Eisengart, 2000; Macdonald, 1997; Rothwell, 2005).

The SFBT approach challenges the traditional structure of mental health services in a variety of ways and may cause dissonance with new SFBT practitioners. As a result, clinical knowledge and beliefs may need to be restructured and familiar clinical methods modified. SFBT is not a series of easily applied techniques but a way of thinking about the process of therapy and how change occurs. Without understanding the assumptions and underlying beliefs of SFBT, techniques will be minimally effective. Learning the SFBT approach is an ongoing process and requires openness, training, observation, mentoring, and practice (Froerer & Connie, 2016; Lee, 2011; Shilts & Thomas, 2005).

A critical element to the success of SFBT is the therapist's belief about the process of change. Beliefs regarding change need to be critically examined because the SFBT approach assumes that change can and does occur quickly without exploring history, diagnosing, and offering ongoing intervention (O'Hanlon & Weiner-Davis, 1989; Reiter, 2010). In contrast, traditional clinical approaches are problem and complaint focused, rely on finding a cause for the presenting problem, emphasize advice-giving, and oriented toward establishing a diagnosis (Froerer & Connie, 2016; Gingerich & Eisengart, 2000; O'Hanlon & Weiner-Davis, 1989; Rothwell, 2005). SFBT is based on empowering the client by drawing on strengths and abilities to construct solutions, rather than the therapist emphasizing the resolution of problems (Gingerich & Eisengart, 2000; Rothwell, 2005; Stevenson et al., 2003). SFBT practitioners also believe that client life struggles and presenting problems are not due to pathology but originate from the patient being overwhelmed and losing sight of their ability to solve problems and mobilize their existing strengths and resources. SFBT practitioners assume clients want to change, have the ability to change, and are already taking steps to change. Therefore, within the treatment structure of six sessions or less, a core duty of the therapist is to amplify change, create hope and expectancy, and co-create a path to change through a collaborative process (Franklin, 2015; Franklin et al., 2016; Gingerich & Eisengart, 2000; O'Hanlon & Weiner-Davis, 1989).

The delivery of the SFBT approach requires specific language skills designed to create hope and expectancy and empower clients to realize inherent solutions (Franklin, 2015). The hope of successful outcomes leads to positive change and the expectation that this will happen is created by the therapist (Reiter, 2010). It is the responsibility of the therapist to shift the client's problem-focused thinking and speech to solution talk and future-oriented thinking. Solution-focused language is carefully used throughout treatment to promote the realization of positive outcome possibilities and ensure clients link their actions to treatment progress and success (Froerer & Connie, 2016; Reiter, 2010; Taylor, 2005). The use of presuppositions is embedded in SFBT language and permeates all SFBT techniques. The use of presumptive language is a type of strategic communication that infers something without saying it directly and is a way to introduce change and promote client acceptance that change is occurring (O'Hanlon & Weiner-Davis, 1989). For example, asking the client "What is better?" instead of "Is anything better?" assumes improvements were made and emphasizes change.

The first session involves developing a strong therapeutic relationship and uses the initial assessment as an intervention. SFBT is a collaborative process and practitioners rely on the expertise of the client. Therefore, a healthy therapeutic relationship is critical for success. Initial engagement requires SFBT practitioners to adopt the language of the client, accept the client's perspective, understand the context of their identified problem, and intentionally reduce the pathology of the presenting problem by normalizing their concerns (Corcoran, 2016). The initial assessment in SFBT is used as an intervention by immediately engaging the client in the process of change. This may differ from traditional binary assessment models where first the objective is to obtain an elaborate history to understand the client's presenting complaint and to develop a diagnosis, and then move forward with the treatment process (Lee, 2011).

At the beginning of the first session, the SFBT practitioner asks the client, "Please tell me what brought you in today." However, after this opening statement, the first session becomes an open and fluid exchange that doesn't follow a rigid protocol (Lee, 2011). Taylor (2005) developed a helpful guide for trainees learning how to implement SFBT for the first session that includes five areas of inquiry. The five areas of inquiry include the major focal points of client engagement with accompanying SFBT techniques. The five areas of inquiry include the client's: (1) awareness of what improvement will look like; (2) recognition of improvements already occurring; (3) acknowledging actions leading to improvements; (4) expanding possible solutions; and (5) establishment of goals.

The first area of inquiry from Taylor's (2005) work is associated with specific SFBT techniques such as exploration of pre-session change, the miracle question, and identification of what improvement will look like. This line of inquiry occurs at the beginning of the first session and challenges the idea that a client's situation is defined by a "problem." Often, exploring pre-session change occurs immediately following asking the client what brought them into treatment. The practitioner may simply ask the client, "What is better since you made the appointment?". Exploration of pre-session change assumes that positive changes have likely occurred between the time of making the appointment and the first session. The focus of pre-session change creates hope and expectancy that change can occur and attributes the change to the client's actions (O'Hanlon & Weiner-Davis, 1989; Taylor, 2005). The miracle question is often asked to promote a future-oriented focus and produce images of living without the expressed problem. The miracle question may be phrased, "What if you wake up tomorrow and the problem is solved, what would that look like?" Asking the client to describe the future without the problem provides insight into potential solutions and can oftentimes be the spark to move toward change (de Shazer & Berg, 1997; O'Hanlon & Weiner-Davis, 1989; Reiter, 2010). Following the client's response to the miracle question, the therapist asks, "What aspects of this miracle are already occurring?". Further intentional questioning can elicit how the client sees themselves behaving or thinking differently without the problem, who will be the first to notice the miraculous changes, and how their life will be different (Franklin et al., 2016; O'Hanlon & Weiner-Davis, 1989).

The second area of inquiry focuses on recognizing when improvements have occurred and exploring what was different or better during these moments (Taylor, 2005). The SFBT practitioner assumes there are always times, places, and circumstances when the expressed problem doesn't occur. Using exception questions examines the times when the problem doesn't occur and elucidates possibilities to solve the problem. A simple exception question is, "What is different during the times when you are not as stressed?". As a reminder, the therapist doesn't ask "Have there been times you have not been as stressed?". As the therapist, you are implying there must be times when the client is feeling less stressed (Franklin et al., 2016; O'Hanlon & Weiner-Davis, 1989; Reiter, 2010).

The third area of inquiry from Taylor (2005) amplifies what the client is doing to create identified improvements to ensure they take credit for the positive changes. When the client provides an exception to their expressed problem, a quick follow-up question is, "How did you make that happen?". The therapist may have to be persistent and insist that the client must have done something to create the exception, no matter how small. Additional questions can include, "What did you do differently?", or "How is what you did different from the way you might have responded 1 month ago?". The underlying assumption of this line of inquiry is once the client recognizes their part in creating the exception, increased self-confidence will occur to do more of the same (Corcoran, 2016; O'Hanlon & Weiner-Davis, 1989; Reiter, 2010).

According to Taylor (2005), the fourth line of inquiry directs the client to acknowledge the positive results from their actions and explore how other areas of their life are impacted. Targeted questions are used to expand potential solutions and explore what occurred following their action. For example, the SFBT practitioner may ask a range of question to include "Who else notices when you do_____ (insert behavior)?", "How do people react differently to you?", "If you were to do _____ repeatedly over the next month, how would it impact your life?", "How is your day different when you_____?", or "What will have to happen for you to do it that same way more often?". Using this line of questioning can expand clients' narrow view of their problem and prompt them to not overlook the positive impact one small exception can have in their lives (Franklin et al., 2016; Lee, 2011; O'Hanlon & Weiner-Davis, 1989; Reiter, 2010).

The fifth and final area of inquiry from Taylor (2005) occurs toward the end of the first session and is focused on the future and the establishment of achievable goals. Collaborative goal setting, scaling questions, and compliments are techniques typically used. Collaborative goal setting involves questioning allowing the client to define treatment goals that drive the trajectory of treatment. Questions such as, "What will indicate to you that your situation is improving?", and "What will indicate to you that things are continuing to improve?" can facilitate the identification of concrete and achievable goals (Bodenheimer & Handley, 2009; O'Hanlon & Weiner-Davis, 1989). Scaling questions are an important technique that can facilitate the identification of specific observable goals that are meaningful to the client. For example, the client may be asked, "On a scale from 1 to 10 where would you place your stress?" An immediate follow-up question might be, "You chose a #6, what would a #8 look like?", and "What will it take for you to reach a #8?" (de Shazer & Berg, 1997; Lee, 2011; O'Hanlon & Weiner-Davis, 1989; Reiter, 2010). Additional scaling questions can focus on the client's level of confidence to achieve a higher number on the scale. The therapist can ask, "On a scale of 1–10, how confident are you that you can reach a #8?", and "What would it take for your confidence to be higher? (Taylor, 2005). The goals identified through scaling questions can also be used for follow-up appointments to monitor progress.

The SFBT practitioner concludes the first session by offering authentic compliments to reinforce successful actions by the client to correct the presenting concern. Compliments accentuate client strengths and should be based on the conversation that occurred during the session. A compliment can be stated as "I appreciate your willingness to seek help. I think you are a person that doesn't give up easily and you are already using this strength to create change." Also, no-fail homework is assigned such as, "Observe the times you feel less stressed" (de Shazer & Berg, 1997; Lee, 2011; Macdonald, 1997; O'Hanlon & Weiner-Davis, 1989; Reiter, 2010; Rothwell, 2005).

Behavioral Health in Primary Care Framework

Early models of behavioral health in primary care began to surface in the 1960s (Robinson & Strosahl, 2009), but complex issues of funding, reimbursement, and the challenges of integrating two different treatment models representing the medical and behavioral health fields have stunted the growth of this innovative approach (Pomerantz, Corson, & Detzer, 2009; Robinson & Strosahl, 2009). The foundation of behavioral health services in primary care is a population health management paradigm. This paradigm is identified by Bryan, Morrow, and Appalonio (2009) as either having a horizontal or vertical structure. The horizontal structure emphasizes providing care to the entire population of primary care patients to better manage the needs of the primary care patient to improve overall health and well-being. In contrast, the vertical structure provides targeted specialty care to a select few of the general primary care population (Bryan et al., 2009). Within the horizontal or vertical structure of population health management, the level of actual integration into primary care exists on a continuum (see Fig. 9.1). On one end of the continuum is coordinated care with primary care that resembles traditional mental health care with a reciprocal referral process in place. In the middle is a co-location model where the behavioral health specialist has a physical presence in primary care, mostly keeps autonomy over the treatment, and has occasional engagement with the primary care team. On the opposite end of the continuum, the behavioral health

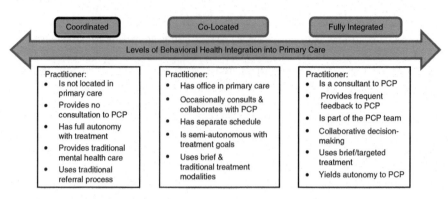

Fig. 9.1 Continuum of Primary Care Integration

specialist is fully integrated into the primary care team, acts as a consultant to the primary care physician, frequently communicates with the entire primary care team, and provides brief and targeted interventions (Bryan et al., 2009; Mauer, 2003; Robinson & Strosahl, 2009).

Integrating mental health services into primary care improves access to care, provides an opportunity for prevention and education, lessens the stigma of seeking mental health care, reduces demand on the primary care provider, and patients can receive short-term and more precise care (Miller & Malik, 2009; Pomerantz et al., 2009; World Health Organization, 2008). According to the National Council for Community Behavioral Healthcare (2002), about 30% of primary care office visits are mental health in nature. Furthermore, 50–80% of people that have a common mental health issue are treated in primary care (Bryan et al., 2009; Mauer, 2003;Miller & Malik, 2009; World Health Organization, 2008). Consequently, primary care providers may not be adequately trained and can feel overwhelmed treating mental health issues and often don't have the time to adequately address these types of patient concerns (Robinson & Strosahl, 2009). However, when patients have direct access to a mental health professional to address their concerns, they can be treated earlier with targeted care and will require fewer medical-related appointments creating less demand on the primary care provider (Miller & Malik, 2009; World Health Organization, 2008). According to Mauer (2003), patients prefer to have mental health care coordinated within primary care because it is more efficient and also reduces the stigma of seeking mental health services. During a medical appointment, a medical provider can accompany a patient down the hall to connect with a mental health provider for a drop-in session. This type of in-house coordination helps to overcome the 30–40% rate of "no-shows" for follow-up appointments when patients are referred to mental health services outside the primary care clinic (Miller & Malik, 2009; National Council for Community Behavioral Healthcare, 2002).

Interventions offered by the mental health specialist complement the care provided by the primary care physician because the mental health specialist can address a wide spectrum of disease management or lifestyle concerns. Moving beyond the biomedical approach and drawing on psychosocial factors of patients, mental health specialist can offer effective health education and utilization of functional interventions to assist patients to adapt to an illness, be compliant with medication or diet, learn stress-management techniques, improve sleep hygiene, and practice improved self-care that impacts the overall quality of life (Mauer, 2003; Miller & Malik, 2009; Pomerantz et al., 2009; Population Health Support Division Air Force Medical Support Agency, 2006). Furthermore, patient outcomes are positive when mental health issues are addressed in primary care. In as few as one to three, 30-min sessions, improvements in symptom reduction, behavioral change, sense of well-being, and improved life functioning can be achieved (Bryan et al., 2009; Cape, Whittington, Buszewicz, Wallace, & Underwood, 2010; Miller & Malik, 2009; Pomerantz et al., 2009; Robinson & Strosahl, 2009).

Introduction to the Case of Jim

In the context of this case, the SFBT practitioner's integration into primary care at the free medical clinic aligns with the horizontal framework as described by Bryan et al. (2009), where the entire primary care population is available for a referral. The level of integration in the clinic includes characteristics of being both co-located and fully integrated. The SFBT practitioner's office is physically located in primary care but full integration into the primary care team is not evident. Referrals are received from the physicians and consultation will occasionally occur to clarify the referral details. Appointment schedules between the SFBT practitioner and physician are not fully coordinated and the SFBT retains significant autonomy with treatment protocol and goals. When appointment schedules do overlap, the primary care physicians can do an on-site referral, and the patient is seen as a walk-in. Behavioral health appointment slots are 30 min in length which follows the brief therapy model.

Jim is a pseudonym to protect his identity. The identifiers of this case have been changed to maintain the confidentiality of the client. Jim was referred by one of the free medical clinic physicians after disclosing his pattern of substance use. Jim was scheduled within a week, and at the time of the appointment, the SFBT practitioner had minimal history about Jim's substance use because there was no access to records and the referring physician did not provide details regarding Jim's substance use. The physician wants Jim assessed and his substance use addressed in treatment.

Jim, a 57-year-old black, divorced, male, presents with an extensive substance use history. On two occasions, Jim has been voluntarily admitted into an inpatient substance abuse treatment facility and has engaged with outpatient counseling on several occasions. However, he has not had any type of mental health treatment for the past 6–7 years. Jim drinks beer daily to help him sleep and he is frequently exposed to drugs because he allows prostitutes to smoke crack in his trailer in exchange for occasional sexual activities. Jim reports using crack cocaine one or two times a week 2 years ago, but he has tried to quit and now uses it about two or three times a month. Specific details about past mental health diagnosis and medical history are insufficient due to his limited recall ability and sparse medical records. However, through the free medical clinic, Jim is being treated for high blood pressure and ongoing headaches. He does not report any current or past legal issues. His education level is a high school diploma. Jim grew up in the south and currently resides in a southern state. He lives alone in a run-down rental trailer, isolated on a dead-end street in an extremely rural part of the county. The street where he lives contains a pocket of small houses consisting mainly of low-income, black individuals and families. Jim describes his neighbors as acquaintances versus friends, but reports they keep an eye out for each other. Details regarding his divorce are unclear but he does not have any contact with his ex-wife. However, he sees his adult daughter and her 13-year-old child about once every 3–4 months. Jim has a sister that tries to be supportive and occasionally provides him rides to medical appointments. Both his sister and adult daughter live approximately 30 miles away which limits their contact. The relationships with his sister and daughter are very meaningful to Jim. He expresses guilt regarding his history with substances that have interfered with developing a deeper relationship with his daughter and grandchild. Jim does not identify with any religion and does not indicate spirituality is integrated into his life. Jim has not worked consistently in the last few years and has primarily worked manual labor jobs. Jim doesn't own any type of transportation which increases his sense of isolation. He relies on friends to take him to work odd jobs and to obtain food at the nearby country store.

Theoretical Integration

SFBT is an excellent fit to use in primary care and is compatible with population health management goals to better manage mental health-related issues commonly seen in primary care such as medication compliance, anxiety, depression, stress management, sleep hygiene, and substance use (Khatri & Mays, 2011). The core tasks of the SFBT approach are consistent with brief healthcare goals to provide patient-centered care while targeting specific behavior change using goal-driven, time-limited solution-focused strategies, follow-up, and support (Bodenheimer & Handley, 2009; Flemming & Manwell, 1999; Khatri & Mays, 2011; National Council for Community Behavioral Healthcare, 2002; Rothwell, 2005).

Providing services in primary care requires flexibility to accommodate characteristics associated with the primary care environment and discard many of the traditional mental health practices. For example, to manage time efficiently to stay within a 15- to 30-min time limit, a more active and directive approach with patients is required. This may be uncomfortable for traditionally trained mental health clinicians. Delicately balancing being empathic and directive without compromising the critical development of the therapeutic relationship is a developed skill. Accomplishing this balance can be facilitated by using the assessment process as an intervention during the first session. Even during a 15–30 min initial session, Taylor's (2005) areas of inquiry can be applied to join with the client, explore exceptions, set goals, and provide homework.

Joining: (10 min) includes being genuine and authentic while engaging in small-talk to quickly connect with the patient. Attention to the development of the helping relationship occurs immediately and undergirds all treatment activities. The role of the clinician and structure of the first session is quickly explained to the client. The clinician inquires if the patient understands the process and asks if they are willing to continue. Open-ended and presuppositional questions are used throughout the session, and thoughts and feelings are validated to normalize their concerns.

The moment Jim is called back to the behavioral health office, efforts begin immediately to positively connect with him to develop the helping relationship and initiate the assessment. Jim's frail physical structure and his slightly disheveled appearance are immediately noticed. Jim slowly walks down the hallway toward the office with an imbalanced gait. Jim has a noticeable smile, friendly disposition, and steady eye contact. Once in the office, Jim is engaged in small talk which involves joint laughter at some of his responses. His sincerity about attending the appointment stood out, but he could only articulate a minimal understanding as to why his medical provider referred him. Uncertainty existed about why Jim believed to be at this appointment. Regardless, careful attention is given to responding to Jim so that he does not feel alienated due to the details of the referral being unclear. Jim is difficult to understand at times because he sometimes mumbles, speaks in generalities, and has several front teeth missing. As a result, a cognitive impairment (substance-induced or biological), or Jim being currently impaired by a substance is immediately considered. The SFBT practitioner speaks slowly and is mindful to keep speech simple and asks specific, clarifying questions that seem to work well with Jim. An explanation is quickly given to Jim outlining limits of confidentiality, the goal of the first session, and the role of the SFBT practitioner being a consultant to his primary care provider. There is a moment of silence to see if Jim wanted to respond, then Jim is asked, "Do you understand what was just explained?" He responds by nodding and mumbling "Yes, I understand." Permission to continue with the session is asked to reinforce his voice in the process. Jim agreed to continue.

Due to the paucity of Jim's responses, the SFBT practitioner recognizes staying within the 30-min allotted time is going to be difficult. Fortunately, there are no patients scheduled immediately following Jim so a little more time can be spent with him. With experience, the SFBT practitioner has learned that being flexible to take advantage of the time with patients is imperative because they may not return due to limited transportation and resources.

Exploration: (10 Min) Exploration includes rapidly identifying patient concerns as the patient sees them, not necessarily as the primary care provider sees them. The clinician may ask, "What brings you in" and then follow-up with questions designed to uncover exceptions to the problem. Careful attention is given to the context and functional impact of the patient's described problem and the associated thoughts and feelings. Listening for areas of pre-session change or when the presenting concern is not present or is less intense allows the clinician to amplify strengths and evidence of existing change already occurring.

The SFBT practitioner acknowledges the brief referral note from Jim's medical provider and explains that she is concerned about his current level of substance use.

He nods in agreement and says, "Yes, I believe she must be concerned." Wanting to know his perspective, Jim is asked, "Tell me what brings you in this evening." He pauses and mumbles a few things and has difficulty articulating why he is at the appointment. The SFBT practitioner quickly asks, "Are you okay talking about your substance use?" Jim indicates he is fine discussing his current use and began telling, "I drink a 40oz beer each night to help me sleep." The SFBT practitioner asks follow-up questions designed to explore patterns associated with his use and search for exceptions to his substance use. A reflective statement is provided by the SFBT practitioner, "You are having trouble sleeping each night and the beer helps with getting sleep." Jim replied, "Yes, I haven't slept in years and drinking helps." An open-ended prompt is stated, "Jim, tell me more about your substance use." He admits, "I do use sleeping pills at times with the beer, but I like my beer better." Based on his matter-of-fact response and tone, it seems Jim's daily drinking is a well-established pattern and the possibility exists of other substances being used. The SFBT practitioner asks, "Jim, I appreciate your honesty regarding the beer and the use of sleeping pills, are you using any other substances?" Jim acknowledges smoking a pack of cigarettes daily for the past 20 years. There is a moment of silence, and then Jim confesses to smoking crack cocaine about two or three times a month. Jim quickly interjected that he is not interested in attending inpatient care or any type of detox services.

Once Jim mentioned his crack cocaine use, the SFBT practitioner began fighting a dismissive attitude and internal dialogue turned negative. A feeling of anxiousness surfaced with the SFBT practitioner because Jim's situation is complex and immediately challenges two of the SFBT goals associated with the first session; abolishing the label that a problem exists and create confidence that the situation can be managed by the client. Jim's extensive substance abuse history and continued use is an overwhelming problem, and the SFBT practitioner begins doubting how Jim is going to feel more confident managing his situation based on his prior treatment attempts, continued use, and limited insight. The SFBT practitioner is apprehensive about Jim's success with the limited resources and time constraints within the primary care setting. Consequently, the SFBT practitioner prematurely assumes that this is a one-session experience resulting in a referral to the local mental health clinic where Jim can have access to more consistent and robust services. However, the SFBT practitioner intentionally focuses on staying connected to Jim and maintains trust in the possibility of change, no matter how small.

Jim exclaims, "I don't like to smoke crack and I know it isn't good for me. I would like to quit." Indicating he would like to quit was the first time Jim expressed willingness to make any type of change. Adhering to the here-and-now focus of the SFBT approach, the SFBT practitioner amplifies his desire to quit and responds by stating, "So, you want to make changes to your crack use", "What does this change look like?" Jim describes that quitting the use of crack is difficult because prostitutes that he befriended frequently come to his house to smoke crack in his trailer. He continues by saying he only uses crack when his female "friends" would come to his trailer. The SFBT practitioner is interested in the context of Jim's described problem, so he is asked, "Tell me more about when the "friends" come to your trailer." Jim verbalizes that he knows they are not his real friends, but they want a place to hang out and smoke crack without being bothered. He admits partially enjoying their company because he gets lonely and on occasion, sexual favors are exchanged for the use of his trailer. A reflective statement is used, "So, you are often lonely and when these "friends" come by, you don't feel as lonely?" Jim replies, "Yes, and I tell myself that I'm not going to use with them and then I get talked into using the crack." Jim continues, "I have told them not to come around in the past but they come back and I let them into my house." In his remark, an exception is noted in his behavior when he told the prostitutes not to come around his trailer. Accentuating this exception is a priority so the SFBT practitioner states, "In the past, you have told them not to come around. How did you do that?" Jim responds with a wry smile, "I just told them to get lost in an agitated way." Jim continues, "They didn't come in and disappeared for a few months, but they came back and I let them in." Despite that he let the prostitutes back into his trailer, the SFBT practitioner stays focused on Jim's efforts to create change and guides him to consider using existing strengths to create future change. Therefore, Jim is asked, "What do you need to do to get rid of them in the future?" Jim replies, "I can run them off anytime, they're no good anyway." The SFBT practitioner quickly asks, "What is better when you are firm with them and don't allow them into your trailer?" Jim notes, "I don't use crack and feel better. I just stick to my nightly beer!"

Goal Setting: (10 Min) Collaborative goal setting is a shared process between the clinician and the patient to establish achievable, concrete, readily understood, and easily measured goals. Scaling questions are often used to illuminate future images of desired functioning to assist with establishing goals. Goals need to start small, described in specific behavioral terms and viewed as manageable by the client.

Based on Jim's past, the SFBT practitioner knows that assuming the expert role and being directive about his need to stop using substances is not going to be successful. Instead, a partnering approach is used and demonstrates respect by allowing Jim to identify what is important to him and then work toward achieving small successes to increase self-efficacy. Therefore, the SFBT practitioner states, "Jim, it seems when you set firm boundaries with the prostitutes, you use less crack and feel better. Is it okay if we focus on ways for you to continue to set good boundaries with them since this aligns with your desire to use less crack?" He agrees, and the SFBT practitioner senses Jim's interest and reasonable comfort level with working on this goal. Scaling questions are commonly used in the SFBT approach to establish a baseline and help identify small, achievable goals. Jim is asked, "On a scale from 1 to 10 (1 low confidence and 10 very confident) how confident are you that you can turn the prostitutes away when they come by again?" Jim indicates he is a #7. Next, Jim is asked, "What does a #9 level of confidence look like?" Jim replies, "I don't know, maybe letting them know how serious I am." The SFBT practitioner responds, "Jim, what will that look like when you are serious?" He fidgets with his hands, looks away in thought, and then replies, "I may have to get angry with them, maybe yell, and slam the door." "Wow", the SFBT practitioner says. "Jim, it seems you have identified a goal that will lead to using less crack." Jim agrees to work on setting stronger boundaries with the prostitutes and verbalizes this is something he feels he can do.

The SFBT practitioner successfully collaborates with Jim to formulate a workable goal and receive buy-in. If a directive or educational stance was used to communicate his need to stop using crack, Jim would have acquiesced to be polite, but not be invested. On the surface, the established goal to set better boundaries with prostitutes might seem minimal in the context of his crack use and use of other addictive substances. However, this was a straightforward, concrete goal that Jim was comfortable with and had confidence he could achieve. This goal provided him the opportunity to self-manage and experience the outcome based on his efforts.

Compliments/Homework: (5 Min) Providing feedback to the patient by offering genuine, relevant compliments and amplifying strengths and efforts already initiated to create change is a goal of this segment. Also, achievable, no-fail homework is given that is designed to alter the patient's behavior or perception of the presenting complaint. For example, the patient may be encouraged to monitor the presenting complaint throughout the week to identify when it does not occur or occurs with less intensity or duration. Regardless of the patient returning for a follow-up appointment, homework is given.

The SFBT practitioner genuinely compliments Jim by stating, "Jim, I appreciate your sincerity about being at this appointment and your willingness to make a change in your drug use. I can tell making a change is important to you." The SFBT practitioner continues, "Also, I want to point out that you have previously told the prostitutes to stay away and it worked. You have the ability to be firm and set good boundaries with them. If it's okay with you, as a homework task, I would like you to continue setting good boundaries with them. If you need to get angry, slam the door, or yell to tell them to stay away and not allow them into your trailer, do it." Jim nods in agreement and says, "Yes sir, I will do it." It is common to see a patient only one session using SFBT in primary care. However, Jim is offered the option for a return appointment. He desires a follow-up appointment but scheduling quickly becomes an issue due to his lack of transportation. In this case, the SFBT practitioner consults with the referring physician and provides an overview of the session, clinical impressions, goals, and plan for follow-up.

Follow-Up Appointment: The SFBT practitioner works with the primary care team to schedule Jim for a follow-up appointment to coincide with his medical appointment. Due to misaligned schedules, Jim is scheduled for another appointment in 6 weeks. The second session with Jim lasts 15–20 min due to his medical appointment going over the allotted time and his ride is waiting to take him home. Nevertheless, the SFBT practitioner completes a brief check-in with Jim by asking a presuppositional question, "Jim what is better since the last time we talked?" He answers, "I'm doing what you have said and I have used less crack." The SFBT practitioner responds, "Wow, excellent news. Tell me how you are doing that?" Jim proceeds to explain that he has deterred the prostitutes from coming into his apartment a few times but let them in on one occasion. Jim is proud of his progress and encouraged that he experienced some success with his goal. Since time is limited during this session, Jim agrees to keep the same goal, and the SFBT practitioner proceeds to amplify his success by emphasizing the skills he has shown to manage this goal. Due to ongoing transportation and scheduling conflicts, Jim is not able to be scheduled for another follow-up appointment at this time.

Several months pass and the SFBT practitioner often thinks about Jim and how he is doing. One evening, Jim unexpectedly appears on the SFBT practitioner's schedule. Immediately, the SFBT practitioner notices a medium-sized lump on the left side of Jim's neck. Jim explains he has been diagnosed with cancer and is currently receiving chemotherapy. The prognosis didn't sound positive based on his report. The SFBT practitioner is shocked that amid his cancer diagnosis and treatment, Jim is still committed to attending a follow-up appointment. Jim states, "I had to come and tell you in person how I was doing and that I achieved my goal." The SFBT practitioner can tell Jim is extremely proud of his accomplishment. The SFBT practitioner is speechless and touched by his commitment to this seemingly small goal but amazed how meaningful this was to Jim.

Cultural Considerations

Several differences in diversity need to be considered in the case of Jim such as issues of race, social-economic status, level of education, and age. The SFBT practitioner is a white, middle class, educated male working in a free medical clinic located in the south. The practitioner must be mindful of his status working with Jim, an older, less educated, lower social-economic, black male. There are many historical and cultural reasons why Jim would not trust the practitioner and question his motivations and investment in his improvement. The practitioner is not from the south, and in fact, there was a moment when Jim asked the practitioner where he was from. The SFBT practitioner assumed Jim was possibly questioning if he could be understood or gauging to what extent he could relate to the practitioner. Furthermore, due to possible distrust and existing differences, Jim may be reluctant to disclose information to the practitioner.

The SFBT practitioner is perpetually sensitive about the significant power differential working with patients at the free medical clinic due to possible feelings of shame related to their life situation and differences associated with their current economic and healthcare status. The practitioner is in a precarious clinical situation to balance being directive with Jim, which aligns with the SFBT theoretical framework and primary care setting, and not coming across as abusing power. To mitigate the power differential, the practitioner diligently works to develop trust in the therapeutic relationship and finds moments to invite Jim's voice to the conversation and empower him to make a change. The SFBT practitioner can connect with Jim quickly by being nonjudgmental, genuine, and sincere about hearing his story.

The challenge of working with Jim using the SFBT approach is not fully understanding his lived experience. Therefore, in this case, the practitioner exercised extreme caution to not react to Jim based on ethnocentric views, negative interpretations, or assumptions. Reacting in this way would have threatened the therapeutic relationship, diminished his voice, and led the practitioner to overlook significant cultural elements. For instance, the practitioner struggled with dismissing or minimizing Jim's battle to turn away prostitutes. From the practitioner's perspective, it should not be that hard to dismiss prostitutes and see that the benefits easily outweigh the cons. However, if this perspective prevailed, the SFBT practitioner would miss seeing the relief from isolation the prostitutes provided Jim and the genuine struggle he has setting healthy boundaries. The practitioner took the time to understand Jim's connection with the prostitutes and how they were linked to his presenting concern.

Due to the brief, directive nature of the SFBT approach and the fast-paced environment of primary care, human difference or cultural issues can easily be overlooked and minimized. The astute SFBT practitioner will recognize the presence of cultural considerations and their influence on treatment. No matter the setting or length of treatment, it is critical to consider patients in the context of intercultural and intracultural factors.

Discussion Questions

1. What is your comfort level improvising and simultaneously adapting to the patient's personality and desires, the demands of the work environment, and the treatment model?
2. How do you respond to defeatist thoughts that challenge your prescribed clinical framework?
3. How do you manage your dissonance between your preferred treatment goals and what the client finds meaningful?
4. What is your comfort level being directive, time, and goal-driven instead of relying on traditional mental health practices?
5. What assumptions does this case challenge regarding your beliefs about change and treatment success?
6. Consider a time when you reacted to a patient based on your ethnocentric views. How did it impact the situation?
7. What framework or model do you use to guide your work regarding intercultural and intracultural factors?

References

Bodenheimer, T., & Handley, M. A. (2009). Goal-Setting for behavior change in primary care: An exploration and status report. *Patient Education and Counseling, 76,* 174–180.
Bryan, C. J., Morrow, C., & Appalonio, K. K. (2009). Impact of behavioral health consultant interventions on patient symptoms and functioning in an integrated family medicine clinic. *Journal of Clinical Psychology, 65*(3), 281–293. https://doi.org/10.1002/jclp.20539.
Cape, J., Whittington, C., Buszewicz, M., Wallace, P., & Underwood, L. (2010). Brief psychological therapies for anxiety and depression: Meta-analysis and meta-regression. *BMC Medicine, 8*(38), 1–13.
Corcoran, J. (2016). Solution-focused therapy. In N. Coady & P. Lehmann (Eds.), *Theoretical perspectives for direct social work practice. A generalist-eclectic approach* (3rd ed., pp. 435–450). New York: Springer Publishing Company.

de Shazer, S., & Berg, I. K. (1997). 'What works?' Remarks on research aspects of solution-focused brief therapy. *Journal of Family Therapy, 19*, 121–124.

Flemming, M., & Manwell, L. B. (1999). A primary treatment method for at-risk, problem, and dependent drinkers. *Alcohol Research and Health, 23*(2), 128–137.

Franklin, C. (2015). An update on strengths-based, solution-focused brief therapy. *Health & Social Work, 40*(2), 73–76.

Franklin, C., Zhang, A., Froerer, A., & Johnson, S. (2016). Solution focused brief therapy: A systematic review and meta-summary of process research. *Journal of Marital and Family Therapy, 43*(1), 16–30.

Froerer, A. S., & Connie, E. E. (2016). Solution-building, the foundation of solution-focused brief therapy: A qualitative Delphi study. *Journal of Family Psychotherapy, 27*(1), 20–34.

Gingerich, W. J., & Eisengart, S. (2000). Solution-focused brief therapy: A review of the outcome research. *Family Process, 39*(4), 477–498.

Khatri, P. & Mays, K. (2011). Brief interventions in primary care. SMHSA-HRSA Center For Integrated Health Solutions. Cherokee Health Systems (powerpoint).

Lee, M. Y. (2011). Solution-focused theory. In F. Turner (Ed.), *Social work treatment: Interlocking theoretical approaches* (5th ed., pp. 460–476). Oxford: Oxford University Press.

Macdonald, A. J. (1997). Brief therapy in adult psychiatry—further outcomes. *Journal of Family Therapy, 19*, 213–222.

Mauer, B. J. (2003). Background paper: Behavioral health/primary care integration models, competencies, and infrastructure. National Council for Community Behavioral Healthcare.

Miller, B. F., & Malik, A. D. (2009). Integrated primary care: An inclusive three-world view through process metrics and empirical discrimination. *Journal of Clinical Psychological Medical Settings, 16*, 21–30. https://doi.org/10.1007/s10880-008-9137-4.

National Council for Community Behavioral Healthcare. (2002). *Background paper: behavioral health/primary care integration models, competencies, and infrastructure.* Rockville, MD: National Council for Community Behavioral Healthcare.

O'Hanlon, W. H., & Weiner-Davis, M. (1989). *In search of solutions: A new direction in psychotherapy.* New York, NY: W.W. Norton & Company.

Pomerantz, A. S., Corson, J. A., & Detzer, M. J. (2009). The challenge of integrated care for mental health: leaving the 50 minute hour and other sacred things. *Journal of Clinical Psychology in Medical Settings, 16*, 40–46. https://doi.org/10.1007/s10880-009-9147-x.

Population Health Support Division Air Force Medical Support Agency. (2006). *Behavioral health optimization project training manual.* San Antonio, TX: Population Health Support Division Air Force Medical Support Agency.

Redpath, R., & Harker, M. (1999). Becoming solution-focused in practice. *Educational Psychology in Practice, 15*(2), 116–121.

Reiter, M. (2010). Hope and expectancy in solution-focused brief therapy. *Journal of Family Psychotherapy, 21*, 132–148.

Robinson, P. J., & Strosahl, K. D. (2009). Behavioral health consultation in primary care: Lessons learned. *Journal of Clinical Psychological Medical Settings, 16*, 58–71. https://doi.org/10.1007/s10880-009-9145-z.

Rothwell, N. (2005). How brief is solution-focused brief therapy? A comparative study. *Clinical Psychology & Psychotherapy, 12*, 402–405.

Shilts, L., & Thomas, K. A. (2005). Becoming solution-focused: Some beginning thoughts. *Journal of Family Psychotherapy, 16*(1), 189–197.

Stevenson, C., Jackson, S., & Barker, P. (2003). Finding solutions through empowerment: A preliminary study of a solution-oriented approach to nursing in acute psychiatric settings. *Journal of Psychiatric and Mental Health Nursing, 10*, 688–696.

Taylor, L. (2005). A thumbnail map for solution-focused brief therapy. *Journal of Family Psychotherapy, 16*(1), 27–33.

World Health Organization and World Organization of Family Doctors (Wonca). (2008). Integrating mental health into primary care: A global perspective.

Chapter 10
Narrative Therapy: The Case of J.J.

So' Nia L. Gilkey

Introduction to Narrative Therapy

The historical narrative timeline, externalizing conversations in the context of landscapes of action and landscapes of identity, mapping the lived experience by key life events, and re-authoring one's story through exceptions and unique outcomes are all key techniques when applying narrative therapy. White (2000) suggests that clinician reflection is a key part of the narrative therapy process, particularly as it relates to practicing conversations beforehand with the client, examining challenges and/or barriers that emerge during the therapy session, and exploring the role of the clinician-client relationship when working toward the re-storying of events that facilitated the therapy experience in the first place. Staying focused on the event and/or events at hand and not becoming distracted by other elements that might be important to consider but should be limited in the narrative exchange if it detracts from the goals of the therapy established by the client and the therapist.

The American Psychological Association describes narrative theory as a theoretical approach to understanding how people structure and make sense of the stories of their lives. Initially, narrative theory came out of literary studies as a way to examine the process of storytelling by storytellers in literature. How they crafted their stories, the knowledge or experiences influencing their stories, and how the storyteller might relate to the story once told offered a framework for how to view the storytelling experience and what could be gained from it. As written about today in the clinical and behavioral sciences fields, narrative theory assumes that people construct their lives through stories in order to make sense of what has/is happening to them (White & Epston, 1990; Coulter 2014). Essentially, it proposes a framework for how people view their lives and tell stories about their lives.

S. N. L. Gilkey (✉)
Walden University, Minneapolis, MN, USA
e-mail: Sonia.Gilkey@waldenu.edu

© Springer Nature Switzerland AG 2021
R. P. Dealey, M. R. Evans (eds.), *Discovering Theory in Clinical Practice*,
https://doi.org/10.1007/978-3-030-57310-2_10

Narrative Theory and the Application of Narrative Therapy

Narrative therapy is a form of psychotherapy that leverages therapeutic approaches designed to support the client's values, skills, and knowledge they use to live their lives, tell stories about their lives, and solve problems that are part of their lived story or experiences (Madigan, 2019). Consider this while also challenging the frames or perspectives that can be confronted through the telling of one's story (Carey & Russell, 2004; Madigan, 2011). Narrative therapy is generally credited to Michael White and David Epston during the late 70s and early 80s at a time when the fields of family therapy and community practice were burgeoning (Madigan, 2011).

The narrative therapist focuses upon assisting people to create stories about themselves, about their identities, that are helpful to them. This work of "re-authoring identity" claims to help people identify their own values and identify the skills and knowledge they have to live these values. Through the process of identifying the history of values in people's lives, the therapist is able to co-author a new story about the person. Narrative therapy reflects the idea that the experiences we have are mapped into stories that we construct as our reality, and further, those stories become seen as "problem-saturated dominant stories" (Merscham, 2000, p. 282).

White & Epston (1999) defines narrative as a storied account of a person's experience in a particular context or situation, told through the unique biographical lens of the client. Narrative theory gives us an ontological framework for deconstructing an individual's experience and then re-authoring or re-storying that experience such that the individual is equipped with a more empowered sense of their reality and thus, better able to respond with improved coping strategies as it relates to the psychosocial impact of traumatic events. The details of the story are not changed, but rather a deeper reflection of the details, feelings, and behaviors associated with the story or event are pursued. As well, how the client experiences the details and the shifting of perspective regarding the details stands to promote a change in the client's internal and external responses to the traumatic event or events, and allows for a safe psychological space for the re-storying of the event. Narrative theory lays the groundwork for such a reflection, and ultimately gives space for the development of narrative therapy as a therapeutic approach to helping clients recall, reflect, reframe, and renew the storying of events that have negatively impacted their lives.

As it relates to the therapist, therapist skills like the reflecting on the role of and practice of externalizing conversations with clients with complex trauma histories, and the application of reflective writing at the conclusion of each session. Each of these can help to inform the clinician's present and future clinical work when using narrative therapy with clients with complex trauma histories; and further aid in how the clinician shapes the therapeutic process such that it is responsive to both the internal (i.e., self-blame, emotion regulation, sense of control over what happens to you) and external trauma reactions (i.e., fighting, destruction of property, challenging authority) that can present in a client when a traumatic experience happens. This is important to recognize to ensure that the therapeutic process does not overlook the cognitive, environmental, and/or cultural influences that impact how the client responds to the narrative therapy approach.

The Case of J.J.

The Substance Abuse Mental Health Services Administration, or SAMHSA (2014) conceptualizes trauma in three potential ways called the 3 E's. They are events, experiences, and effects. The following is a case study that presents a clinician's work with a client who has experienced persistent trauma in childhood, adolescence and early young adulthood, to the point where he was hospitalized for psychosis after an arrest for stealing a car and assaulting a police officer. This case study considers the client's traumatic experiences and resulting effects as a key framework for the use of narrative therapy in dealing with the client's history of complex trauma experiences, self-loathing identity, and with a recent diagnosis of PTSD with psychotic features. The client's identifying information has been changed for confidentiality. Merscham (2000) observes that when working with a client with complex trauma experiences, the clinician should create a therapeutic environment where the client feels safe, engage the client in opportunities to retell and later, re-story the event in a psychologically safe way, and support the client in re-engaging his/her/their environment in a way that feels safe for them, while also promoting a sense of being empowered to engage the environment that the client sees as harmful, uncertain, and untrustworthy in terms of his/her/their safety.

J.J. is a 20-year-old male whose parents are White and African American. J.J. presented with a significant history of early childhood adverse events. Since he was about 3 years old, J.J. recalls a history physical abuse, domestic violence in the home, persistent juvenile arrests for delinquent behaviors, past history of suicide attempts, dropping out of school at age 13, and past substance use although he stopped using drugs at age seventeen after a friend over-dosed from heroine. J.J. reported being brutally beaten by gang members to the point he thought he was going to die. He also reported a history of being removed from in the home at least three times, and that each time he was returned back to his abusive parents. He was age 7 when he first attempted suicide. J.J. tells the story of seeing a lot of community violence including seeing dead bodies as an almost daily occurrence in his community due to gun violence. This caused him to often fear for his life.

The client had just turned age 20 at the time he started therapeutic work with his therapist. He had been kicked out of the home of his mother for the fifth time in 3 months for violent outbursts and was couch surfing (staying with different friends for a few days at a time) to avoid having to live on the streets. He reported a recent break-up with a girlfriend about a week prior to attempting to steal a car. During the attempted theft of the car, the client was involved in an altercation with the police faced going back to jail not only for fighting with the police officer, but as a result of this altercation, he has violated his probation for a past domestic charge related to a fight with his mother.

Over the course of ten sessions with the client, the client reported hearing voices since age 11. He indicated that the voices often told him that he was worthless, ugly, dumb, didn't deserve to live, and that no one would ever love him. J.J. believed these voices but says they would only come when he felt overwhelmed with things that were happening in his life, or if he felt his life was at risk or threat of harm was imminent. J.J. dropped out of therapy at session 13, after the incident involving the assault against the police. About 2 weeks prior to the incident with the police, J.J. stated in his session with the therapist that he was beginning to see some progress in terms of how he managed his emotions when he thought about past events and could imagine a time when he would feel like he has some control over what happens to him. Of course, the break-up with the girlfriend a week later, resulted in J.J. feeling as if he needed to resort back to maladaptive coping behaviors. In previous sessions, J.J. stated that when he felt stressed, he would escape in his mind and try to shut everything out. He reported that he would become stressed out and unable to shut out negative voices in his head, as well as escape from overwhelming feelings of his demise. J.J. reported hearing voices in the past, and that this had resulted in suicidal attempts and violent outbursts. He says the voices often told him to kill himself and that everything would be okay if he was dead. J.J. indicated that he had attempted death by suicide at least three times in the past 18 months because he felt like he just couldn't take it anymore. J.J. had previously indicated that he knew the police was looking for him for a probation violation involving his mother, and that "death by cop" seemed like a good action to take, at least that is what the voices in his head advised him. Death by cop is often described as an individual recognizing that if he waves a gun at a police officer or demonstrates behavior that could be particularly threatening to a police officer, it is highly likely that the person will be shot by the police. J.J. believed if he attacked a police officer while in the act of stealing a car, for sure, he would be shot and killed. Since his suicide attempts had not worked, he believed this would be the only way to assure his death.

J.J. agreed to enter therapy as part of a diversion program to keep him out of jail for past offences. Before therapy was abruptly terminated because J.J. assaulted a police officer, he actively participated in therapy and was very open to the changing his life's narrative. The clinician used narrative therapy approaches like mapping, externalizing, deconstruction, establishing unique outcomes and re-storying (Madigan, 2011; White & Epston, 1990) to help J.J. deal with his past and current trauma experiences. J.J. stated that he often felt disempowered in his family and community, and that "being a young Black male in America, who can you trust to have your back. A black man's life means nothing, and neither do I. Who is going to care if I live or die?" J.J. identifies as Black/African American. J.J. had been engaged in some form of therapy since the first removal from the home at age 6 but had not seen a therapist since his last recognized suicide attempt at age 19. J.J. initially believed that therapy could not help him, and that he had never had anyone to really "see and hear" his side of his story. He was responding well to the narrative therapy model, and although treatment was interrupted, J.J. showed great promise in being able to use this intervention approach to aid in his psychological healing of the various life traumas he has experienced.

Theoretical Integration

J.J. has had a range of diagnoses from childhood PTSD, major depression, ADHD, ODD, schizophrenia, and most recently, PTSD with psychotic features after a full review of his psychological history and environmental trauma experiences. Although the last noted diagnosis for J.J. was PTSD with psychotic features, upon further clinical assessment and review of the current diagnostic literature, the more probable diagnosis for J.J. is C-PTSD (complex post-traumatic stress disorder) (Herman, 1992). J.J. symptoms particularly reflected issues of negative self-image, significant problems with emotion dysregulation, risky behaviors, and some personality disturbances along with the traditional indicators of PTSD (Herman, 1992).

J.J.'s case has great utility for the application of narrative theory in the context of narrative therapy as an appropriate intervention approach because J.J. is able to view his trauma experiences as something that he can now "re-author" and have greater control over how he experiences his trauma. With the help of the therapist, he is guided through an emotional and cognitively safe deconstruction of his trauma experiences; is able to identify unique aspects of his experience that can be viewed differently and give him more power over how he recalls the experience; and allows him to establish a re-storying of his trauma experiences that recognizes and acknowledges his trauma from his point of view, while also encouraging a shift in how he experiences the thoughts, emotions, and behavioral reactions to his trauma. J.J. through the use of narrative therapy is able to shift the narrative of his trauma experiences from one filled with negative thoughts, overwhelming feelings of disempowerment, and distorted perceptions of self to one that creates a more empowered identity and sense of control in his environment. Narrative therapy gives him the freedom to express the range of emotions, cognitive distortions, and behavioral reactions he experiences as a result of his trauma, and gives his experiences validity through a safe emotional space of re-storying of the past and present; this with the help of the therapist who is skilled to guide J.J. through the narrative therapy process. This can lead to the unpacking of multiple trauma layers and allow the therapist and client to co-construct a therapeutic approach that engages the client from an empowered position throughout the intervention. This can be critical for a client like J.J. who has had a prevailing experience of invisibility and feeling muted to tell his story of trauma (excluding states of psychosis).

Larkin and Morrison (2006) in their edited book, Trauma and Psychosis: New Directions for Theory and Therapy, offer critical discussions of the relationship between trauma and psychosis, the experience of traumatic life events and its impact on cognitive processing, and how assessing the effects of the traumatic experiences on clients can be used to determine a therapeutic approach that best fits the worldview of the client, and thus identify a therapeutic approach that works best for the client. Larkin and Morrison (2006) subsequently frame narrative therapy as a thera-peutic approach that aligns with the client's natural or intuitive approach in telling his/her/their story and thus supports the client and therapist in being better equipped to leverage narrative therapy techniques like externalizing, deconstruction, unique outcomes, and re-storying. It is essential that the clinician establish a pathway to helping the client understand his/her/their perceptions and processing of present and past trauma experiences, as well, identifying the current problems that have come out of the past and present trauma experiences in order to successfully identify and apply a trauma-informed therapeutic approach like narrative therapy.

Narrative Therapy Techniques

The hallmarks of narrative therapy include the four key techniques of externalizing, deconstruction, unique outcomes, and re-storying or the re-telling of one's story from a different framework. When the therapist engages in these techniques the individual is able to follow a pathway that supports their ability to experience and manage emotions, thoughts, and behaviors that might be difficult to confront in the moment, but give the individual a better understanding of how their trauma experi-ences can be re-storied so as to inspire a different perspective of the trauma experi-ences. Hence, the individual is able to achieve more control regarding internal and external responses to trauma experiences and thusly, yield healthier coping and improved trauma reactions to the traumas the individual has experienced.

When working with the client to use externalizing, the therapist is essentially challenging the client to consider their current problems or problem situations as external to them; that is the individual is encouraged to reframe the problem or negative experience in such a way that they have control to change something about how they deal with or approach the negative situation or problem rather than trying to get the problem or negative situation to change. The individual learns to focus on changing his/her/their reaction or response to a problem situation or problem envi-ronment rather than expecting the problem or problem situation to change. The individual learns that internal processes can be leveraged to change the outcome such that negative thoughts and behavioral reactions that used to result in unwanted consequences are averted.

Deconstruction requires that the therapist help the client to reduce the problem experience or situation to different parts, focus on what really is the main issue, then reorder the parts to either include or exclude those elements that do not serve the individual. The focus is instead on those aspects of the problem or situation that the individual has the greatest chance to influence and exert some personal power.

Unique outcomes allow the therapist to help the individual craft a story about their lived experience, particularly as it relates to past trauma experiences, in a way that tells the individual's story from a positive lens. The individual and therapist together identify those unique aspects of who a person is to create a stronger func-tional identity that supports positive self-imaging, self-confidence, personal control and authority over one's lived experience; and thusly develop a story-line that affirms the individual as valuable, worthy, and capable of creating a different lived experience for themselves.

Re-storying or the re-telling of one's story involves telling the individual story through the eyes of the individual as he/she/they see their story. The therapist helps the individual to tell their story in a way that is uninterrupted by others' point of view and subsequently encourages the individual to view their story with ownership (Beaudoin, 2015). "This is my story as I see it" essentially is the goal of this process. As the individual tells the story of their lives, they are able to identify spaces where the story can be altered to support a more empowered, self-efficacious narrative with meaning that can only be determined according to the person telling his/her/their story. The individual is helped to identify what meaning they make of their life and discover a new meaning and re-storying of those experiences that have impacted them so greatly (White, 2007; White, 2011).

When working with individuals to leverage these techniques in the context of trauma, the therapist is always looking to center the individual and the individual's perceptions of their trauma at the forefront of these techniques (Beaudoin, 2015; Etchison & Kleist, 2000). The traumas the individual has experienced play a key role in this process, but only as a means to help the individual confront those traumas and develop a different emotional, cognitive, and behavioral response to said traumas (Beaudoin, 2015). Helping the individual be better able to do this gives the individual authority and control over how he/she/they confront and eventually respond to the traumas that have impacted the individual so negatively and creates opportunities for the individual to identify healthier coping responses when trauma triggers arise.

Cultural Considerations

Therapists who work with clients with a history of complex traumatic experiences will want to give special consideration to aspects of the individual's intercultural experience that impact how the individual navigates their trauma psychologically, socially, and behaviorally. The experience of trauma and how it is portrayed in a family system, as well, how it is portrayed in social discourses within a specific cultural community can impact greatly how the individual relates to his/her/their experience with trauma; and further what behavioral, psychological, and social responses the individual deems as acceptable reactions to trauma. Oftentimes the individual's trauma response and how the client makes sense of the trauma experienced is rooted in their perceptions and realities about what the environment expects. African Americans have a cultural experience with trauma that is complex, particularly if you position historical or transgenerational trauma at the forefront of the trauma discussion (Denham, 2008; Leary, 2005). In direct relationship to that, the therapist must then recognize and understand how coping in a historical trauma context across generations affects how the individual, family system, and the

ecological environment of which the client is challenged to survive and accommodate can become a space of normality rooted in daily survival strategies that often
work against the individual's ability to leverage healthy coping behaviors and cognitive and emotional wellbeing.

When there are daily risks from the environment and daily experiences that
either trigger negative trauma reactions or pose significant risks to the individual's
sense of wellbeing and protection, helping the individual to use an intervention like
narrative therapy with tools like externalizing, deconstruction, identifying unique
outcomes, and re-storying can enable to the therapist to offer strategic therapeutic
guidance that better supports a trajectory of successful therapy outcomes over the
course of the therapy experience. The therapist is charged in the case of J.J. to position the therapeutic experience in a way that culturally centers J.J.'s view of the
world, and culturally locates the process of narrative therapy in order to promote
J.J.'s ability to relate to concepts like externalizing or re-storying. Culturally locating an individual's trauma means getting to know the community of which the individual is challenged to survive and thrive in the past and present; getting to know
how the client relates historically to the lived experience of trauma (in the case of
J.J. as an African American in the United States), both for him/her/their self and the
family system; and understanding those cultural nuances that dictate how an individual views trauma. African American males often are less able to express their
traumas through traditional means (like therapy for example), and thus have adapted
their coping in many instances to the internal and/or external demands and expectations of the environment (Denham, 2008; Oliver, 2006). This is important to consider as trust and relatability of the therapist can present as a significant challenge
when the individual has different socio-cultural rules to dealing with life stressors
including significant trauma experiences.

In the case of J.J., how the individual views trauma experiences, the therapist's
ability to understand trauma experiences from the vantage point of the individual
lived experience, and having a cultural understanding of what behavioral and emotional reactions that are either normalized or considered taboo as it relates to trauma
experiences for the individual are particular cultural considerations the therapist
will want to be skilled to explore. The therapist must be willing and skilled to
explore complex dynamics like the environment, internal sensibilities of the client,
family coping and functioning, family trauma history, socio-culturally accepted
reactions or coping as it relates to trauma, and the impact of historical trauma on the
client systems which can be just as complex of a conversation as traumas rooted in
the family and community system (Denham, 2008; Leary, 2005). Because there is
often a distrust of healthcare services and stigma associated with mental health care
for many African Americans, particularly males (Rich, Grey, et al., 2005; Oliver,
2006), the therapist will want to acknowledge and validate the client's perceptions
of engaging mental health services. As well, the therapist will need to give particular attention to ensuring trust and personal and psychological safety while also recognizing the unique needs of the African American male client when it comes to
engaging the therapeutic process and an intervention model like narrative therapy.

Discussion Questions

Consider the following questions if you were the clinician working with J.J.

1. Using the case example of J.J., which aspect of his childhood experience would you use to introduce J.J. to the idea of a narrative therapy approach? Explain.
2. How does narrative theory aid in the clinician's understanding about how people tell their stories and changes they can make to their stories of the lived experience when given the opportunity to do so?
3. Consider some typical trauma reactions. How might the clinician use narrative therapy to support the client in normalizing such reactions?
4. How might the therapist use the techniques of unique outcomes and deconstruction to help the client begin to re-story some aspects of her/his/their trauma experiences?
5. What are some key practice considerations when engaging African American males in the therapeutic process should therapists keep in mind?
6. If you consider a client's socio-cultural experiences and complex realities in the world, in what ways does narrative therapy promote culturally responsive approaches as it relates to a client like J.J.?

References

Beaudoin, M. N. (2015). Agency and choice in the face of trauma: A narrative therapy map. *Journal of Systemic Therapies, 24*(4), 32–50.

Carey, M., & Russell, S. (2004). *Narrative therapy: Responding to your questions*. Dulwich: Dulwich Centre Publications.

Coulter, S. (2014). The applicability of two strengths-based systemic psychotherapy models for young people following Type 1 trauma. *Child Care in Practice, 20*(1), 48–63.

Denham, A. R. (2008). Rethinking historical trauma: Narratives of resilience. *Transcultural Psychiatry, 45*(3), 391–414.

Etchison, M., & Kleist, D. M. (2000). Review of narrative therapy: Research and review. *The Family Journal, 8*(1), 61–67.

Herman, J. L. (1992). Complex PTSD: A syndrome in survivors of prolonged and repeated trauma. *Journal of Traumatic Stress, 5*, 377–391.

Larkin, W., & Morrison, A. (2006). *Trauma and psychosis: New directions for theory and therapy*. New York, NY: Routledge Publishing.

Leary, J. D. (2005). *Post Traumatic Slave Syndrome: America's legacy of enduring injury and healing*. Milwaukie, Oregon: Uptone Press.

Madigan, S. (2011). *Narrative therapy: Theory and practice*. New York, NY: American Psychological Association.

Madigan, S. (2019). *Narrative therapy* (2nd ed.). New York, NY: American Psychological Association.

Merscham, C. (2000). Restorying trauma with narrative therapy: Using the phantom family. *The Family Journal: Counseling and Therapy for Couples and Families, 8*(3), 282–286.

Oliver, W. (2006). The streets: An alternative black male socialization institution. *Journal of Black Studies, 36*(6), 918–937.

Rich, J. A., Grey, C. M., et al. (2005). Pathways to recurrent trauma among young Black men: traumatic stress, substance use, and the "code of the street". *American Journal of Public Health, 95*(5), 816–824.

Substance Abuse and Mental Health Services Administration. (2014). SAMHSA's concept of trauma and guidance for a trauma-informed approach. HHS Publication No. (SMA) 14-4884. Substance Abuse and Mental Health Services Administration.

White, M. (2000). Reflections on narrative practice. Dulwich Centre Publications.

White, M. (2007). *Maps of narrative practice*. New York, NY: W.W. Norton & Company.

White, M. (2011). *Narrative practice: Continuing the conversation*. New York, NY: W.W. Norton & Company.

White, M., & Epston, D. (1990). *Narrative means to therapeutic ends*. New York, NY: W. W. Norton & Company.

Chapter 11
Relational Cultural Theory: The Case of Monica

Ashley Davis and Nina Aronoff

Introduction to Relational Cultural Theory

In this chapter, the case of "Monica" will be used to illustrate Relational Cultural Theory (RCT) principles in action. All names and identifiers of this case have been changed to maintain the confidentiality of the client. Monica is a 32-year-old Latina woman who sought therapy in an outpatient mental health clinic. During her childhood and now within her workplace, she has felt unseen, misunderstood, and held back from advocating for herself and fully investing in relationships. Several cultural and social factors add complexity to this case, including often passing as White due to her light skin color, a family history of immigration, and resisting her parents' traditional gender expectations. Using RCT, the therapist–client relationship is explored for its salience in moving from disconnection to connection, healing empathic failures, nurturing relational competence, and promoting individual growth.

Self-in-Relation Theory

Traditional psychological development theory, as well as Western civilization values are value-based and focused on achieving certain developmental aims. Maturity requires obtaining a sense of self and identity that is measured through one's capacity to separate, be autonomous, and achieve through competition. These are the primary values of a specific, *dominant* culture (White, middle class, patriarchal), and *dominant* psychological theory (White, Western, male, heterosexual). These

A. Davis (✉) · N. Aronoff
Social Work, Boston University, Boston, MA, USA
e-mail: Davisash@bu.edu; NAronoff@bu.edu

© Springer Nature Switzerland AG 2021
R. P. Dealey, M. R. Evans (eds.), *Discovering Theory in Clinical Practice*,
https://doi.org/10.1007/978-3-030-57310-2_11

theories/paradigms also underemphasize, or even devalue, connection as central and too much emphasis on relationship as a relative inability to individuate.

The traditional Western model of psychological health is not entirely without merit. However, it is limited in scope when considered from a more inclusive perspective that considers gender, race, class, and other structural variables, as well as connection as a primary site of growth. The specific risk of a non-inclusive perspective is seen in how connection is pathologized or treated with a paternalistic gaze; that is, being "too connected" is seen as enmeshment or being less well developed, psychologically. Western models pathologize connection at another level, which is by predominantly locating "the problem" in individual pathology. Problems are seen as individual deficits to be addressed and changed, rather than breakdowns in connections.

In 1976, Jean Baker Miller published the first edition of *Toward a New Psychology of Women*, describing a distinctly *alternative* approach to understanding development, particularly women's psychological development. Miller saw how the broader cultural context of Western societies (and Western psychology models) was based on principles of dominance and subjugation; maturation is based on competition and individualism versus connection and collaboration, and the goal of development is separation and autonomy. In this paradigm, she recognized that certain groups are both socialized differently and also denigrated for not achieving those specific markers of achievement and maturity that are typically assigned to men with power.

Her primary focus was on women's development in this phase of the theory's development, although over time the theory highlighted how these dynamics pertain to other groups marginalized by factors such as race, class, and sexual orientation. Seeing the inherent gendered organization of society, where men, the "ideal," are socialized and rewarded for separation and disconnection, and women are socialized to be connected and responsive to others, Miller's theory applied a different, critical approach to human development. She described how women's socialization goals reinforced what aspects of character and functioning were simultaneously expected of women and in that sense "valued," while also being seen as "less than" that of males.

Miller reframed developmental goals of connection as strengths rather than weaknesses. This "reframe" was by no means a method for justifying women's second-class status, psychologically, politically, or economically. Miller's constructs, instead, cast light on society's distorted views of power, in which "good" power was *power over* others, relying on the establishment and maintenance of a dominant/subordinate basis for all social relations. She brought a radically different view to the purpose of therapy and how to understand the kinds of psychological and emotional injuries that brought many people to therapy in the first place.

Throughout the 1970s, 1980s, and 1990s (until her death in 1996), she collaborated with a group of colleagues (Judith Jordan, Alexandra Kaplan, Jean Stiver, Janet Surrey, Wendy Rosen, Maureen Walker, and others) to develop and articulate ideas of women's development and therapy based on what women valued and expressed as substantive elements of their own lives. Along with other feminist psychology scholars at the time, Miller and her colleagues explored the processes by which women develop and what constituted the priorities of a mature self. These priorities, even necessities, define the development of self, sense of self, and identity as a *process that occurs in connection with others* (beginning with caregivers and continuing throughout life), as well as the importance of relational competency to healthy development. These scholars saw that women's development throughout life is oriented to the emergence, development, and maintenance of relationships, based on early connections with primary, female caregivers and later transferred to friends and to all other intimate relationships through care and nurturance of connection.

Disconnections, and the devaluing of women's priorities, strengths, and resilience, could then be seen as a cause for many of the troubles women brought to therapy, often without a way of seeing the problem as anything but themselves. Consequently, therapy could be seen as the ideal, relational context in which to activate authentic and empathic connections as a place of healing and empowerment. Through a therapeutic relationship that would ideally be based on mutuality and a *power-with* rather than *power-over* model, change would occur on a different scale, both within the therapeutic context and beyond. Lastly, and important in contrast to many developmental theories, relational growth does not occur in stages but as a process that embodies the possibility for one's capacity to change and develop across the lifespan (Jordan, 2013).

This work resulted in the identification of the "five good things" (Miller, 1976/2012) in growth-fostering relationships: "a sense of zest; a better understanding of self, other, and the relationship (clarity); a sense of worth; an enhanced capacity to act or be productive; and an increased desire for more connection" (Jordan, 2018, p. 25). The principles of authenticity, empathy, and mutuality are central aspects of growth-promoting relationships that facilitate connections and healing (Jordan et al., 1991; Walker, 2004). Authenticity can be described as "a person's ongoing ability to represent her−/himself in a relationship with increasing truth and fullness" (Miller & Stiver, 1997, p. 54). Empathy is "the dynamic cognitive-affective process of joining with and understanding another's subjective experience" (Jordan, Kaplan, Miller, Stiver, & Surrey, 1991, p. 15) and also underpins the capacity to move out of disconnection, separation, and isolation into connection and healing. Mutuality is the capacity to move, and be moved by, relationship. In healthy relationships, the participants are authentically engaged, empathically connected, and mutually empowered.

By contrast, what occurs for people when the "five good things" are missing, is "a drop in energy, decreased sense of worth, less clarity and more confusion, less productivity, withdrawal from all relationships" (Jordan, 2008, p. 3). Relational disconnections lead to a sense of isolation, confusion, and shame about one's sense of self and value, worthiness to be in relationship, and abilities in life. These effects result from relational contexts in which one (or one's group) is disempowered and devalued, is faced with lack of clarity or confusion in relationships and has repeated experiences of disconnection. Disconnections are recognized as inevitable and potentially provide the necessary platform on which to rebuild connection and vitality.

Relational Cultural Theory

Relational cultural theory developed out of a growing recognition that self-in-relation theory needed to more fully integrate the widespread structural dynamics of unequal power and difference in society, emphasizing the reality that each of us lives in specific cultural contexts that affect development, and that some of those contexts have damaging effects on individual and collective health and wellbeing. The development of RCT re-centers Miller's original ideas about power and its implications across all systems of society as dysfunctional constructs, based on inequality and therefore, profound disconnection in all spheres of lived experience, in individual lives as well as structural systems. In Miller's original thinking about the *power-over* model inherent to societies based on colonization and slavery, the relational and social norms are aimed at maintaining structures that allow certain groups to dominate and therefore, require other groups to remain subordinate. As a result, all marginalized groups experience both internalized oppression and continuous overt oppression in daily life. In a relational context, people with more power become invested in defining others as different or inferior, and to using that power (directly or indirectly) to disconnect from people defined as "other." People from marginalized groups often feel disconnected and demoralized, and may internalize sense of being "less than," especially if disconnected from the strengths of their culture. Noting that relationships and disconnections are constructed within specific cultural contexts (Miller & Stiver, 1997), RCT more wholly delineates an understanding of inequality and injustice and provides a pathway for moving toward healing at multiple and more effective levels.

Turning the focus to injustice/justice, it becomes necessary in our work then to understand and be accountable to the costs of injustice, as it is meted out in individual, family, group, and community experience, to foster connections through which some of those injuries can be healed, and to re-center and reclaim marginalized perspectives and values in order to change not just individual lives but also society. Indeed, as Jordan noted, "Social change and social justice have always been at the center of RCT. Some people have said, 'Diversity is great and wonderful,' and everybody believes in it, but, in fact, diversity is a code word for differential stratifications around power" (in Trepal & Duffey, 2016, pp. 440–441). Alternatively, a justice-based approach requires a reorganization of power relations and an amelioration of disconnections.

RCT is applicable to contemporary practice in multiple ways. For one, the goals of therapy include a strong focus on individual and collective strengths and resilience as forces to be activated for connection and empowerment. Secondly, RCT highlights the dysfunction inherent to holding the individual accountable for social structures that are unjust, allowing the therapy to focus on the outcomes of living with the dynamics of oppression and privilege, and supports the idea that difference is a primary ground from which to grow and enhance connection and relational competence. Thirdly, RCT asks practitioners to review the issues we see in therapy critically, by not adhering solely to the paradigms of Western psychology that still dominate and that often focus on a deficits perspective, but instead to understand the social constructs and relationships that affect people's lives through disconnections. Similarly, if psychological problems emerge out of disconnections in relationships or patterns of disconnection, psychological health emerges out of relationships and contexts that are growth-enhancing and acknowledges the full range of clients' experiences in context.

The anticipated experience of cycles of connection and disconnection is understood on a much deeper and broader scale, encompassing the everyday weight and injury of oppression for all marginalized groups in the dominant culture, as well as the resilience and defenses required to survive in such conditions, which RCT refers to as "strategies of disconnection" (Miller & Stiver 1997, p. 106). Including in our scope of treatment these "strategies of disconnection" empowers us as clinicians to be of greater service. Therapy can aim to avoid the risk of not helping the client and, in some cases, being a site of oppression in and of itself, and instead, provide a context for healing that is both broad and deep. As Walker (2008) emphasizes, "In a culture that valorizes power-over as the means to physical survival, emotional safety, and material wellbeing, openness and uncertainty are dangerous options indeed" (p. 98). Therapeutic work aimed at enhancing relational capacity is indeed a "counter-cultural process" (Walker, 2008, p. 98).

Principles of RCT Theory

As with any socially conscious approach, different knowledge, values, and skills are demanded of the practitioner, beyond the competencies expected of any good client-centered therapy. This model must use a justice-based lens to shift away from deficits-based paradigms and toward strengths-based, relational paradigms that are based on understanding structural inequality and its effects on clients (including, perhaps, in previous therapy). Our process must include cultural humility and responsiveness, and increased empowerment and collaboration in practice.

First, practitioners must learn about the ways in which structural racism and other forms of cultural oppression manifest in Western society, as well as how those manifestations affect people individually, in groups, and in systems. Knowledge of oppression must include an understanding of privilege, the unearned advantages that dominant groups have by virtue of unequal social structures, not merit.

Second, practitioners must develop awareness about their assumptions, biases, and other unconscious forms of oppression and privilege they have internalized about themselves and others. Practitioners have to be increasingly open to learning about their own unconscious ways of behaving so as to avoid microaggressions, and to review their practice continuously for these effects. Additionally, this process necessarily entails awareness of one's own racial and cultural identity and development, as well as that of the clients with whom they meet (Malott & Schaefle, 2015).

Third, practitioners need to develop skills for holding the knowledge of oppression and privilege, in general and as applied to particular groups and their history, as well as skills for how to listen to the specific client and her experience. Following the principles of intersectionality theory (Collins, 1991; Crenshaw, 1991), social identities are understood to be multiple, intersecting, and often mutable depending on the immediate context and over time. Even after gaining knowledge, the practitioner will always be limited, to a certain extent, by their own lived experience. Consequently, the practitioner needs to stay open and curious about the very specific lived experience of the individual, couple, family, or group before them (Ruiz, 2012).

Fourth, practitioners need to be aware that the client's experience of the dynamics of oppression and privilege (as well as their own) may have resulted in certain beliefs, behaviors, defensive stances, and forms of resilience. In the client's presentation, these features may manifest as an abiding sense of distrust, shame, humiliation, frustration, numbing, or other expressions that can be easily mischaracterized but ought to be understood as a means of surviving in a world structured around inequality. These mechanisms can be seen as forms of strengths and resilience, as well as strategies of disconnection, that could be amenable to shift within the relational context of appropriately attuned therapy.

The very disconnections that bring people to therapy can be, over time, the basis for moving out of that disconnection, if the therapy both preserves the pace and dignity of the client and the therapist is themselves fully engaged, self-aware, and empathic. As Walker (2008) describes, "It is a fundamental premise of the Relational-Cultural Model that acute disconnection can lead to a deepening of connection. In other words, we learn to see acute conflict as the source of growth and possibility. Chronic disconnection, on the other hand, can lead to isolation, stagnation, and hopelessness" (pp. 89–90). Our orientation, as practitioners, must be toward connection.

Fifth, practitioners must be committed to ongoing growth and development of these skills and bodies of knowledge, including continuous reflection on ourselves in the work. This reflection is both an individual and relational process, as practitioners must engage in ongoing supervision or consultation about their work in order to grow.

Keeping these principles in mind, we will discuss a case based on one of our own practice experiences, applying these five principles, noting that some of them become visible only by critically thinking about them after the fact.

Introduction to the Case of Monica

Monica is a 32-year-old, bilingual, Latina woman who grew up in New York City. She works as a line cook at a popular Mexican restaurant and hopes to attend culinary school and open a restaurant of her own someday. Eight years ago, she met her partner, a White man named Tyler, age 34, at a neighborhood pub where they were both regulars for trivia and karaoke nights. Given the high cost of rent in the area, they opted to move in together and share living costs sooner than they otherwise might have. Their respective parents often inquire about marriage and grandchildren, but Monica and Tyler are uninterested in planning a wedding or becoming parents. They enjoy being active outdoors and volunteering with local organizations that support youth, build community, and promote social justice.

Monica is the eldest of three daughters. Her father worked a union job in construction, and her mother did not work outside the home. She cared for her children as well as elderly family members and was active in their local Catholic Church. Her parents immigrated to the United States from El Salvador in the 1980s. As part of the largest wave of El Salvadoran migrants, they came to escape the poverty and violence that resulted from the El Salvadoran civil war. Her father was successful in obtaining a work permit so the family would have documentation to stay in the country. Monica was the first family member to be born here. Compared to the rest of the family, she has a light skin tone and often passes as a White person. Monica's parents instilled the importance of education in their children and opted to send the girls to selective public schools that required entrance exams. All three girls took honors courses and participated in college-readiness programs.

Growing up, Monica's parents spoke to their daughters about their bodies and sexuality in a way that conveyed a sense of shame, danger, and fear. The sisters were admonished to dress modestly and avoid socializing with boys, and were told that dating could interfere with their education and ruin their futures. As a hard-working student, Monica worked diligently throughout high school. Even so, her parents—particularly her mother—expressed skepticism and concern about her whereabouts and choices. Monica recalled a time in high school when she had not yet completed a major assignment. In a panic, she and a friend skipped school to finish their homework together. When her parents learned of the unexcused absence, they were livid and assumed that she had violated their rules and had been promiscuous, despite her explanation and evidence to the contrary. For the next month, they required her to check in every hour and inform them of her whereabouts. She felt shamed and alienated, and worried that other adults would mistrust or doubt her integrity and intentions.

As adults, Monica and her sisters have not maintained close relationships with each other. Her sisters made similar life choices—in whom they married, what careers they pursued, and where they lived—that were expected and pleasing to their parents. They still live in New York, as do their parents. Monica feels unable to relate to their choices and feels judged by her decision to leave New York City, live with her White partner before marriage, and work toward becoming an entrepreneur in an industry dominated by men. She identifies as less religious and more politically liberal than the rest of her family. The entire family shares an uneasiness about recent anti-immigrant sentiments, despite the United States being their home for decades. At various points, Monica tried to reconnect with each sister separately, but gave up the effort when her interest in their lives was unreciprocated. She assumes that her parents and sisters are emotionally close and enjoy regular time together. While she did not want to be a part of that life, she also feels loneliness and lacks a solid sense of home, family, and culture.

Monica's job as a cook requires long shifts and leaves little time for friends. She spends most of her downtime with Tyler. She finds that their relationship feels more like considerate roommates at times, instead of romantic partners. Recently, Monica devoted a weekend to volunteering with a self-defense and empowerment training program for girls of color from low-income backgrounds. The instructor was a Black woman who related easily with the girls, used humor to diffuse tension, and commanded respect in the classroom. Monica, on the other hand, struggled to connect and build trust with the girls, and was unsure how to handle their repeated assumptions that she was a well-off White woman who could not relate to their lived experiences. As the class assistant, Monica found herself uneasy in the role of disciplinarian, in which she was to remind the kids to pay attention and stay on task. Her most gratifying experience was providing one-on-one support to a girl who only spoke Spanish and needed a translator to participate fully.

Monica has been struggling with increased anxiety and depressive symptoms, including low mood, poor energy, ruminative thoughts, and a loss of interest and pleasure. She called a local mental health clinic that provides outpatient counseling, and explained that she was interested in weekly therapy with a strong preference for a female therapist. Over the phone, she told the intake worker that she felt isolated and lonely, and wanted to feel closer to family, friends, co-workers, and others in her life. She worried that she had low self-esteem and difficulty trusting herself and others. Monica was matched with a similarly aged, White, female social worker who also happened to be from New York City. This social worker, Hanna, was relatively new to the practice and had a particular interest in women's and cross-cultural issues in therapy.

Theoretical Integration

Relational-cultural therapy offers a strengths and empowerment-based lens for understanding Monica's decision to enter treatment. Even in the face of disconnection and confusion, Monica has motivation, through therapy, to connect and improve her sense of wellbeing. It is important for all therapy to begin with relationship-building. The therapeutic relationship provides a solid foundation in which the work of therapy can unfold. From an RCT perspective, the relationship is not just the pre-requisite to the work of therapy. The relationship *is* the work itself, as growth occurs in therapeutic relationships oriented to connection (Miller & Stiver, 1997), and then potentially can manifest throughout the client's life.

With time and concerted effort, Monica and Hanna developed a solid relationship that reflected Miller's (1976/2012) criteria of the "five good things." Hanna paid attention to her own experience in the therapeutic relationship as one source of knowledge about the quality of connection. She also felt that their shared gender and having roots in New York might make for good points of connection. She was particularly attuned to shifts in how Monica spoke of connections and disconnections, how she showed up in the therapeutic relationship, and how her relational sense of self began to shift over the course of their work together.

Monica's relationships outside of therapy were important to explore as well. Monica had hoped for closer relationships with her sisters, partner, and friends. When these relationships stalled or were limited, she felt ineffective in forming and maintaining close relationships, and withdrew into isolation rather than potentially facing more rejection. She held back from connections as a way to protect herself from the pain of inauthentic relationships; this dynamic is called the central relational paradox (Miller & Stiver, 1997). In addition, it became clear that Monica had mostly become cut off from her culture. These disconnections had resulted in a terrible sense of isolation, loss of vitality, and a pull toward indifference that felt habitual but also deeply unlike herself.

Monica carried relational images, or mental constructs not entirely within her awareness and formed out of her ongoing and cumulative experiences in relationships (Miller & Stiver, 1997), that reflected her feeling of failure and resignation to disconnection. Through these images, Monica had come to define what she could expect in relationships and of herself, forming beliefs about her lack of worth and competence (Eldridge, Surrey, Rosen, & Miller, 2008). Hanna took a nuanced and strengths-based approach to interviewing Monica about her relationships. With whom did she feel most authentically herself? What told her that she could fully be herself in that relationship? In what relationships did she experience empathy? Who truly saw her, and how did she know she was seen and known? Had her experiences had an influence on other people's perspectives or choices? How did she know, and what did this mean to her? What feelings were evoked in reflecting on her relationships?

These questions helped Monica recover some positive and empowered memories, of her family, friends, and early relationship with her partner. She began to see new relational possibilities and strengths. They uncovered relationships that Monica had not thought of in these terms, including non-immediate family members and current acquaintances and coworkers that could be deepened into friendships. Monica also explored the sadness that arose from relationships that were cut-off or that did not feel satisfying. On her own, Monica could easily fall into a spiral of shame; in therapy, Monica experienced Hanna's empathy, authenticity, and connection as a supportive context in which to explore her life. Together, they considered her losses empathically and also with some new perspective. Through the therapeutic relationship, Monica began to shift her relational images and her sense of herself as able to form meaningful, authentic connections.

Working Through Disconnections with a Cultural Lens

Hanna formulated that Monica's distress, sadness, and anxiety arose, at least in part, from feeling shut out of relationships with family members and her culture. Monica had faced the central relational paradox with family members: stay in relationship in an inauthentic or disempowered way, or withdraw from those relationships for psychological self-protection. Disconnection had become a protective strategy for

Monica. When she was unable to bring her whole self to relationships with family members, she created necessary geographic and emotional distance (Comstock et al., 2008). Such an approach, in part, reflected healthy boundaries and a strong sense of self. At the same time, Monica appeared to internalize a sense of being unwanted in relationships, for being "different" from the expected norms of her own culture, along with feeling different from the majority culture. In her early life, she found a way to be her authentic self in connection to family, yet in her adult life, had no way to replace that familial and cultural experience elsewhere, leading to feelings of grief and ineffectuality.

One early disconnection that had an overshadowing influence in the present related to experiences with her family and gender socialization specific to her culture. Growing up Monica felt she was not always seen authentically or believed when she shared parts of herself. In one incident, she skipped school to finish an assignment. When her parents learned of this, she was disbelieved, shamed, and punished. Her mother made value-laden assumptions about her sexuality and the risks involved with this transgression. Even now as an adult, Monica did not feel her choices were understood or accepted, especially about moving in with her White partner and being disinterested in marriage and children. In the therapy, Hanna was able to reframe the incident along culturally specific lines, helping Monica to see that her reaction was valid, as well as helping her to understand her mother's sense of responsibility for her as a young woman. Hanna made a point to honor times when Monica shared openly and authentically, particularly about topics that could evoke shame or stigma. Their exchange allowed Monica, over time, to engage with increasing vulnerability, develop compassion and acceptance of herself, and see greater possibilities in her present and future.

Another topic central to Monica's experience of disconnection from both the majority and Latinx cultures was her repeated experience of having her race misidentified as White due to her light skin color. She resented that most people did not recognize the diversity of skin tones among Latinx people, and the work of educating others became exhausting and led to "erasing" her cultural identity because she could pass as a member of the dominant group. These moments were isolating and alienating, whether the assumptions were made by White people or people of color. Over time, these moments added up to a sense of inauthenticity and disconnection from the world. She also felt confused from the paired denial of her identity and relief from some discrimination, with which she was all too familiar. It was crucial for Hanna to engage Monica with empathy and reaffirm the experience of disconnection, while also connecting to the real feelings of loss and anger that accompanied those moments. As a White woman herself, Hanna needed to work inside and outside of the therapy room to understand the presence and effects of colorism (Burton et al., 2010), and to grasp the lived experience of oppression and discrimination, including the mixed feelings about "passing" and the consequences for Monica, both within and beyond the therapy. She needed to anticipate and be attuned to how their racial difference and racial identities manifested in the therapy. In this regard, Hanna raised the possibilities inherent to their therapeutic relationship at appropriate moments, when empathy and a sense of connection allowed for this issue to be directly addressed. Most importantly, Hanna practiced cultural humility and engaged in supervision to explore the racial and cross-cultural issues, so as not to derail or burden Monica with her own personal and professional development.

As they continued to work on disconnections in cultural contexts, Hanna and Monica unpacked her confusing experience as an assistant in the self-defense class. The girls had assumed Monica was a White woman who would not understand their lives. Together, Monica and Hanna explored how the girls' lived experiences of encounters with White women led to these beliefs, and how these assumptions created disconnection between the girls and Monica. Since individuals may turn to strategies of disconnection as a protective stance, when unable to bring their whole self to a relationship (Comstock et al., 2008), Hanna explored more deeply Monica's lifelong experiences of cultural disconnections, brought on by incidents of discrimination, ambivalence about "passing," and ultimately, the experience of the self-defense class. Hanna inquired about whether there were times when Monica needed to disconnect as a protective strategy and listened empathically for the pain that often accompanies those experiences. Monica used this opening to share more about herself, particularly times when she was marginalized as a woman, a Latina, and a second-generation American.

Hanna's direct and empathic questioning invited Monica to have empathy for the girls and to see herself in their experience, rather than simply feeling mis-seen in the encounter. Monica and Hanna also explored how the girls' assumption about Monica was incorrect and was based on incomplete information and a narrow definition of who is Latinx. Monica described the toll that it took to explain her actual background so she could be known more authentically and fully. It was not surprising that she felt most comfortable supporting a Spanish-speaking girl who otherwise would have been isolated. Monica helped the girl empower herself to have a voice, literally and figuratively, and thus rejected the idea that anyone needed to be marginalized for being different than the norm. In reflecting on this role, Monica recalled, with sadness and disappointment, times in her own life where a cultural connection had been missed and she had turned away. By feeling safe to be more authentic in those moments now, she could grapple with those feelings and reintegrate them as part of her story.

Hanna was curious, respectful, and validating in engaging Monica about her experiences of connections and disconnections, with particular attention to the ways their different perspectives reflected their respective social locations. Hanna could be another well-meaning White woman who was out of touch about the lives of the girls of color in the self-defense class, and out of touch about the reality Monica's lived experience. Staying close to Monica's experience, she resisted a singular perception of the racial dynamics, especially knowing that as a member of the dominant group, her socialization differed from Monica's. Their respective standpoints allowed for the development of mutuality, or "a creative process in which the contributions of each person and openness to change allow something new to happen" (Miller & Stiver, 1997, p. 13).

Since relationships are seen to occur along continuums of connection and disconnection (Comstock et al., 2008), therapeutic relationships are no exception. It may feel threatening or overwhelming for Monica to experience disconnection within the context of therapy, as it may evoke a fear that the relationship is like others in her life: not solid enough to withstand the rupture. Disconnections, however, are simply unavoidable and inevitable. These incidents are opportunities to explore the feelings of disconnection, to respond with empathy and mutuality, and to work toward deeper connection.

Knowing Monica's history with disconnections that were never repaired satisfactorily, Hanna anticipated with her that disconnections would occur in therapy at some point. Using the concept of anticipatory empathy (Jordan, 2018), she wondered with Monica about how they might work through those moments. Wanting to know, understand, and to be influenced by Monica's experience, Hanna invited Monica to give voice to experiences of disconnection within their relationship. Rather than shaming or distancing, Hanna's presence and empathy could encourage a deeper, stronger connection between them (Miller & Stiver, 1997) and, subsequently affect Monica's relationships outside of therapy.

Cultural Considerations

To apply the five principles framework described earlier in the chapter, we would need to look at each element for a better understanding of the therapeutic process in this case. The first principle—to understand racial and cultural oppression in Western society—can be seen in a number of ways. One critical piece is the need to understand Monica's experience as a Latina in the United States and her family's immigration history. In this regard, Hanna had work to do. Monica's parents immigrated to the United States during the revolution in El Salvador. They arrived under complicated circumstances, as the United States was lending support to the violent and oppressive regime from which they were fleeing. Although 20% of Salvadorans live in the United States (U.S. Census Bureau, 2017), they do not constitute one of the three main Hispanic cultural groups—Mexican-Americans, Cuban-Americans, and Puerto Ricans—and thus, often experience a sense of invisibility and not-belonging (Millar, 2004). Her parents' immigration story, like countless others, is rooted in violent struggles over power and trauma, resulting not in peace and stability but disconnections and relocation to a foreign environment. They endured forced disconnections from El Salvador and forged new connections in the United States, where they received assistance and were also thrust into a society in which they were suddenly a minority, linguistically and culturally. In a new and unfamiliar country, her parents had to re-build community through work, their church, and having a family in which to instill their values and hopes for their daughters' futures.

Despite its history as a nation of immigrants, the United States has been inhospitable for many who seek refuge and a new life here. From an RCT perspective, when immigrants are expected to assimilate or acculturate to the dominant culture, they are expected not to be their authentic selves; they may be true to their culture and language only within their own communities. Dominant groups have a long history of creating divisions based on race, gender, class, and immigration status, among other aspects of social identity, to harness and maintain economic, social, political, and cultural power (Miller, 2008). Within this structural hierarchy, the dominant group has "more resources and privilege and thus, has more capacity to force or control others" (Miller, 2008, p. 147). For many immigrants, this sets up a struggle about how to maintain their traditional culture while also trying to make their way successfully in the new culture, a balance often difficult to maintain as their children assimilate.

One way in which dominant cultural power is exerted is through controlling images, images that "define for each group what is acceptable and what is not, what people can and cannot do" (Eldridge et al., 2008, p. 33). Explicitly and implicitly, dominant groups circulate controlling images through social institutions to "suppress less privileged groups, restricting minorities' access to upward mobility, self-efficacy, and power of self-definition" (Vasquez-Tokos & Norton-Smith, 2017, p. 913). Thus, controlling images are a "major instrument of power" that provide the ideological justification of oppression (Collins, 1991, p. 68). Although Monica's parents had lived in the United States for more than 30 years, and Monica had been born here as a U.S. citizen, they were faced continuously with controlling images about Latinx immigrants. For example, there is a pervasive controlling image of Latinx immigrants as coming to the United States to "steal our jobs." This xenophobic sentiment fuels fear and resentment reflects a scarcity model, and results in discrimination. As a light-skinned Latina, Monica is simultaneously oppressed by the controlling images *and* buffered by the privilege of passing as White. In addition to her lighter skin, she is in a relationship with a White man whose access to sources of power and privilege is greater than that of her parents and sisters. Such a pairing is more common for light skinned Latinx people than those with darker skin (Burton et al., 2010). These conflicting realities may evoke guilt, confusion, and ambivalence, among other feelings, for Monica as she grapples with her bicultural identity.

Additionally, Monica's formative years were spent as the first child born to immigrants who ascribed to traditional roles and values for their family. As Monica grew up, she made decisions based on her personal and professional ambitions, rather than following traditional cultural scripts that may have felt right to her mother and sisters. One such script, *marianismo*, derived from a strong Catholic belief in the Virgin Mary, was reflected in her mother's identity and views on marriage and motherhood, as well as the messages she imparted to her daughters about their bodies and sexuality (Ruiz, 2005). When Monica skipped school to work on an assignment, her mother's reaction may have come from genuine concern that, without supervision, teens could have sexual relationships that could result in pregnancies and might derail their education and their futures. This fear may be rooted in her knowledge of disparities seen within her community; among Latinas, the teenage pregnancy rate is nearly double the national average (Aparicio, Pecukonis, & Zhou, 2014).

Her mother's reaction may also have reflected her sense of responsibility to instill values about sexuality in her daughters, and her urgency and fear about what it would mean or how it would reflect on her mothering, if her daughters did not heed these messages. Latinx immigrant parents who closely monitor their adolescents' peer group and appear "overprotective" may subscribe to the belief that "the degree of social success for Latino adolescents in this critical phase of development will ultimately determine the total family's success in the new society" (Quinones-Mayo & Dempsey, 2005, p. 658). The assumption, however, left Monica feeling un-seen and alienated, rather than trusted and believed. As an adult, Monica adopted a different script—or simply made pragmatic choices given the current financial reality for young adults living in expensive cities—by sharing an apartment with her partner without plans to get married or have children. Another possibility, that this move was a defensive strategy related to her relationship with someone White, was also important to explore. These are all major areas of knowledge that Hanna, who may have known some of them, would have needed to educate herself to, in order to best inform her work with Monica.

The second principle pertains to self-awareness and continuous reflection on her own assumptions, biases, and sociocultural location. As a professional with a long-term commitment to cross-cultural practice, Hanna was invested in this practice of self-questioning and openness to growth. However, there were areas of knowledge that were new to her. Although she had worked with LatinX clients previously, this was her first experience of a client from El Salvador. As such, she needed to question her assumptions about knowing the culture, as well as intercultural dynamics specific to El Salvadorans. She also needed to be sure she was prepared to respond empathically to the presence of intergenerational trauma. Hanna has explored her own intersectional identity; yet knowing it is an ongoing process helped her be open to increasing her knowledge and awareness without resistance and seeking additional supervision to support this process.

The third principle—the need to understand the dynamics of oppression and privilege in general as well as listening acutely for individual experience—is one that Hanna has been practicing for some time. She strives to remain attuned to the specific experiences that Monica has had, and the ways in which Monica embodies her own struggle with racial and cultural identity. Monica's struggle reflects the tensions between cultural and generational differences that arise when she reflects on her life choices (e.g., partner, career, etc.), as well as the positive and negative consequences of being able to disconnect from her family of origin. Hanna must hold both the general and specific cultural information about Monica in her ongoing process of connecting with her client, while being careful not to assert her assumptions or values about these choices.

The fourth principle involves understanding how Monica's experience and expression may have been molded by her varied experiences and ensuing choices based on being in several marginalized groups in U.S. society: a first-generation, heterosexual, Latinx female from El Salvador who is light-skinned, living with a White partner at a distance from her family, and disconnected from her two younger sisters. What defensive strategies might she have incorporated as a means of survival in those contexts? In many contexts, she has made choices that reflect a sense of agency and empowerment, yet those choices have also resulted in disconnections that appear drain her vitality and result in stagnation (Walker, 2008). In her day-to-day living, exemplified by her experience with the girls' group, she experiences exchanges that reinforce her privileged *and* marginalized statuses, in a variety of contexts and in a variety of ways, positive and negative, and ultimately confusing in some respects. She has mixed feelings about how closely she wishes to claim her racial and cultural identity and what might be the costs of those decisions, including the moments in which she decides to "pass" as White. Hanna witnesses Monica's meaning-making about her world, values, and experiences on her own terms, without reframing them in her own language or according to her own lenses and, in that ongoing process, creates a space for empathy, mutuality, and authentic engagement.

In terms of principle five, Hanna remains aware of how her own lived experience and worldview can intrude on the connection she is forging with Monica. Her work on herself and in understanding cross-cultural practices help in this effort. She also uses supervision with a practitioner who has many years of experience in cross-cultural practice to explore her own vulnerability and process questions about her strategies for creating a growth-promoting relationship with Monica. As the final principle of the framework, Hanna demonstrates a commitment to her own ongoing growth and development. That process alone, however, is not enough, as she has to bring herself fully and authentically to the therapy with Monica, thereby engaging her own openness to connection and the real process of collaboration with her client to be successful.

Through their intentional and sustained work, Monica felt seen and understood by Hanna in ways unlike what she had experienced with many people in her life. She left sessions feeling many emotions and ultimately less confused and more energized and hopeful. Monica could tell also that she was having an impact on Hanna's thinking and understanding. She responded to a particularly empathetic comment by saying, "Yes! You get it. Can I carry you around so you can vouch for me?" Monica felt believed and trusted in her relationship with Hanna. Her playful and poignant comment conveyed that Hanna's empathy resonated deeply, and provided a needed, powerful, and transformative relational experience. Both women came to know that they had taken risks and built a healing connection. Ultimately, their process reflected the sense of mutuality at the heart of growth-promoting connections.

Discussion Questions

1. To what aspects of the therapy does RCT draw our attention? What does it neglect to focus on?
2. What are ways that a therapist can demonstrate empathy, authenticity, and mutuality in their relationship with a client?
3. What would you do if you found yourself in a cross-cultural disconnection with a client?
4. Given the importance of the identity(s) of the therapist, how would who *you* are have an impact on the relationship you would form with Monica?
5. If your practice is with couples, families, groups, communities, or organizations, how would you apply the concepts of RCT in those contexts?
6. In therapy, how might you see the effects of *power-over* and *power-with* cultures?

References

Aparicio, E., Pecukonis, E. V., & Zhou, K. (2014). Sociocultural factors of teenage pregnancy in Latino communities: Preparing social workers for culturally responsive practice. *Health & Social Work, 39*(4), 238–243.

Banks, A. (2015). *Wired to connect: The surprising link between brain science and strong, healthy relationships.* London: Penguin.

Burton, L. M., Bonilla-Silva, E., Ray, V., Buckelew, R., & Hordge Freeman, E. (2010). Critical race theories, colorism, and the decade's research on families of color. *Journal of Marriage and Family, 72*(3), 440–459.

Collins, P. H. (1991). *Black feminist thought.* New York: Routledge.

Comstock, D. L., Hammer, T. R., Strentzsch, J., Cannon, K., Parsons, J., & Salazar, G. (2008). Relational-cultural theory: A framework for bridging relational, multicultural, and social justice competencies. *Journal of Counseling & Development, 86*(3), 279–287.

Crenshaw, K. (1991). Mapping the margins: Intersectionality, identity politics, and violence against women of color. *Stanford Law Review, 43*(6), 1241–1299.

Eldridge, N. S., Surrey, J. L., Rosen, W. P., & Miller, J. B. (2008). What changes in therapy? Who changes? *Women & Therapy, 31*(2–4), 31–50.

Jordan, J. V. (2008). Recent developments in relational-cultural theory. *Women & Therapy, 31*(2–4), 1–4.

Jordan, J. V. (Ed.). (2013). *The power of connection: Recent developments in relational-cultural theory.* Routledge.

Jordan, J. V. (2018). *Relational-Cultural therapy.* New York: American Psychological Association.

Jordan, J. V., Kaplan, A. G., Miller, J. B., Stiver, I. P., & Surrey, J. L. (Eds.). (1991). *Women's growth in connection: Writings from the stone center.* New York: Guilford Press.

Malott, K. M., & Schaefle, S. (2015). Addressing clients' experiences of racism: A model for clinical practice. *Journal of Counseling & Development, 93*(3), 361–369.

Millar, M. (2004). Odyssey to the North: Salvadoran identities-American lives. *Dialogos, 8*(1), 49–51.

Miller, J. B. (1976/2012). *Toward a new psychology of women.* Boston: Beacon Press.

Miller, J. B. (2008). Telling the truth about power. *Women & Therapy, 31*(2–4), 145–161.

Miller, J. B., & Stiver, I. (1997). *The healing connection: How women form relationships in therapy and in life.* Boston: Beacon Press.

Quinones-Mayo, Y., & Dempsey, P. (2005). Finding the bicultural balance: Immigrant Latino mothers raising "American" adolescents. *Child Welfare, 84*(5), 649–667.

Ruiz, E. (2005). Hispanic culture and relational cultural theory. *Journal of Creativity in Mental Health, 1*(1), 33–55.

Ruiz, E. (2012). Understanding Latina immigrants using Relational-Cultural Theory. *Women & Therapy, 35*(1–2), 68–79.

Trepal, H., & Duffey, T. (2016). Everything has changed; An interview with Judy Jordan. *Journal of Counseling & Development, 16*(4), 437–441.

U.S. Census Bureau. (2017). Facts for features: Hispanic Heritage Month 2017. Retrieved from https://www.census.gov/newsroom/facts-for-features/2017/hispanic-heritage.html.

Vasquez-Tokos, J., & Norton-Smith, K. (2017). Talking back to controlling images: Latinos' changing responses to racism over the life course. *Ethnic and Racial Studies, 40*(6), 912–930.

Walker, M. (2004). How relationships heal. In M. Walker & W. B. Rosen (Eds.), *How connections heal: Stories from relational-cultural therapy* (pp. 3–21). New York, NY: Guilford Press.

Walker, M. (2008). How therapy helps when culture hurts. *Women & Therapy, 31*(2–4), 87–105.

Chapter 12
Systems Theory: The Case of Esperanza

Madeline Pérez De Jesús, Enitzaida Rodríguez, and Gladis Anaya

Introduction to Systems Theory

Systems theory calls practitioners to examine the relational dynamics between individuals, and between and within groups, organizations, or communities, as well as mutually influencing factors in the environment (Leighninger, 1977). While systems theory is commonly used in social work, the authors argue that the profession would benefit from expanding its scope to intentionally explore issues of diversity and the impact of trauma. This chapter demonstrates how systems theory supports culturally informed clinical practice by highlighting the case of "Esperanza," a 16-year-old ninth-grade student who, with thousands of others, migrated from Puerto Rico to urban cities in the Northeast and other areas in the United States after being displaced by Hurricane Maria in 2017. Two Latinx social workers enter Esperanza's life in her new high school setting in Hartford, Connecticut.

The authors' overview of systems theory includes a perspective on how problems arise, how systems theory facilitates understandings of the change process, and implications regarding complementary interventions that are can be used based on this theory. The case study of Esperanza details her demographics, family dynamics, and various ecological factors that influence her situation. Theoretical integration

M. P. De Jesús (✉)
Department of Social Work and Equitable Community Practice, University of Saint Joseph, West Hartford, CT, USA
e-mail: madelineperez@usj.edu

E. Rodríguez
School Social Worker, University of Saint Joseph, West Hartford, CT, USA
e-mail: erodriguez@usj.edu

G. Anaya
University of Saint Joseph, West Hartford, CT, USA
e-mail: ganaya@usj.edu

© Springer Nature Switzerland AG 2021
R. P. Dealey, M. R. Evans (eds.), *Discovering Theory in Clinical Practice*,
https://doi.org/10.1007/978-3-030-57310-2_12

follows the case example, with the authors demonstrating how systems theory informed social workers approach to treating the client and understanding the client's response. Important considerations regarding intracultural and intercultural factors that influenced clinical intervention effectiveness are described. The authors note that systems theory also served as a tool for resolving a practice conflict for the social workers. In the concluding section, the authors pose discussion questions to support readers in thinking critically about the usefulness of systems theory and the process of integrating theory into clinical practice.

The overarching premise in systems theory is that there is *reciprocity* in the interlocking relationships between people, families, social networks, neighborhoods, and other related systems (Leighninger, 1977). This reciprocity includes elements in the environment such as nature, encompassing physics, chemistry, biology, and social relationships. While the origins of systems theory come from Charles Darwin's notion of "the survival of the fittest," the theory has broadened and supports social work by offering a balance between biological, psychological, and sociological roots. Systems theory had a significant impact on social work during the 1970s, when its contributions included general systems theory, and family therapy developed into ecological theory and the importance of networking (Payne, 2002). This theory is particularly useful to social workers, as they are trained to have a person-in-environment lens.

Leighninger (1977) identified three main contributions of systems theory to the field of social work: (1) it expands the practitioner's focus beyond the client to the client *and* their environment, (2) it allows for a better account of social change, and (3) it has the potential of having social workers reflect on issues of power and control. Social workers are not strangers to examining ourselves as agents of social change, and in his discussion of the applicability of systems theory, Leighninger reminds us that we must also examine the other side. In other words, just as we explore how social workers are agents of change, it is also central to look at how we might operate as agents of social control or even social oppression.

Systems theory offers a specific perspective on how problems arise. This perspective is evident in a definition of social work that was put forward by the International Federation of Social Workers in 2000, and subsequently reinforced by the International Association of Schools of Social Work (as cited in Hutchings & Taylor, 2007, p. 382):

> The social work profession promotes social change, problem-solving in human relationships, and the empowerment and liberation of people to enhance well-being. Utilizing theories of human behavior and social systems, social work intervenes at the points where people interact with their environments. Principles of human rights and social justice are fundamental to social work.

Systems theory assumes individuals are part of overlapping or intersecting multiple networks and defines problems within this overlap. No individual lives in a bubble; our families, our communities, the related systems with which we engage, and the broader sociopolitical and economic climate impact us all. Just as the problem is found in these overlapping systems, this is also where potential solutions lie.

Payne's (2002) reminder of the importance of networking is applicable to our clients, as the people in their systems shape the types of information they receive and their beliefs, which in turn impact their actions. For instance, a client may have access to accurate or inaccurate information, and may operate in the world with a sense of entitlement or a sense of despair.

Various interventions emerge from the foundational principles of systems theory. Visual aids provide a concrete way for clients and those who work with them to digest how systems theory helps make meaning of a client's life. Ecomaps and genograms are examples of visual aids that can be particularly useful during the early stages of rapport building and assessment. Ecomaps are visual representations of the interconnected systems of an individual's life that show the relationships between the client and their environment (Hartman, 1995). Whereas ecomaps display a more comprehensive arrangement of systems, genograms fix the gaze specifically on family dynamics across generations, allowing client and practitioner alike to examine family dynamics with particular focus on behavioral patterns and quality (Altshuler, 1999). The relationships between systems, people, and the client are represented by lines drawn on the visual aid. A thick solid line represents a meaningful positive connection. A broken line symbolizes a weak connection. Lines drawn with crosses through them indicate stress. Some lines might also include arrows to suggest that a relationship appears to be mutually beneficial, mutually toxic, or one-directional. Pope and Lee (2015) are a good starting point for further direction on the creation of genograms.

Systems theory helps social workers understand that it is not only individuals who serve as stressors or supports to a client; the processes of bureaucratic institutions that represent education, religion, political, and economic entities can stress or support a client, as well. Understanding the client's supports and stressors is a prerequisite to engaging with the client therapeutically.

Cognitive behavioral therapy (CBT), a psychological treatment model in which the treatment provider helps the client become aware of their thought processes, belief systems, and antecedent behaviors, is one approach being increasingly used by social workers to treat clients with a range of problems, including but not limited to anxiety, depression, and post-traumatic stress. CBT as an empowering model aligns well with systems theory, as clients from underrepresented groups are frequently subjected to discrimination and intergenerational trauma. CBT can be trauma-focused, and typical techniques for child and adolescent survivors of trauma include cognitive reprocessing and reframing, exposure, stress management, and parental treatment (Cohen, Mannarino, Berliner, & Deblinger, 2000).

Mutual aid groups, another intervention model, situate individuals who are undergoing similar social problems as providers of support to each other, in the context of a group working on solutions. Such groups provide opportunities for clients to share their lived experiences while witnessing each other's accounts of interactions with various systems, and subsequently influencing each other (Gitterman, 2004).

Social workers frequently engage in a role traditionally referred to as case management, a process of assessing the client's needs and then securing (in some cases advocating for) a package of services. Consistent with a focus of engaging clients with institutional actors, resource referral is an intervention in which social workers secure assistance for clients to supplement supports that are limited or unavailable from their personal agency standpoint. All the heretofore mentioned types of interventions help ground understandings of the case study of Esperanza.

Introduction to the Case of Esperanza

Esperanza is a 16-year-old Puerto Rican heterosexual female. All names and identifiers of this case have been changed to maintain the confidentiality of the client. A ninth-grade student at her local urban high school, Esperanza lives with her 7-month-old baby, 34-year-old mother (Ms. Colon), and two adolescent siblings in an apartment in Hartford, Connecticut. While neither Esperanza nor her family currently attend church services, they identify as Catholic and were all baptized as infants. Ms. Colon, the primary income-earner, works as a home health aide for the elderly. Both of Esperanza's parents stopped their formal schooling after eighth grade. The family unit receives some public assistance and financial contributions from Esperanza's siblings; also high school students, who both hold part-time jobs. The family's primary language is Spanish.

Esperanza was referred to the school social worker last year, initially for academic reasons. As an "over-age student," Esperanza was required to undergo a series of educational evaluations. While Esperanza did not have any learning disabilities, she was 2 years behind grade level due to gaps in her school attendance and limited English-language proficiency. Her social work referral expanded beyond academics after her classmates informed teachers that Esperanza was pregnant. Because she was a pregnant minor, a referral to the state child welfare agency was also made. Despite being polite and cooperative with the social worker, Esperanza initially refused the involvement of school and state officials, stating she "tenia todo el apoyo en su familia" ("had all the support she needed within her family"). Esperanza previously received counseling services from a school social worker as an elementary school student in Puerto Rico, to support her coping with her parents' divorce. Counseling services then involved 6 months of weekly individual sessions, which Esperanza described as supportive. She has since developed and maintained healthy relationships with both parents, who appear to collaborate well in their co-parenting of Esperanza and their other children. Esperanza's relationally healthy and loving family, as well as her personal resilience, prove to be strengths in her treatment.

Esperanza's presenting concern was her increase in trauma-related symptoms, including increased anxiety, depressive mood, difficulty concentrating, and lowered frustration tolerance. These symptoms were interfering with her ability to maintain effective, positive communication with others both in school and with her personal relationships. Esperanza also stated she was fearful of "engaño" (Spanish for trickery or fraud) from institutional officials such as social workers and teachers.

During the first 5 years of her life, Esperanza lived with both of her parents. At the age of five, her parents divorced. Although her parents terminated their marriage, Esperanza reports that her parents speak about each other in cordial ways and engage in healthy co-parenting. This cooperative co-parenting engagement is a family strength, especially since she has gone back and forth living with each in the years since their divorce. Back and forth is also a larger pattern for Puerto Ricans, as it references travel between the island and the mainland in a circular motion facilitated by U.S. citizenship. Despite having legal recognition as U.S. citizens, Puerto Ricans who have spent time in both places often experience cultural discrimination and feelings of not belonging to the island or the mainland. Acevedo (2004) references this dilemma as belonging "neither here nor there."

Between the ages of 5 and 12, Esperanza lived intermittently with each of her parents and migrated back and forth between Connecticut and Puerto Rico on at least three separate occasions. When Esperanza was 12 years old, her mother moved to Connecticut in search of employment with two of her children (the eldest and the youngest). Esperanza remained in Puerto Rico with her father for three years until her mother could "send for her" to move to Connecticut.

When Esperanza was 15 years of age and still living with her father in Puerto Rico, she experienced the devastating impacts of a hurricane that led to a mass exodus from the island to the United States. Esperanza is a survivor of sexual abuse. While she described having a "boyfriend," she clarified that this person was a man 10 years her senior. Despite this being a relationship that felt like a courtship for her and was approved by her family, it is a situation of abuse. She was not within the legal age of consent to engage in a sexual or emotional relationship with this adult.

Esperanza's mother and older sister appear to be affectionate and reliable positive supports for her. They care for Esperanza's baby while she is at school. On days that Esperanza does not have family childcare, she does not attend school. This accumulation of absences (an average of one day a week) impacted Esperanza's academic progress and was brought to the attention of the state child welfare agency as potential educational neglect. The engagement with child welfare also revealed that Esperanza had been impregnated at 15 by a 25-year-old man, which raised concerns. Esperanza assured social workers that she was not raped and was "in a relationship" with her child's father. Despite her description of her child's father as an attentive partner and active father to their child, he was arrested on multiple counts, including statutory rape for his involvement with Esperanza. Esperanza interpreted her boyfriend's arrest and her social service involvement as unjust, and she experienced the state and judicial system as preventing her and her infant from receiving his emotional and economic support.

Upon migrating back and forth from Puerto Rico to the mainland United States, Esperanza had to learn to navigate two distinct cultures and languages. She also had to adapt to two separate family structures and dynamics of interaction. She showed signs of anxiety and depression and made statements about how she struggled being a teen mom while desiring to engage in typical adolescent activities, and the ramifications of those tensions in a social context. For example, the social worker noted that Esperanza lamented about missing the junior prom and other social activities due to her caregiver responsibilities. Despite these difficulties, Esperanza stated that her baby is "mi cariño" ("her love") and speaks about the child with much affection.

After Hurricane Maria, there was little evidence of support for the mental health impacts of this natural disaster on the many students migrating and integrating into mainland American schools. As Puerto Rican students increasingly enrolled in urban high schools, social workers scrambled to address these challenges and meet the needs and demands of newly arrived families that had been deeply impacted by the hurricane. In the scope of this distressing event, the school social worker and her MSW intern worked with Esperanza.

During the initial phase of working with the client, the workers administered psychological first aid, a set of support actions aimed at reducing post-traumatic stress related to natural disasters often offered in schools. Psychological first aid centers around the core actions of contact and engagement, safety and comfort, stabilization, information gathering, practical assistance, connection to social supports, information on those supports, and linkages to collaborative services (Ruzek, Brymer, Jacobs, & Layne, 2017). Psychological first aid was offered both individually and in group settings for Esperanza and her classmates, as the enrollment of displaced Puerto Ricans increased in their high school. The efforts of the social workers were to help Esperanza feel assured, connected, and supported in her current environment. Within a few weeks of working with Esperanza, it was clear that the experience and aftermath of the hurricane had severely impacted her. She had reported nightmares and trouble sleeping, and appeared to have decreased frustration tolerance despite remaining polite to those in authority.

Theoretical Integration

Systems theory was a useful tool both in supporting the social workers with their treatment of Esperanza and in understanding the client's response. By focusing on the notion that there is reciprocity in the relationships between individuals, groups, organizations, and communities, as well as the larger sociocultural and political environment, the social workers were not only better equipped to identify factors that hinder Esperanza but potential solutions, as well.

Esperanza received treatment from the school social worker (a bilingual Latina of Puerto Rican descent) and a social work intern (a bilingual Latina of Mexican descent). The clinician (and the clinician in training) approached their work with Esperanza from a stance of cultural humility, in which they were able to incorporate Latino cultural values such as *personalismo*, which refers to the significance Latinos place on positive rapport with others (Mogro-Wilson, 2013; Mogro-Wilson, Rojas, & Haynes, 2016). More than merely engaging with Esperanza in her native language, Spanish, personalismo involved asking Esperanza about her extended family members and engaging in informal exchanges to establish rapport.

It is important to differentiate for emerging social workers the differences between an informal exchange (which facilitates trust) and unprofessionalism (which diminishes trust). These informal exchanges included brief, playful debates over whose brand of Puerto Rican coffee is better and who is the favorite participant in *La Voz* (the Spanish-language version of the singing competition, *The Voice*). Establishing rapport with Esperanza in this way was vital during the engagement process. Rapport is the entry point to the client–worker relationship. More than comfort, receptiveness, and respect, rapport is a commitment to display warmth, interest, and caring in a way that encourages the client's trust and confidence. Choosing a highly viewed talent competition as an initial conversational prompt proved to be an excellent choice, as it provided at least 20 weeks of continuous narrative from which to build a relationship ("Can you believe Tania was eliminated in week three? Did you text your vote for the semi-finals of *La Voz*?"). Moreover, selection of a show that was popular in Puerto Rico allowed for cultural affirmation, a sense of familiarity, ease of communication in the native language, and joy. Personalismo sustained and supported the therapeutic alliance, as it built trust, confidence, and respect while diminishing Esperanza's worry about potential "engaño" (trickery).

Systems theory allowed the workers to expand their view of trauma as being a component of the environment for this youth. With this in mind, they continued their work with Esperanza using ACEs (Adverse Childhood Experiences) screening to assess how many types of maltreatment a client has experienced prior to the age of 18. This tool covers ten types of trauma within three categories: abuse, neglect, and household dysfunction.

Trauma-informed approaches recognize that there have been potential traumatic experiences in the lives of our clients. Social workers must explain to clients why they are asking sensitive questions rather than just ask them as a matter of protocol. These explanations demonstrate mutual respect and cultural humility. Recognizing that sensitive questions may be misunderstood as "engaño" (trickery), in this case, the social workers began by informing Esperanza that they needed to ask her some "preguntas intimas" (intimate questions) to support her in maintaining healthy personal and academic relationships. They explained this was part of a screening tool to help people and apologized in advance if they made her feel uneasy. By offering this apology, the social workers were rebuilding trust with Esperanza. The onus is on the social workers to create, sustain, and/or repair the client–worker relationship, and systems theory taught these social workers that they inherited Esperanza's distrust from previous incidents experienced as betrayals from institutional actors. These incidents include the involvement of child welfare services because of teachers disclosing "her private life," as well as a slow relief response from the U.S. government to assist Puerto Rico during and after the hurricane.

Systems theory helped the social workers see how betrayals such as the incarceration of Esperanza's boyfriend also took place at a macro level. In Esperanza's eyes, her relationship was legitimate, and this perspective was further confirmed for her because she had the consent of her parents. There may thus be traumatic stress from the hurricane experience coupled with the type of trauma that arises for groups of people who have experienced disparate treatment (Matheson, Foster, Bombay, McQuaid, & Anisman, 2019). The apology for asking about intimate matters is one of several ways the social workers sought to affirm Esperanza's legitimate feelings of distrust.

Esperanza agreed to answer the ACEs questions. The MSW intern facilitated the questionnaire in a conversational tone, rather than administering the tool as a formal survey. The intern, speaking in Spanish, framed the questions in ways that supported the therapeutic alliance and empowered Esperanza to respond candidly. ("Esperanza, we know these questions may make you feel uneasy and we are sorry for that. We need to know if a parent or other adult in the household often or very often … cursed at you or insulted you? Think about it. Take your time."). Here, the MSW intern sandwiches the ACEs question between a statement that affirms the client's feelings and reassurance that she does not have to rush through this process.

Esperanza's overall score was two out of a possible ten. She scored yes to questions #4 (feeling unloved or unimportant from her family) and #6 (parents ever separated or divorced). Esperanza was hesitant about answering question #3 (did an adult or person at least 5 years older than you ever touch or fondle you or have you touch their body in a sexual way?). She struggled to understand the age of consent law in Connecticut (as well as throughout all of the United States and Puerto Rico). It was incomprehensible to her that the father of her daughter was held legally responsible for a sexual relationship with her as a minor, resulting in 3 months in jail and a court order to pay child support after his release. Esperanza struggled with the conflictual way the court ordered her boyfriend to pay child support, when prior to his arrest he had been both emotionally and economically supportive of her and the child.

Her family described Esperanza and her co-parent as a loving couple with joint plans for the future. Through the conversational facilitation tool of ACEs, the social work intern learned from Esperanza that she knew many couples with a 10-year age gap, and early-age pregnancy was an intergenerational pattern in her family. Despite this, it was critical for the social workers to be mindful of the imbalance of power between Esperanza and her child's father. Power imbalance is what allows an adult to take advantage of an underage person in ways that meet the American Psychological Association's definition of sexual abuse. The MSW intern made a note in the questionnaire about the circumstances of Esperanza's "relationship" and the client's belief that she is not a victim of abuse.

While her ACEs score is relatively low, systems theory helped the workers explore Esperanza's perspective and understand that she has experienced more trauma than her score displays. Additional traumas not represented in this assessment include Esperanza's displacement from her family/country, her early pregnancy, surviving as a teen parent, her status as a sexual abuse victim (related to a consensual sexual relationship with 25-year-old adult male who was viewed as a sexual predator), DCF involvement (educational neglect), and her mental health diagnosis (anxiety, depression, PTSD). For example, Esperanza experienced trauma in the loss of the person she identified as her boyfriend, whose incarceration was directly connected to her disclosure to someone that he was the father, as well as incidents in her macro environment related to surviving a natural disaster and various forms of cultural assault from government officials.

As a result of the ACEs assessment, not only have the workers continued their work with Esperanza through a trauma-informed lens, but they also made the realization that trauma was a component of the environment for Esperanza. While Esperanza's ACEs score was two, the mutually influencing factors in the environment are trauma-infused, providing a comprehensive understanding of her lived experience. From a macro lens, understanding Puerto Rico's commonwealth status as neither a U.S. state nor an independent country sheds light on the territorial limbo that migrants experience in their "host" country. Mental health professionals have highlighted the colonization of Puerto Rican as a factor to consider when treating Puerto Rican clients (Teichner, Cadden, & Berry, 1981).

As mentioned, ecomaps are visual representations of all the systems at play in an individual's life, while genograms show the relationships between a client and their family members. The MSW intern engaged Esperanza to collaborate on creating ecomaps and genograms to support an understanding of the interconnected systems in her life. Before inviting the client to create visual representations of her own life, the intern first focused on developing trust by collaborating on an ecomap based on a fictional character. They collectively chose the movie *Real Women Have Curves*, a 2002 comedy about a Latina teen and her dynamic with school and family. The intern's engagement strategy included the small but significant detail of preselecting the menu of movies and ensuring that all the films were comedic and based on Latino culture. Utilizing a Latinx-focused movie both affirmed the client's heritage and was a trauma-informed strategy to minimize any potential triggering that might occur from watching a drama that centrally focused on adverse childhood conditions. Choosing the movie together also temporarily suspended the worker–client hierarchy. The shared decision making of the therapeutic intervention allowed Esperanza and the intern to work together to understand the main character and her relationship to the family and systems around her. In that exercise, Esperanza was able to see how one is not only influenced by people and systems, but can also take actions to be the influencer.

Ecomaps and genograms visually demonstrate the relationships between systems, people, and the client, which are represented by the intensity and direction of lines drawn on the visual aids. In drawing the relational connections in the genogram of the main character, Esperanza communicated her understanding of systems theory as the interrelatedness of a person and their environment. In drawing these lines for herself, Esperanza expressed a significant amount about her life without needing to say much verbally. The intern learned that Esperanza experienced high school to be a source of stress. (The workers had differing views on Esperanza's school attendance.) While her teachers worried that Esperanza would be missing significant instructional time, Esperanza viewed herself as a responsible mother who cared for her child when family members were not able to step in. The representations serve as prompts for the intern to use at follow-up meetings.

The social work intern was forthcoming in asking Esperanza if they could talk about her family as a way for her to better understand herself. Esperanza agreed. The intern then utilized a strengths perspective as she tapped into Esperanza's passion for art to make the activity more engaging and student focused. Social work interns are often limited in how they can assist a client. However, this scenario proved to be a win-win. While the school social worker was unable to dedicate time to such detailed visual aids due to her large client case load, the intern was available. The intern happened to be learning about these tools in her Master of Social Work program and appreciated the opportunity to further develop her skills. Most importantly, Esperanza benefited from the creative activity.

While the under-resourced high school had limited supplies, the intern was able to take advantage of a recent donation of art supplies such as poster board and vivid paint colors to make the activity creative and fun. As Esperanza drew thick solid lines to represent strong relationships and faint lines to represent weaker bonds, the intern was able to ask questions such as, "How would you describe your neighborhood?" and "In what ways do you rely on professionals to help you and in what ways do you rely on family?" Her answers provided further evidence of Esperanza's reliable family network, which supports her with childcare and ensures that she and her child are cared for in their home.

Esperanza's healthy baby, her determination to be a good mother, and her hardworking family were all strengths identified in this activity. Esperanza noted that her language and culture were strengths. She discovered that not being fluent in English was a present challenge, as was being a teen single parent and having limited economic resources. However, she reclaimed her power in being able to engage in this analysis of herself rather than being talked at by professionals. Over time, Esperanza was able to identify her situation as temporary. She was able to reframe her situation and articulate how she can work on developing into a bilingual and bicultural communicator and identify some life goals by using the supports provided by her family and institutions. The reclaiming of her personal agency is an example of a powerful outcome of working with a culturally attuned social worker and MSW intern.

The intern took this art ecomap project one step further by asking Esperanza to do a separate ecomap for her life in Puerto Rico. It was in that activity that Esperanza illustrated the significant differences with respect to time, method of communication, and cultural expectations in social service care on the island versus a mainland urban city. This visual representation served as a tool to help explain Esperanza's point of view to new service providers and those who were still developing their cultural awareness (an outcome discussed further in the cultural considerations section of this chapter).

The social workers then focused on securing supports for the two parental figures in the family: 16-year-old Esperanza and 34-year-old Ms. Colon. These supports were in the form of mutual aid groups. The social workers acknowledged to Esperanza the reality that while she has the desires and responsibilities of a teenager in high school, these dynamics are complicated by her role as a mother. Therefore, she needed a space that was specifically designed to aid her in these simultaneous, and at times conflicting, roles.

Esperanza benefited from a Spanish-language teen mother's support group embedded in her high school. Receiving mutual peer support from students who shared her situation created the conditions for Esperanza to seek out more resources as friends vetted them. She was able to see how her peers benefited from state-subsidized childcare and parenting classes and began to let go of the initial reservations she had about receiving such aid.

The workers, as well as the members of the mutual aid group, encouraged Esperanza to have regular communication with her father to strengthen his role, which had been weakened after the divorce and displacement. While Esperanza's future with her child's father is unclear due to his incarceration and the power imbalance between them, she recognizes that healthy bonds with her parents, siblings, and extended family will provide her with support and perspective on how to proceed with healthy relationships. She has committed to supporting her child by maintaining a positive relationship with the child's father.

During a debrief session with Esperanza, the social worker explained statutory rape and age of consent. Esperanza had difficulties understanding why the father of her baby was seen "like a criminal" when, according to Esperanza, he was emotionally and economically supportive towards the baby. She shared that his incarceration caused additional emotional trauma and economic family stress. Esperanza shared that she willingly chose to have sex with her boyfriend out of love and emphasized that she never felt forced. In trying to advocate for herself and the father of the baby, Esperanza inquired if the court would allow her to make a statement in defense of her boyfriend. She expressed that she would tell the judge she acted freely and voluntarily and was knowledgeable about what she was doing. The social workers had to reframe Esperanza's relationship for her. While they acknowledged that she consented to the relationship, they explained to her that due to her age there is a power differential between her and her child's father. This was one of the more challenging cognitive reframes that became part of Esperanza's longer-term treatment plan.

Ms. Colon was offered the opportunity to participate in *Madres de Madres* (Mothers of Mothers), a support group for grandmothers under 40 years of age. Unfortunately, due to Ms. Colon's need to manage two jobs and take care of her family (including serving as a childcare provider for her granddaughter), she was unable to make herself available to attend the group. Ms. Colon also clarified for the social workers that even if she did have the time, she would not attend *Madres de Madres* because "de esas cosas no se hablan afuera de la casa" ("These types of things are not spoken of outside the home"). The intern continued to forward information to Ms. Colon and intermittently reminded her that since it was an open group, she was welcome to join at any time.

The social worker recommended a state-subsidized childcare agency for Esperanza's daughter and successfully secured a spot for the child. Utilizing the childcare agency would have provided relief to the family by minimizing Esperanza's school absences, freeing up some time for Ms. Colon to consider attending *Madres de Madres* or engage in self-care, and allowing Esperanza's baby to engage with other children and participate in developmentally appropriate play that is not always available in contexts of overworked caregivers. Unfortunately, Esperanza refused the childcare resource, claiming "nadie cuide lo de uno mejor que uno" ("No one care for your own, like yourself"). This statement, which points to Esperanza's suspicions about anyone outside her nuclear family caring for her child, is related to the theme of fear of experiencing trickery from institutions. Further exacerbating her distrust in systems, the local news had recently reported the arrest of several staff members at a subsidized daycare center for their physical abuse of toddlers.

Rather than contradict Esperanza's beliefs, the social workers deferred to Esperanza, acknowledging her agency and right to self-determination, which further empowered Esperanza and fortified the therapeutic alliance between them. The social workers then reframed the childcare conflict for Esperanza. Specifically, they supported her in seeing that chronic absenteeism is strongly linked with low academic achievement and school non-completion. Therefore, activating the childcare resource would allow Esperanza to focus on school, which in turn would create employment opportunities that directly impact her own and her daughter's future. While this did not work immediately, over time the social workers were able to help Esperanza view childcare support as a resource for her to be able to better provide for her child for the long term.

Once Esperanza established months of consistent and engaged participation in the young mother's support group, the social worker explored her interest in cognitive behavioral therapy. Esperanza agreed. The social worker met with Esperanza in a private, quiet room and guided her with a series of questions to tap into her emotions. Upon Esperanza articulating a fearful thought, the social worker gently inquired about the thought with questions asked in a gentle tone, such as, "I hear you. Why do you think that is true?" This gentle questioning of Esperanza's fearful thoughts eventually helped her develop alternative narratives. These changes in thought then led to more positive emotions, which can support new and different behaviors that ultimately support change.

The technique of gently challenging fearful thoughts allowed new thought patterns to emerge. Initiating the CBT approach via Cognitive Behavioral Intervention for Trauma in Schools individual sessions, the social worker helped Esperanza address underlying symptoms of stress and trauma. Through this process, Esperanza was able to understand that her underlying thoughts and feelings are interrelated and were influencing her actions and behaviors.

While the social work intern was not able to lead the CBT sessions, she was able to learn in other ways. For example, the intern completed the online Cognitive Behavioral Intervention for Trauma in Schools training and discussed these themes at length in supervision. Furthermore, the intern utilized some individual cognitive-behavioral approaches with Esperanza, including but not limited to psycho-education discussions and relaxation and mindfulness strategies that supported the cognitive restructuring work led by the social worker. The tasks of the social work intern and her contributions to this case are highlighted to illustrate ways social work supervisors can carve out meaningful assignments for interns who might have limited ability to lead a case, and provide social work students with ideas of how they might initiate such roles in supervision.

Cultural Considerations

Cultural considerations must always be taken into account; even in situations of shared heritage, social, cultural, and economic contexts may still differ. In this case, the social workers of Latinx descent had also undergone their own migration journeys, intensifying their mindfulness of the client's sudden transition from a relaxed island community to the hustle and bustle of urbanity. Other service providers might misunderstand this mismatch of pace as the client's disinterest in receiving services. However, the social workers knew from both professional and personal experience that Esperanza's follow-up delays were related to her being unaccustomed to urgency and immediate agency responses. As such, they affirmed Esperanza's lived experience while orienting her to new communication expectations from Hartford's school, child welfare, and criminal justice systems. To prompt their client to secure resources, the social workers often used a gentle tone to remind Esperanza, "Things are done differently here."

While many social workers may take on the task of informing their clients that there are rules and regulations they must follow, culturally affirming social workers take this task to the next level and actively offer themselves as a human connection to what may feel, at times, like faceless bureaucracy. In this case, the workers used the metaphor of a bridge to describe how they are links between Esperanza and the institutions with which she must interface. Positioning themselves as "the bridge" was another active attempt to (re)build trust. Although the distrust they experienced was inherited, as opposed to earned, the social workers knew it was their responsibility to earn their client's confidence. In addition to serving as liaisons and coaches, they took on a "clinician-activist approach" (Walz & Groze, 1991), recognizing that Esperanza was not always able to articulate cross-cultural misunderstandings and they were needed to advocate on her behalf.

It bears repeating that sharing a cultural background with one's clients does not eliminate cross-cultural conflict. For instance, these social workers understood that Esperanza's family endorsed her romantic relationship with her child's father. The 10-year age difference did not render it illegitimate, from their perspectives, as they believed Esperanza was old enough to consent to the relationship as a teenager. This dynamic was conflictual for the social workers, who understood that Esperanza and her family consented to the relationship but also understood this relationship to constitute sexual abuse. The genogram helped the workers identify an intergenerational pattern of sexual abuse; Esperanza, her mother, and her aunts were all underage mothers with children fathered by men much older than them. While the social workers have not yet established a strong enough foundation with the family to explore this sensitive topic, they have identified as potential areas to expand upon in family therapy the multi-faceted dimensions of abuse and the difficult reality that family approval does not preclude abuse.

Currently, there is a debate about distinguishing between PTSD and complex stress disorder (the latter not yet in the DSM 5) in order to acknowledge the pervasive negative outcomes (social determinants) of long-term exposure to IPV, neglect, childhood abuse, and other traumas that do not fully meet PTSD criteria. It is worth noting that Esperanza and other immigrants/migrants might fall under this category as a result of having faced natural and human-caused catastrophes in Puerto Rico, as well as "host" country discrimination, cultural violence, etc.

Systems theory helps social workers tease out the diversity of the Latinx experience. For example, the intern (who was of Mexican descent) viewed Esperanza's U.S. citizenship as an asset, given that she herself had undergone significant legal and economic hurdles to secure citizenship status. Esperanza, on the other hand, was unable to identify her ability to migrate as a privilege. While this may be related, at least in part, to Esperanza's youth, the affordances of systems theory to allow concerned parties to delve deeper and identify that while Esperanza's move from the island is defined legally as migration (traveling within the same country), she has experienced it culturally, socially, and linguistically as immigration (traveling from one country to another).

Discussion Questions

These questions challenge the reader to think critically about the theory and integration of the theory in practice.

1. What are some of the assumptions of systems theory? How are these assumptions aligned with the work of social workers?
2. How might systems theory serve as a tool to help social workers create strategies to build trust with a client who explicitly shares their legitimate disappointment with how institutions have responded to their prior needs?
3. Social workers might work under policies and political climates that perpetuate injustice. What conflicts might this raise for you? How will you support yourself should this occur?
4. In this example, both the client and the workers were Latinx and there were cultural differences to consider. How might systems theory support social workers to prepare to engage in cultural-informed work with clients of different backgrounds?
5. Systems theory emphasizes the interconnectedness of systems. Name some examples of strategies and tactics you would use to collaborate with social workers from other institutions who are attempting to aid the same client.

References

Acevedo, G. (2004). Neither here nor there: Puerto Rican circular migration. *Journal of Immigrant & Refuge Services, 2*(1–2), 69–85.
Altshuler, S. J. (1999). Constructing genograms with children in care: Implications for casework practice. *Child Welfare League of America, LXXVIII*(6), 777–790.

Cohen, J. A., Mannarino, A. P., Berliner, L., & Deblinger, E. (2000). Trauma-focused cognitive behavioral therapy for children and adolescents: An empirical update. *Journal of Interpersonal Violence, 15*(11), 1202–1223. https://doi.org/10.1177/088626000015011007.

Gitterman, A. (2004). The mutual aid model. In C. D. Garvin, L. M. Gutierrez, & M. J. Galinsky (Eds.), *Handbook of social work with groups* (pp. 93–110). New York: Guilford Press.

Hartman, A. (1995). Diagrammatic assessment of family relationships. *Families in Society, 76*(2), 111–122.

Hutchings, A., & Taylor, I. (2007). Defining the profession? Exploring an international definition of social work in the China context. *International Journal of Social Welfare, 16*(4), 382–390.

Leighninger, R. D. (1977). Systems theory & social work: A reexamination. *Journal of Education for Social Work, 13*(3), 44–49.

Matheson, K., Foster, M. D., Bombay, A., McQuaid, R. J., & Anisman, H. (2019). Traumatic experiences, perceived discrimination, and psychological distress among members of various socially marginalized groups. *Frontiers in Psychology, 10*, 416. https://doi.org/10.3389/fpsyg.2019.00416.

Mogro-Wilson, C. (2013). Parenting in Puerto Rican families. *Families in Society, 94*(4), 235–241.

Mogro-Wilson, C., Rojas, R., & Haynes, J. (2016). A cultural understanding of the parenting practices of Puerto Rican fathers. *Social Work Research, 40*, 237–248.

Payne, M. (2002). The politics of systems theory within social work. *Journal of Social Work, 2*(3), 269–292. https://doi.org/10.1177/146801730200200302.

Pope, N. D., & Lee, J. (2015). A picture is worth a thousand words. Exploring the use of genograms in social work practice. The New Social Worker. Retrieved from www.socialworker.com/feature-articles/practice/a-picture-is-worth-a-thousand-words-genograms-social-work-practice/.

Ruzek, J. I., Brymer, M. J., Jacobs, A. K., & Layne, C. M. (2017). Psychological first aid. *Journal of Mental Health Counseling, 29*, 17–49.

Teichner, V., Cadden, J. J., & Berry, G. W. (1981). The Puerto Rican patient: Some historical, cultural and psychological aspects. *Journal of the American Academy of Psychoanalysis, 9*, 277–290.

Walz, T., & Groze, V. (1991). The mission of social work revisited: An agenda for the 1990s. *Social Work, 36*(6), 500–504.

Chapter 13
Bowen Family Systems Theory: The Case of Juliette

Robin Shultz

Introduction to Bowen Family Systems Theory

The term "family systems therapy" implies that the clinical work being conducted involves more than one person in the therapy room. But when practicing from a Bowen Family Systems Theory perspective, therapy often begins with a single motivated individual seeking help with managing personal problems or dealing with "difficult" people or relationships. Clients are often experiencing anxiety, depression, or other emotional or physical symptoms from which they cannot move beyond.

Bowen Family Systems Theory (BFST) is an evolutionary-based theory built on the premise that problems develop, not within people, but from the back and forth interactions that occur between people. Clients presenting for therapy typically have little understanding of this concept and arrive at the initial session either blaming themselves or blaming someone else for the problems in their lives. Clinicians practicing from a Bowen Theory perspective have the view that in relationships, each participant holds a share of the responsibility for what is occurring between the two of them, whether positive or negative, contributing to the relationship "process."

Process in a relationship might best be characterized as the unspoken relationship "rules" that define how each person is supposed to behave or respond in a given situation or interaction, and the spoken or unspoken reactions of the other in response. In short, process is a reciprocal, bidirectional interaction between two people that communicates either verbally or nonverbally, (a) the "rules of the game" for that relationship, (b) whether or not these [largely unspoken] rules have been adhered to by the other, and (c) how each reacts internally to the other's actions.

Systems practitioners, like their psychodynamic counterparts, understand that it is impossible for any one individual to change another. Where BFST thinkers differ however, is in their understanding that all systems, relational or otherwise, function

R. Shultz (✉)
Geneva, IL, USA
e-mail: RShultz@NewLegendsCounseling.com

© Springer Nature Switzerland AG 2021
R. P. Dealey, M. R. Evans (eds.), *Discovering Theory in Clinical Practice*,
https://doi.org/10.1007/978-3-030-57310-2_13

in a self-reinforcing manner that serves to maintain the stability of the system. In terms of human functioning, this means that when one individual in a system changes their behavior, others in the system will likely shift to accommodate the change and sustain the system's stable functioning. In open systems (i.e. living relationships systems) this unconscious, subtle movement allows for the potential change in one person to inadvertently impact the behavioral functioning of others in the system (von Bertalanffy, 1968).

Given this unique understanding, clinicians practicing from a BFST perspective often consider working with a single individual rather than the entire family system sufficient for facilitating change in a person's life. As transformation in a client relationship system is never guaranteed, individuals learning to focus on assuming responsibility for their own thoughts, feelings, and actions in lieu of attempting to change others can gain a sense of personal agency as they embark on the journey of differentiating a self (Bowen, 1978). Focus on the individual rather than the couple or family may seem contrary to what might be expected from a family systems treatment model, but Bowen Theory scholars recognize that the real work in families often begins with one motivated individual who, working on self, becomes a catalyst for the growth and change in others, even if those others never attend therapy.

Bowen Family Systems Theory emerged from extensive family research conducted by psychiatrist Murray Bowen, MD, beginning in the 1940s and lasting well into the 1980s. Bowen's earliest work started in 1946 at the Menninger Clinic in Topeka, Kansas, where he began studying schizophrenic families. Bowen's interest in this work grew from his observations that in families with a schizophrenic child, an intensity existed between mothers and the identified child. In an effort to better understand these relationships, a research study was designed allowing Bowen to observe the family's day-to-day interactions as they lived together in a hospital setting. These observations, lasting up to 14 months at a time, revealed predictable, repeated, and enduring patterns of interaction between family members not only in schizophrenic families, but in all families to a certain degree (Bowen, 1978).

Bowen characterized the intensity of the relationship observed between mothers and their schizophrenic children as "symbiotic" due to its tendency to be maintained well beyond the reality needs of the child, to the point of appearing to inhibit the child's development (Bowen, 1978, p. 5). This intensity was hypothesized to manifest from the mother's unresolved attachment to her own mother which later became focused upon her child (Bowen, 1978). Bowen considered these and other reciprocal, patterned interactions occurring between family members to be "family emotional process" (Kerr & Bowen, 1988, p. 277), and key in understanding how problems developed and were maintained in families. An important outcome of this research was the hypothesis that family problems manifested from interactions and dynamics occurring between family members rather than from any one single individual (Bowen, 1978).

How Problems Arise

One interaction pattern Bowen found particularly prevalent in families was the "triangle" (Bowen, 1978, p. 307). Bowen defined this as a relational arrangement between parents involving the passive exclusion of one parent from the parent/child relationship by the other. Bowen found that in many cases, the excluded parent contributed to his or her own exclusion by actively maintaining an over-involvement in activities external to the marriage (Bowen, 1978).

Bowen's research interests eventually expanded beyond the family unit to include (a) the effect of stress on human functioning, and (b) the conceptualization of a science of human behavior. In this investigation, Bowen began to explore how family functioning might play a role in the development of psychiatric disorders in its individual members. Applying his own experiences working within medical and mental health organizational settings, Bowen was able to more clearly articulate how emotional processes, emotional fusion, and triangles operated in real time within groups of interconnected individuals. From these personal experiences, Bowen concluded that his original hypotheses indicating prevalence for patterned and reciprocal interactions to exist within families, also pertained to workgroups, organizations, and to society as a whole (Bowen, 1978).

Another significant contribution Bowen Theory made to the field of mental health was the observation that anxiety is a key factor in the development of dysfunctional interaction patterns among individuals. The combination of research, personal experiences gained through professional work, and the ability to view group functioning through a broader systems lens contributed to a fuller conceptualization of the impact that workplace anxiety has on individuals in workgroups. This research leading to the development of Bowen Theory also indicated that when people become anxious in the workplace, similar to families, triangles form and anxiety gets expressed within the group as gossip, "side-talking" about absent colleagues, and "diagnosing" others as those who "understand" individuals not present, analyzed and discussed them (Titelman, 2008, p. 6).

Furthermore, observations indicated that when individuals moved away from the workgroup or the family, they experienced a clearer sense of self, and in return, experienced an emotional "pull" toward "togetherness" from coworkers or family members. Bowen Theory sees this "pull" as an attempt to draw the individual back into the fold in order to be on the "inside" of a triangle. Individuals are then silently expected to merge with colleagues (or family members) in the jointly held notion that "we understand each other perfectly and are in agreement about this 'pathological' third person" (Titelman, 2008, p. 6).

From this point forward, Bowen Theory viewed the triadic (triangular) relationship as the basic building block of families. Bowen Theory attributed emotional distancing within marriages, "emotional divorces," the family projection process, and over/under-functioning reciprocity, to triangles existing in the family, crediting mother/father/child triads for the stabilization of relationships and particularly, the marital relationship (Titelman, 2008, p. 9).

Rather than a treatment "model" or set of techniques, Bowen Theory represents an understanding of human behavior that emerged directly from the observation of nuanced, moment-to-moment interactions between people that develop into established relationship patterns. Bowen Theory observed that in both "normal" and non-normal families, people unconsciously worked together to maintain the status quo, or as systems thinkers describe, "homeostasis" (von Bertalanffy, 1968). This information in addition to family research and personal experiences were used in the development of Bowen Theory. This theory opened the door to a new way of thinking about how problems develop and are maintained in individuals by applying systems principles to the patterned interactions of living things, including human behavior.

Bowen Theory is composed of eight interlocking concepts that broadly describe the ways in which human systems function. These include (1) Differentiation of Self, (2) Triangles, (3) Nuclear Family Emotional Process, (4) Family Projection Process, (5) Emotional Cutoff, (6) Multigenerational Transmission Process, (7) Sibling Position, and (8) Societal Emotional Process (Bowen, 1978). Each of these concepts, while offering its own interpretation of an aspect of human behavior in relationships, fits with the others to create a comprehensive picture of how individuals and families function during times of high anxiety and how people work together unconsciously, to maintain the stability of the family system over time.

Differentiation of Self

Differentiation of self, the central concept in Bowen Theory, is characterized by two abilities. These include (1) the degree of maturity or emotional autonomy an individual attained over the course of development, and (2) the degree one can distinguish between thoughts and feelings. These two processes are seen as related (Bowen, 1978).

Variations in this capacity are related to (a) the level of "solid self" the individual possesses, and (b) the amount of acute anxiety he or she experiences (Bowen, 1978, p. 364). Solid self is depicted by an ability to calmly stick with one's own values and opinions in the face of disagreement with others without veering from one's own principles in order to be accepted or, not rejected by, the other(s). Individuals functioning from a position of less solid self or "pseudo self" (Bowen, 1978, p. 473) experience an internal pressure to feel, think, and behave as others are during situations of disagreement.

According to Bowen Theory, within each family line, individual children emerge with higher, lower, or similar levels of differentiation from a baseline, determined by their position among siblings and the level of anxiety occurring within the family at the time of their birth. Differentiation of self can be tracked back through the generations over time, showing that families produce lines within themselves that lead to higher and lower levels of functioning (Bowen, 1978, p. 362). Bowen Theory also suggests that individuals choose marriage partners with similar levels of differentiation to themselves.

Bowen Theory hypothesizes that people at higher levels of differentiation are more able to maintain a solid self during highly stressful situations allowing for the implementation of mindful decisions about how they will handle themselves when experiencing emotional reactivity. People with lower levels of differentiation manage themselves in less productive ways during highly charged situations as reasoning skills become fused with emotion and the anxieties of the moment.

Triangles

Triangles, or three-way relationships, are considered the basic building blocks in human relationship systems according to Bowen Theory. Triangles occur when a two-person relationship becomes unstable due to an increase in anxiety between the two people, and one or both pulls a third party into the relationship in order to relieve some of the felt pressure (Bowen, 1978, p. 307). The triangle's purpose is to keep the original two-person relationship stable by redistributing its anxiety among three people.

Bowen Theory observes that individuals seek to relieve tensions within relationships when the relationships themselves become too intense and including the presence of a third person can bring momentary relief. If tensions persist in the newly formed triangle, additional interlocking triangles often develop in order to hold all of the tension and stabilize the relationship system. Although a stabilized system is more comfortable for those involved, unspoken conflict or subversive disagreement between individuals can develop manifesting in unconscious responding as people react impulsively to what others say and do. An antidote to this automatic functioning is an individual's growing capacity to utilize cognitive processes to manage emotions experienced within the relationship system.

Nuclear Family Emotional Process

Bowen Theory views problems developing in families as emerging from one of three unconscious relationship patterns. These patterns serve the purpose of diverting people's attention away from the anxiety within the relationship toward an external problem, often a more comfortable dilemma with which to deal. Three common patterns serving this purpose include (1) marital conflict, (2) dysfunction in a spouse, and (3) impairment in a child (Bowen, 1978, pp. 475–476).

Marital Conflict

Marital conflict as defined by Bowen Theory is an interactional process between spouses in which partners argue, fight, blame, and criticize each other in lieu of focusing on themselves. Manifesting as externalized anxiety, each individual becomes focused on the other as the source of the relationship problem. This gridlock-like stance results in a paradoxical situation where both partners feel powerless to facilitate change (in the other) on the one hand, and powerful in each of their abilities to stoically hinder resolution by avoiding personal responsibility for their part in the problem, on the other. A prerequisite to breaking this cycle is the ability for one or the other to step back from the problem and observe one's own role in maintaining it. Once achieved, this partner can begin to make changes in their functioning which can systemically impact the functioning of the other over time if these changes are implemented with consistency.

Dysfunction in a Spouse

A second problematic relationship pattern in families is "dysfunction" in one of the spouses. From a Bowen Theory perspective, dysfunction is characterized by the development of a symptom. According to BFST, the spouse most likely to develop a symptom is the one most adaptive or dependent upon the other. Dysfunction in this sense is a chronic condition such as a long-term physical, emotional, or social impairment. Substance abuse, alcoholism, or other emotional or behavioral manifestations that might meet criteria for a mental health diagnosis would fall into this category (Bowen, 1978, pp. 378–379).

Factors predicting whether or not a symptom will develop in a relationship are related to each spouse's perception about which partner needs to change in order for things to improve. If either believes that only one partner needs to change, the likelihood that a symptom will develop is greater, but if both partners believe they both need to change, symptom development is less likely (Kerr & Bowen, 1988, p. 187).

Impairment in a Child

A third relationship pattern leading to family dysfunction is impairment in a child. Bowen Theory suggests that emotional distance in the marital relationship can lead to the over-involvement of a parent with one of the children in the family. Furthermore, this over-involvement can be inadvertently reinforced as the other parent is now absolved from having to try to meet the needs of the other spouse (Bowen, 1978, p. 197). This "Child Focus Process" and can result in the identified child functioning at a level beneath capability level in one or more areas. Two factors contributing to the intensity of the Child Focus Process in a family include (a) the level of emotional "cutoff" family members have from extended family, and (b) the degree of anxiety which exists in the family (p. 379).

The Family Projection Process

The Family Projection Process is a group of processes that operate simultaneously as parents and an identified child actively co-contribute to the transmission of a parental problem to the child (Bowen, 1978, p. 127). This transmission is unconscious on both parents and children's parts, unfolding naturally as reciprocal, systemic functioning occurs during interactions between them. Stemming from one or both parents' feelings of anxiety, their fears and worries are inadvertently projected onto the child through overconcern. The child may also initiate this process as he/she unconsciously attempts to stabilize friction or distance in the parent's marriage by providing them, through development of a problem, a common focus and therefore, opportunity to interact amicably with each other. This diversion serves the dual purposes of (a) allowing parents to be more comfortable within their relationship and (b) providing the child a sense of calm, seeing and knowing that the parents are more comfortable.

The Family Projection Process further provides parents the ability to avoid looking more closely at their own relationship. If marital conflict has become an enduring pattern in the family from which neither parent can extricate oneself, the Family Projection Process allows some relief as parents can now focus on a problem outside their relationship where they are able to influence an outcome. This problem is one that exists either with, or within, their child.

Systems theory's assumptions that (a) all systems, relational included, function in a self-reinforcing manner that maintains the system's stability, and (b) unconscious, subtle movement in one person in a relationship system manifests in changes in another person in the system (von Bertalanffy, 1968), support the main premise in Bowen Theory which is the idea of reciprocal functioning in relationships. Patterns of contextual, self-reinforcing, bidirectional functioning become established as individuals experience either positive outcomes or relief from negative experiences.

Albert Bandura's Social Learning Theory (1986) confirms this process in its explanation of how social learning occurs in children. According to Bandura, children learn vicariously by observing their parents' behaviors, attitudes, and responses to situations, which teaches them how to respond to similar events or interactions in life. Furthermore, children observe not only the actions of others, but also the consequences experienced by them as a result of their actions. Given the observational manner in which children develop their knowledge about patterns of interacting, interpreting, thinking, behaving, and being (within the family), once these patterns are learned and established, they are sustained throughout a person's lifetime and passed down through the generations unless efforts are made by individuals along the way to change them.

The Family Projection Process follows three typical phases. First, one of the parents has a "feeling" about the child that becomes an all-consuming fear of a specific problem the child may have. The parent, experiencing growing anxiety, begins to treat the child as if the feared problem already exists. In an effort to alleviate this anxiety, the parent seeks a diagnosis that supports the condition the child is believed to have. As the symptoms demonstrated frequently meet criteria for a diagnosis, the parent feels calmer inside, which results in a shift in how they interact with the child. This shift in feeling from anxious to calm is imperceptibly communicated to the child who in turn sees the parent calmer. Feeling calmer himself, the child learns inadvertently that the "symptoms" (behaviors) he has demonstrated in the past now make the parent calmer, which in turn, make him feel calmer. BFST does not view this Child Focus Process as a dysfunctional, manipulative, or mindful action on the part of the parent or child, but rather as an unconscious externalization of the parent's already existing anxiety. Nevertheless, the Child Focus Process can contribute to further difficulties for a child later in life.

Emotional Cutoff

Emotional cutoff in Bowen Family Systems Theory is a mechanism used by family members to handle unresolved emotional attachment to their parents as they attempt to prepare themselves to leave home, often for the first time. The term "cutoff" refers to emotional disconnection in a relationship whereby meaningful contact becomes limited or nonexistent between two or more people. Bowen Theory suggests that the more people are "cut off" from their pasts, the more likely they are to recreate it in their current and future relationships. Furthermore, if emotional cutoff is not addressed, it will be passed down to children and future grandchildren (Bowen, 1978, p. 535). Three common ways emotional cutoff manifests include (1) isolating from parents while continuing to live close to them, denying the importance of the emotional attachment; (2) distancing from parents physically by moving far away for no purpose other than to be away from them, and (3) any combination of the above (Bowen, 1978, p. 382).

Multigenerational Transmission Process

Bowen Theory suggests that certain family functioning information is passed down from one generation to the next through the multigenerational transmission process. Ways in which family members interact with each other during times of high stress can develop into patterned interactions between the individuals which define how they are "supposed" to act and respond to each other under specific circumstances. These interaction patterns are largely unspoken and learned by observing and experiencing how others respond to one's own behavior.

Each family has its own unique expectations for what is considered acceptable behavior within the family. This behavior or expected ways of acting and responding is unrelated to societal or cultural norms, determined instead by the "family process" which is prevalent in a particular family line. Family process refers to the interconnected manner in which family members relate and respond to each other that, due to reciprocity and bidirectional interacting, impact the other's next emotional and/or verbal response. When an individual does not respond in an expected manner (a way which maintains the family's status quo), anxiety tends to increase for the other as a result of the relationship predictability being upset. The "other" will then likely try to re-stabilize the relationship by attempting to get the person to "change back" to behaving in the way that is expected (Bowen, 1978, p. 416). Understood as a paradox between the desire for individuality and a desire for togetherness, this process is, according to Bowen Theory, an automatic process that occurs as a result of the systemic functioning present in all human relationships.

These interactional processes within a specific family line, (a) the automatic and unconscious manner in which family members react emotionally and respond behaviorally to each other and to anxiety-producing situations and (b) the relational interaction patterns of the family that contribute to, and have an impact on, each person's development of a "self," are transmitted through the Multigenerational Transmission Process (Bowen, 1978, p. 477). The Multigenerational Transmission Process contributes to people's level of "Differentiation of Self" over multiple generations as the children in each generation mature to higher, equal, or lower levels of "differentiation" than their parents.

Bowen Theory views these multigenerational interaction processes as manifesting from anxiety within and between individuals in the family and become "bound" in one of four distinct patterns of interaction known as "anxiety binders." These include (1) Conflict, (2) Reciprocal Over- and Under-Functioning, (3) Distancing, and (4) the Child Focus Process (Kerr & Bowen, 1988, p. 226).

Sibling Position

Sibling position, or the birth position individuals hold within their families of origin, profiles the personality characteristics that each individual will possess, "all [other] things being equal" (Bowen, 1978, p. 385). Incorporating research by Walter Toman (1961), Bowen Theory recognizes ten sibling position profiles found to predict whether each child in the family might be the child most "projected upon" (Bowen, 1978, p. 478).

Bowen Theory further suggests that when individuals learn as much as possible about the sibling positions of family members from previous generations, they can begin to understand the personalities of those members. Information found pertinent to this endeavor includes (a) knowledge of one's parents' level of differentiation of self and (b) awareness of the particular projection processes that occurred in the nuclear family of the previous generation. Bowen Theory views this information as reliably accurate and effective in determining how a prior generation's functioning level might likely impact the functioning levels of future generations.

Societal Emotional Process

Finally, Bowen Theory (1978) suggests that all of the systemic concepts detailed above are applicable beyond families to the functioning of society as a whole. Bowen Theory observes parallels between how family members function when in a state of heightened anxiety, and how individuals in society function in the midst of threatening or frightening social challenges. Both react to situations in which they feel out of control in one of two ways, which are to either avoid, or attempt to control the situation in order to relieve immediate discomfort. Bowen Theory views "cause and effect" thinking (rather than systems thinking) as contributing to inaccurate beliefs that the absence of symptoms indicates a problem has resolved, when in fact, it has not. This misunderstanding, according to Bowen Theory, can be particularly prevalent in the treatment of children as at times, a Child Focus Process is occurring (Bowen, 1978, p. 450).

How Change Occurs: Clinicians practicing from a Bowen Theory perspective use the Family Diagram to assess individual and family functioning. Information gleaned from the Family Diagram includes not only the "rules," roles, beliefs, and expectations (both spoken and unspoken) within relationships, but also the "symptoms," coping patterns, emotional reactivity, functioning, triangles, and child-focus processes that exist across generations. Levels of individuality and togetherness, sibling positions, marriages, divorces, deaths, diseases, and differentiation of self for all individuals become talking points for therapy as they are used to increase awareness of how the family functions. During this process, the clinician asks thought-provoking questions as clients pragmatically describe interactions and events that have occurred within the family line over time. The therapist's light-hearted, non-judgmental, and non-caretaking demeanor allows the client to take the lead in providing information for the diagram.

Methods Used in Bowen Theory: Clinicians practicing from a Bowen Theory perspective frequently refer to themselves as coaches or mentors. One aspect of the clinician's role in coaching is to highlight instances where a client has become emotionally "cutoff" (Bowen, 1978, p. 382) from specific family members and to educate him/her about how this cutoff may impact current and future relationships. Possibilities for re-connection are discussed and its purpose clarified. At this time, a Bowen Theory clinician might emphasize that the purpose of bridging emotional cutoff is not to resolve problems or differences (or even to discuss them), but rather to provide opportunities for practice in remaining calm and non-reactive in the presence of significant others who typically provoke anxiety in the client. This between-session practice allows clients to experience in real time, their abilities to use cognitive processes to manage emotional reactions—a key element in the concept, Differentiation of Self (Bowen, 1978, pp. 362–363).

As skills in self-management and awareness of family processes which are occurring in their families grow, clients are coached in understanding their own role and participation in the family process as well as possible changes they may choose to make in themselves that might lead to their own improved functioning. The properties of systems functioning are also taught as clients begin to contemplate how changes in themselves may influence changes in the functioning of significant others. The Family Diagram and other visuals depicting bi- and multi-directional processes in relationships are revisited and used frequently, serving as tools for ongoing conversation between client and clinician as clients take steps to implement changes in their lives.

Introduction to the Case of Juliette

Juliette is a 59-year-old Caucasian woman who came to therapy for help in dealing with the recent refusal by her 26-year-old son to remain in contact with her. All names and identifiers of the case have been changed to maintain the confidentiality of the client. Juliette had been married six times, divorced for the last time in the mid-1990s, the year her son was born. Juliette had not been in a relationship since that time and had no intention of entering into one or marrying again in the future. Juliette was an accomplished career woman, having earned her bachelor's degree at age 38, living, until she began therapy, with her only child, her son.

Juliette reported that she and her son had been close since the day he was born and that she had done "everything for him." Throughout his life, Juliette's son had maintained a strained relationship with his father but did not enjoy seeing him for their monthly visits. Juliette maintained strained relationships with her own family of origin, seeing her mother once every month and her brother with whom she was estranged, only when she "had to," which was when her mom told her to. Juliette's father died of cancer 2 years prior to the first session. Juliette reported that he drank every day and smoked cigarettes. Juliette stated that over the past 25 years, she had demonstrated clingy and submissive behaviors in her relationship with her son while at the same time, experiencing extreme pressure from her mother to take care of her, emotionally and physically. Juliette's son's rejection of their relationship had left her feeling panicky, anxious, and "worthless," unable to sleep, and drinking more than her usual daily cocktail. After the third session, Juliette reported that she drank alcohol more than she had originally admitted, having used it regularly throughout her life to calm herself down and that she had made a suicide attempt when in her early twenties after leaving home to travel across the United States with a boyfriend. Juliette did not inform her parents about this attempt and when her boyfriend called them, they did not come to visit her.

Multigenerational Information from Family Diagram

A Family Diagram of Juliette's family was completed over the first three sessions and this tool became a working document that was revisited at each session. In examining the two preceding generations (Juliette's parents and grandparents), it was determined that Juliette's paternal grandmother had successfully completed a suicide after several failed attempts, when Juliette's father was 14 years old. Juliette's paternal grandfather remarried within a month after the death of his wife. Her father's dad worked as an over-the-road truck driver and was away from home for weeks at a time. Within 2 weeks of his remarriage, Juliette's paternal grandfather was killed by a drunk driver in a city far from home while at work 1 day. As transporting the body home was expensive, Juliette's dad never saw his father again.

Juliette's dad had two brothers. His oldest brother left to fight in World War II soon after his dad died and his younger brother was institutionalized during his teenage years due to having schizophrenia. Juliette reported that his younger brother had lived a life of resentment directed at their father and had refused to see him when he came to visit him at the institution. Juliette's mom was the only child of a father who had been an "angry alcoholic" who, although well known by his wife and daughter that he drank, never did so in front of them. This "family secret," according to Juliette, was never discussed but was clearly understood. Juliette's maternal grandmother was the youngest of fifteen and a celebrated "saint" in the family who was seen as a stabilizing force in the home. Juliette reported that her grandmother always had a renter living in the home so she was not alone while her husband was out on the road. Juliette's mother, an only child, experienced many physical symptoms throughout her life including cancer and back problems, but was a dedicated career woman and dutiful to her mother. Juliette's mom had horrific memories of her father, but loved her two children, (Juliette and her brother) unconditionally, no matter how they behaved. She was also addicted to alcohol and prescription drugs, but this was never acknowledged or discussed.

Nuclear Family Information from Family Diagram

Juliette left home at the age of twenty and married a man whom she had known for 2 months. She was married for less than a year before divorcing him and marrying a man 10 years her senior. This marriage lasted a year and was followed by a 2-year marriage to the father of her son, a bartender. After divorcing her son's father, Juliette married a wholesale liquor business owner and after 8 months, divorced him and married a musician. When this marriage ended a year later, Juliette had spent 10 years of her life in and out of marriages. Feeling lost and hopeless, Juliette made a suicide attempt that her parents, after learning of it from a friend, ignored. Juliette's son was 11 years old when she left the hospital a month later. Juliette reported having made up her mind at this point to get her life together, returning to college, dedicating her time to studying, and raising her son. Juliette reported drinking moderately, albeit daily, but never openly in front of her son. Juliette's drinking was never discussed. Juliette said she believed her son did not know she drank as she never told him and never appeared intoxicated. After starting school and moving back to her home state, Juliette visited her parents as infrequently as her mother would allow as she experienced extreme resentment about her mother's coddling, protection of and lying for, her older alcoholic brother.

Juliette's brother had been married four times, experienced difficulties with the law, and was unable to hold a job. He moved in and out of Juliette's mother's apartment in her assisted living facility, often staying for weeks on end. Juliette's mother supported his drinking, refusing to acknowledge that it occurred each time Juliette confronted her about it. When Juliette visited her mother, she, her mother, and her brother all secretly drank alcohol without any of them acknowledging the fact.

Juliette presented for therapy requesting to explore her situation through the lens of Bowen Theory. In an effort to understand her son's rejection of her, Juliette had performed an Internet search of different types of therapy, looking for a model that explained why one person would reject another with such vehemence. In this effort, Juliette found information on Bowen Theory, reading about the concept, emotional cutoff. Juliette searched clinicians near her that provided treatment from the perspective of Bowen Theory. At the intake session, Juliette reported experiencing sadness, shame, and hopelessness, presenting with the treatment goals of (a) learning how to better understand family dynamics in general, (b) finding a way to bring her son back into her life, and (c) achieving and maintaining sobriety.

Theoretical Integration

Information taken from the Family Diagram identified several themes and relationship interaction patterns in Juliette's family of origin that had been transmitted across the generations. These included:

- Distancing, characterized by suicide attempts, overuse of alcohol with avoidance of responsibility for its use, and leaving relationships abruptly either through death, divorce, or "disease" (i.e., mental or physical problems).
- Conflict, characterized by multiple marriages followed by cutoffs.
- Reciprocal over- and under-functioning, characterized by enabling behaviors between Juliette's mom and her brother and between all nuclear family members as they pretended not to know that others were drinking.
- Child Focus Process, evident in the relationship between Juliette's mom and Juliette's brother and between Juliette and her son.

Creation of the Family Diagram allowed Juliette to see visually, the ways in which she had learned as a child to adapt to her environment by watching her parents and grandparents use alcohol and emotional cutoff to manage feelings of anxiety related to relationships. Juliette also learned unfortunately, to seek a sense of "self" (Bowen, 1978, p. 364) through others' validation of her, an unconscious, unobtainable goal that eluded Juliette throughout much of her life and likely contributed to the emotional cutoff of her son. Throughout this exploration, Juliette came to better understand the obstacles faced in the lives of her parents and grandparents, providing her the ability to move beyond anger, resentment, and hopelessness to a position of acceptance as she began making changes in what she could actually control in her life, which were her own behavior and choices.

Juliette was also able to examine the part she herself had played in maintaining the status quo in both her family of origin and nuclear family using avoidance. Through her own internal work with the clinician, Juliette eventually began to comprehend the toll that these actions had taken on her son. By examining her parents and grandparent's patterns of hidden drinking, emotional cutoff, and emotional fusion, Juliette was able to see more clearly her own rationalization that her son was unaware of her drinking since she did not drink in front of him. Juliette began to see her unsuccessful marriages as her way of cutting off emotionally when situations became anxiety-producing and eventually, started to understand that her son likely experienced her emotional fusion with, and focus upon, him in a way similar to how she experienced her own mother.

Juliette attempted to make contact with her son for many months, once showing up at his doorstep and pleading with him to allow her back into his life. After several failed attempts and 6 additional months of working on managing her own anxiousness about being alone, Juliette decided to make two changes in her life. First, she decided to quit drinking and join Alcoholics Anonymous. This step allowed Juliette to develop a network of friends, which took her mind off attempting to contact her son. Juliette also decided that she would no longer support the secret drinking of her mother and brother and informed them of this.

The second step Juliette took was to make a concentrated effort to establish an authentic relationship with her mom by initiating and spending time with her each week and refusing to feel resentful toward her for coddling and enabling her brother. After a few months of being with her mom and practicing remaining internally nonreactive when with her, Juliette began to truly enjoy her mom's company and looked forward to seeing her. Juliette then decided to try to develop a genuine relationship with her brother, an endeavor eventually met with similar success. Juliette began talking with her brother and mom about family dynamics in general as she elicited information to add to her Family Diagram.

Throughout this timeframe, Juliette's unwavering focus on reconnecting with her son weakened and she appeared to be moving toward acceptance that her son might choose never to have a relationship with her again. As there had been no opportunity for conversation between them since he had left, he was unaware that Juliette had begun therapy, stopped drinking, and started working on self. Juliette often arrived at therapy calm, happy, and excited about the new sense of internal independence she was experiencing for the first time in her life. Juliette began to contemplate and discuss the possibility that her son likely learned to deal with his anxiety regarding important people in his life by cutting off from them emotionally and indicated that she no longer wanted to handle anxiety in her own life in this manner.

Juliette made good progress in her treatment but eventually stopped attending therapy. Approximately 1 month prior to her last session, Juliette reported that her mother had begun to criticize her therapy and had started to avoid spending time with Juliette. Juliette had found out that her mom and brother had, after canceling a lunch planned for the three of them, gone to lunch together. The Bowen Theory construct of "change back" (Bowen, 1978, p. 416) was introduced to Juliette after she discussed the hurt feelings she experienced when her mother "accidentally" let it slip that the lunch had taken place without her. This construct, common when individuals begin to make changes in their lives that "upset the apple cart" (disrupt the homeostasis of the family system), is characterized by subtle pressure being placed on the changing individual to abandon the recent changes made and resume to a functioning level more comfortable for other family members. While Juliette could understand this idea intellectually, its occurrence in her own situation was upsetting and she once again began to feel like an outsider with her mother and brother. Juliette planned on discussing the event and the pain it caused her at her next A.A. meeting.

Juliette presented for therapy one more time. At this meeting, she informed the clinician that she had begun experiencing a great deal of reassurance at her AA group as members there were increasingly sympathetic to the pain she was experiencing as a result of the recent rejection by her mother and brother and the prior rejection by her son. Juliette spent the majority of the session discussing the value she had found in the newly developing supportive relationships at her A.A. meeting, indicating that these relationships might replace her counseling sessions. Juliette chose not to schedule another appointment. As she rose to exit the therapy room at the end of the session, Juliette informed the clinician that she had relapsed within the past week.

Unfortunately, Juliette did not return to therapy. While she had been on the path to differentiating a self, two things are hypothesized. One is that her mother's subtle "change back" message reignited Juliette's feelings from childhood that she was only valuable when found so by others. The other is that if this hypothesis was true, the "support" offered by her friends at AA, particularly at this time, may have resembled the more comfortable feelings that Juliette experienced in the past each time she entered into a new romantic relationship after the prior one's failure.

Although Juliette had begun to develop a "solid self" (Bowen, 1978, p. 473) prior to her relapse, the support offered to her at A.A. meetings may have overshadowed the newer, less developed feelings of an evolving but not fully matured, differentiated self. If Juliette had risked continuing with individual therapy, she may have reached a level of maturity that enabled her to withstand being in disagreement with her mom as she calmly stated her own thinking and principles regarding their relationship and what Juliette was, and was not, willing to accept from it. This action, had it been taken, might also have provided Juliette the ability to take this same position when and if she reunited with her son. Doing so would not only break the multigenerational pattern in Juliette's family of cutting off emotionally when one's anxiety becomes too high in relation to significant others, but also would likely impact her son's perception of his mother as being needy, clingy, and overwhelming.

Cultural Considerations

Bowen Family Systems Theory has as one of its main tenets the "individuality vs. togetherness" force (Kerr & Bowen, 1988, pp. 59–88). While these two principles, "individuality" and "togetherness," could be interpreted through the Americanized values of rugged individualism and/or conformity to societal norms, these two culturally driven principles do not accurately depict the functioning of individuals from the perspective of BFST. In Bowen Theory, the individuality and the togetherness forces are biologically driven, operate outside of consciousness, and occur in reaction to others' behavior as one individual automatically leans toward individuality as the other is seeking togetherness.

Neither societal nor cultural expectations are viewed as influencing people's tendencies toward independent thinking or compliance. BFST views both of these forces as emerging from the togetherness force with individuality seen as a response to it, and compliance viewed as an anxious reaction resulting from its potential loss. This view in Bowen Theory pertains to both individuals and society as a whole, superseding the idea that culture itself shapes people's decisions. According to BFST then, individuals make choices that either will, or will not, increase their togetherness with others.

What this means for the Bowen Theory clinician is that people are viewed not primarily from a cultural perspective, but from a human perspective. Potential clients are seen as responding in their lives to significant others' current proclivity toward togetherness with them. In the case of society, clients are responding to their own perceptions of society's willingness to accept them and allow their participation as valued equals.

Given this therapeutic position, when Juliette sought therapy from the clinician after having gained some understanding of Bowen Theory, cultural factors typically considered at the onset of a therapeutic relationship were not seen as a primary treatment consideration. Beyond explanation of the Family Diagramming process, frequency, and format of sessions, the clinician followed the lead of the client in the course of therapy. Education was a key component of the therapy as the client learned more about Bowen Theory and how its concepts pertained to her own life.

Discussion Questions

1. How do other approaches reviewed in this book address similar concerns within their own theoretical frameworks? Would you call the approach used in this chapter an individual or a family approach? Do you think it matters?
2. When an individual is making progress in therapy and then makes a spontaneous decision to stop therapy, what can you as the therapist do to intervene? Should you intervene or accept the client's decision to end therapy?
3. When using a family systems approach to therapy, do you think it would be more or less beneficial to have multiple members present in the therapy room during sessions? What would be the advantages of having more than one member present? What would be the disadvantages?
4. What do you know about systems thinking as a clinician and what might you still learn? Do you think that looking at an individual from a systems perspective might broaden understanding of why relationships can be difficult for some people? What does the impact of family of origin interaction patterns have on individuals' functioning later in life?
5. What opportunities does Bowen Family Systems Theory provide individually oriented clinicians in terms of helping people better understand themselves?

What can people learn about themselves that might make a difference in their lives?

6. What are the implications for our society if more clinicians better understood Bowen Family Systems Theory? Given the concepts, Emotional Cutoff, and Societal Emotional Processes, could broader understanding of these two ideas have an impact on our society as a whole? If so, would this impact emerge from the micro, macro, or mezza levels of practice?

References

Bandura, A. (1986). *Social foundations of thought & action: A social cognitive theory.* Englewood Cliffs, NJ: Prentice-Hall, Inc.

Bowen, M. (1978). *Family therapy in clinical practice.* Northvale, NJ: Jason Aronson, Inc.

Kerr, M. E., & Bowen, M. (1988). *Family evaluation* (1st ed.). New York, NY: W.W. Norton & Company.

Titelman, P. (Ed.). (2008). *Triangles Bowen family systems theory perspectives.* New York, NY: The Haworth Press Taylor & Francis Group. https://doi.org/10.1300/5490_01.

Toman, W. (1961). *Family constellation* (1st ed.). New York: Springer Publishing Company, Inc.

von Bertalanffy, L. (1968). *General systems theory foundations, development, applications* (1st ed.). New York, NY: George Braziller, Inc.

Chapter 14
Experiential Therapy: The Case of Sam

Wendy Seerup, Jennifer Anderson, and Joan Fedota

Introduction to Experiential Theory

Therapeutic work can be more than an idea or concept, but instead an understood experience, felt at the emotional level. The experience can be a new reality to the consumer that "buys-in" so deeply, that their entire world shifts and new insights emerge. These are the ideas embraced by experiential theory—that consumers can effectively approach change as insight, clarity of thought, and emotional catharsis through their therapeutic experiences.

Mullings (2017) defines experiential theory as an integrated approach that "shares a set of core qualities, such as eliciting and exploring reflective experiences in-session, using empathy within the therapeutic relationship as a curative factor, and helping people to explore and make meaning of their own inner lives" (p. 6). Thus, experiential theory is interwoven within the application of experiential therapy, which emphasizes the intimate quality of therapeutic relationship.

Applications of experiential therapy are posed to have unique synergistic merits for consumers with diverse needs and intersectional identities. The next section will review the premises of experiential theory and the application of metaphoric transfer.

W. Seerup (✉)
George Williams College at Aurora University, Williams Bay, WI, USA
e-mail: WSeerup@aurora.edu

J. Anderson
University of Wisconsin at Whitewater, Whitewater, WI, USA
e-mail: andersoj@uww.edu

J. Fedota
Social Work Program, George Williams College at Aurora University,
Williams Bay, WI, USA
e-mail: JFedota@aurora.edu

© Springer Nature Switzerland AG 2021
R. P. Dealey, M. R. Evans (eds.), *Discovering Theory in Clinical Practice*,
https://doi.org/10.1007/978-3-030-57310-2_14

Premises of Experiential Theory

The value of experiential theory is its application within experiential therapy—and the wide range of therapeutic activities available to the provider and the consumer. It is important to clarify the use of two specific terms—provider and consumer. First, the term consumer means the person who will be receiving the service. Yes, the use of this word is intentional in that it affirms the role that self-determination plays in the therapeutic process. It also provides a foundation-level orientation for the reader, which is free from any preconceived notions associated with the more synonymous associations of patient, client, beneficiary, and recipient. Second, this writing uses the term provider in the same manner—as an emancipatory act to free the reader from pre-conceived associations with the more synonymous terms of social worker, therapist, case manager, clinician, and case worker.

The helping process is a relationship-centered experience that merges tasks with process and is facilitated through the therapeutic roles of consumer and provider-as-witness. In experiential therapy, the provider demonstrates a non-judgmental consumer-centered approach (Simms, 2017). This approach allows consumers to express themselves in their own unique manner. Providers are prepared for and validate the socio-cultural components (Tucker, Norton, Itin, Hobson, & Alvarez, 2016) that may emerge in an experiential session such as, but not limited to the consumer's use of specific vocabulary, spiritual beliefs, values, heritage, celebrations, views on life, thoughts or feelings about change, grief/loss issues, and bereavement.

The ensuing facilitation relies on the theoretically unique extensive use of reflective questions and processing, before, during, and/or after the experience (Herrick & Duncan, 2018). Centering on the experience also requires that providers incorporate a wide array of materials (toys, books, games, poems, quotes, pictures, and an array of art supplies). Materials, such as toys and games, can be created or enhanced to target a specific therapeutic goal. Creativity for developing experiential activities is required—and recognition that therapeutic outcomes can occur within and outside of a physical office space is essential.

Aims

Experiential therapy has robust aims as experiential therapies aid consumers in developing insight, resilience, recovery, and resolution, which result in better adjustment, increased coping skills, and enhanced perspective (Baggerly & Parker, 2005). The roots of experiential therapy can be traced to the person-centered humanistic approach developed by Carl Rogers (Rogers, 1951). Thus, experiential therapy can include emotion-focused, existential, person-centered, and expressive therapies. Experiential therapy aims to elicit and explore reflective experiences (Kordeš & Demšar, 2018), uses empathy within the therapeutic relationship as a curative factor

(Malin & Pos, 2015) and helps consumers make meaning of their own inner lives (Zepke & Leach, 2002).

The provider exhibits unconditional positive regard and empathic understanding, which are necessary facilitative relationship building skills (Brubacher, 2017). These are essential for the consumer to feel safe to approach their experience and express themselves fully.

Metaphoric Transfer

The central component of experiential therapy is the therapist's understanding of the *Metaphoric Transfer*—the use of activities within the therapeutic setting or relationship to reflect upon and make meaning and to drive change in a safe and trusting environment (Allen & Hoskowitz, 2017; Shipman & Martin, 2019). The historic *Challenge by Choice* (Schoel, Prouty, & Radcliffe, 1988) experience, such as the use of a high ropes outdoor adventure course where a consumer can try difficult activities in a supportive and caring environment, serves as an example of a metaphor for life's difficult challenges. The consumer may refrain or pause during an activity if it becomes too emotionally or physically demanding, knowing that there will be an opportunity to try it again. The consumer has an opportunity to attempt a difficult task knowing that the attempt is more important than the completion and in the process is shown respect, and affirmation in their choice and ideas. The climbing tower may serve as a metaphor for overcoming obstacles and reaching goals (Grenier, Fitch, & Colin Young, 2018).

Ultimately, the aims of experiential therapy are anchored in the process of metaphoric transfer. It is this transfer that allows experiences to transition into life change. The next selection will highlight the unique definitions of an office space.

Redefining the Use of an Office

The organization or structure of experiential activities and space is based on the needs and abilities of the consumer (Fukui et al., 2011). As such, the options available for experiential therapy are numerous and not limited to a traditional office space.

Settings

Given the creative nature of experiential therapy, the potential professional settings include but are not limited to mental health facilities, behavioral health care facilities, counseling agencies, public libraries, private practices, schools (Martin, 2015), veterinary clinics, correctional institutions, residential treatment centers, addiction treatment centers, group homes, recovery programs, after-school programs, and assisted living facilities (Haller & Capra, 2017). Ultimately, experiential therapy is being incorporated with various populations, in traditional and non-traditional settings, and experiential therapies are producing positive and lasting outcomes with consumer populations with various diagnoses including attention-deficit hyperactivity disorder, autism, post-traumatic stress disorder, traumatic brain injury, dementia, depression, abuse, Alzheimer's disease, anxiety, and trauma recovery within specifically structured community-based programs.

Options

Expressive modalities include but are not limited to art, music, drama, poetry, play, photography, storytelling, horticultural, wilderness, adventure (Harris, 2017; Lariviere et al., 2012; McNish, 2013) and/or animal-assisted therapies (Beetz, 2017; Jones, Rice, & Cotton, 2019). Storytelling can be used with grieving consumers in maintaining healthy identification with the deceased by continual expression of memories, emotions, and thoughts through a familiar process (Glazer & Marcum, 2003). Dance and movement work can encourage consumers to communicate their feelings and thoughts through their actions (Woolf & Fisher, 2015).

Providers can incorporate art-based exercises using various mediums with texture, color, and juxtaposition, to help consumers identify and understand their emotions associated with trauma and loss (Edwards, 2017) and art can even be extended into photography. Underwater photography combined with a poetry writing project undertaken by adolescents reported significant insights for participants. In that,

> "Racing minds achieved profound focus under the surface. Powerful, trusting relationships were built. The water became a stage for kids' deep connection to others, to nature and to the best versions of themselves. And these connections began transforming their pain. Stories were changing" (Thwaits & Mosher, 2016, preface).

The options for experiential activities have increased dramatically over the last decade, and as such, a wealth of opportunities to meet the ever-complex needs of our consumers. It is important to note that this rapid growth in experiential therapy has extended concurrently into the field of neuroscience.

Numerous neurological studies demonstrate how the brain fires familiar circuits in unfamiliar settings, like a developing life narrative. This life narrative will dominate until therapeutic events challenge it (Makinson & Young, 2012). In other words, people tend to repeat patterns of behavior and understanding across settings, until new neurological connections are made. As such, these claims support the reworking of automated neurological connections through both new and repeated experiences available within experiential therapy (Messina, Sambin, Beschoner, & Viviani, 2016). It is now known that neurological connections made at the experiential level can most effectively be changed at the same level (Cozolino, 2010). Leading a client through experiential activities, chosen specifically for the client's unique needs, can promote new neurological connections to offset the old ones and promote growth and change.

Selecting an Experiential Activity

For a client to engage in a specified activity, an evaluation process must occur to decide the goodness-of-fit of the activity for the consumer. First, both parties must agree to engage in the experiential activity and the activity must be aligned with the care plan. For example, a consumer who is open to meeting animals would potentially thrive in an animal therapy setting as opposed to a consumer who is fearful of animals. Second, the consumer needs to possess the knowledge, skills, and resources to safely and successfully carry out the activity. Lastly, performance anxiety, on the part of both the provider and the consumer, must be addressed.

Performance anxiety is a clustered experience of nerves, fears, and concerns about performing something out of the realm of what is usual. As such, consumers new to therapy can be nervous about a range of things—new locations, new experiences, and/or the newness of the questions, activities, and processes. It is important to clearly explain expectations, instructions, and how experiential therapy functions, and reaffirm the role of choice and self-determination.

In truth, performance anxiety can be experienced by new providers as well as established providers that are new to experiential therapy. Much in the same way providers would support, encourage, and empower their consumers to work through their nerves, fears, and concerns, providers may need to observe experiential therapy sessions, co-facilitate experiential therapy sessions with established experiential therapy providers, and then be observed facilitating experiential therapy sessions (Nye, Connell, Haake, & Barkham, 2019). Thus, it is important for new providers or established providers new to experiential therapy to attend, engage, seek out, and collaborate with others in the field of experiential therapy (Berdondini, Elliott, & Shearer, 2012).

Therapeutic processes may be guided by the practitioner but are ultimately the choice of the consumer. Practitioners must remain cognizant that the work of therapy exists as equally in session as well as outside of session and support opportunities for their consumers to self-determinate whenever possible. A critical piece of any experiential therapy activity is to provide an overview of the inherent risks and rules. This often includes outlining the level of choice available to the consumer and includes a mindful presentation of any inherent safety risks—real or perceived. Second, practitioners need to embrace the principle of life-long learning. This is especially true in experiential work where additional training, supervision, and credentialing are required (Barker et al., 2019).

Each modality may contain unique access barriers for consumers. As an example, animal-assisted therapy barriers include consumer fear, allergies, requirements to sign safety risk forms, and lack of referrals from service providers (Legge, 2016).

Therapy animal organizations carry liability risk insurance. However, obtaining consumer health insurance coverage for animal-assisted session fees may result in a barrier to service. Health insurance providers are looking for a licensed counselor to facilitate and bill the session, whereas a trained animal instructor may instead lead the session. Similar barriers exist in outdoor adventure activities.

Steps in Experiential Therapy

Experiential steps are an interwoven process of sequential stages. The steps of experiential therapy include experiencing, reflecting, generalizing, and applying/transferring. These steps are interwoven and do not represent a linear process. See Fig. 14.1 as an example of the interwoven process. Thus, they exist and can be integrated within social work practice. It is important to understand the components of each of these steps.

Fig. 14.1 Conceptualization of experiential therapy steps

Step 1: Experience

Experiencing occurs when an individual participates in an activity. This is the data-generating phase of therapy. Before this step consumers have already been matched with specific therapeutic activities. The provider and consumer participate in the activity together. The provider will provide the materials, prepare the setting, and facilitate the activity with the prompts needed to help the consumer understand their choices. The consumer will participate in the activity in the ways that they choose, using their own creative and decision-making processes. During this step, for example, the consumer might make art, do a ropes challenge, or groom a horse.

Step 2: Reflect

Reflection involves creating opportunities for consumers to think about what they felt, thought, did, and/or observed during an activity. This can be done through discussion, journaling, or other processing tools. The main question in reflection is "*What?*", as in "*What just happened?*" In this step, the provider asks: How did you show-up in the experience? How was this for you? What did you do? What did you feel? What choices did you make? It is in this step of reflection that awareness happens, and the consumer identifies mental and physical states, and observations that occurred in the experiencing step. Without reflection, a consumer's insight into the process of the activity will remain shallow.

Step 3: Generalize

Generalizing is about how THIS experience relates to an aspect of their life that they are working on outside of the experience, such as school, home, work, spirituality, marriage, and/or their own identity. The provider helps the consumer recall observed behaviors that were displayed during activities and reflect upon whether these behaviors occur in other contexts. This is an active phase of introspection. The main questions in generalization center on "*So, what?*", as in "*So, what does this say about me?*" In many ways, this step focuses on insights gleaned from questions such as, but not limited to: So, what did you learn about yourself in this process? So, what are you taking away from your process? So, what do you think this means for you?

Step 4: Apply and Transfer

Applying, which is also known as transferring, is when the consumer takes observations about their experiences in an activity and applies them to "real life." This is a pivotal stage! The underlying question moves from the "*So, What?*" and becomes, "*Now, What?*" Herein lies the skill of the provider as the consumer transfers their experiences into an insight and forward-thinking opportunity (Tremblay, Kingsley,

& Gokiert, 2019). The closing of the therapeutic activity becomes the consumer's own generated action plan for what to work on next: *Now, what will you do differently in your life as a result of this knowledge?*

The therapeutic process of experiential therapy is fluid in nature. Once the steps are completed, the consumer and provider may start over at step one, and experience a new activity, taking with them the information learned from the last activity, in a process of activities scaffolding upon one another. Next, we will discuss special considerations that arise in the therapy process.

Provider Considerations

Social workers share common values, including valuing the dignity and worth of the person. Social workers are mindful of individual differences, cultural and ethnic diversity, the client's right to self-determination, and (the responsibility to) seek to enhance the client's capacity and opportunity to change and address their own needs (NASW, 2017). Experiential therapy as a treatment choice by social workers is reflective of the wide variance in clients' interest in and capacity for change models (such as traditional "talk" therapies). Safety and training are considerations of practitioner competence when choosing a modality.

Safety

Safety precautions must also be included in any treatment planning and goal setting. For example, the consumer may be susceptible to sunburn (or be taking medication that cautions against exposure to the sun), may be allergic or sensitive to smells or animal fur, or may need protection from sharp objects being easily accessible. Allowing the consumer to drive the decisions about their own safety is critical and is an extension of their right to self-determination.

Safety can be a subjective experience in that an experiential therapeutic activity might generate feelings of being unsafe or at-risk for one, while the same experience is welcomed by another (Helbig-Lang & Petermann, 2010). So, choice in activities can manifest differently across consumers and should be viewed as potential safety concerns. Certainly, experiential therapy activities are designed to foster consumer's growth and insight, which can be experienced as challenging and generate uncomfortable feelings (Bailis, Fleming, & Segall, 2005). However, it is important to acknowledge that no experiential therapy activity should ever place a consumer at-risk or in an unsafe situation.

Training and Credentialing of Providers

Experiential therapy can be incorporated into a vast number of practice settings. A creative provider will continually create activities and scenarios to represent the needs of the client. Some activities may require more assistance or training, such as when incorporating animals and activities that incorporate risk, such as outdoor adventure activities.

In equine-assisted therapy, horses serve as catalysts and metaphors to allow clinical issues to surface. The sheer weight of a horse creates potential safety risks for consumers and providers. For this reason, therapists work closely with a horse handler, who is responsible for ensuring safety as well as providing proper instruction for interacting with horses. The equine activities include choosing a horse, horse grooming, mounted work, and other gestalt activities. Horses elicit a range of emotions and behaviors in humans which can be used as a catalyst for personal awareness and growth. They offer a wide variety of opportunities for projection and transference. Clients can often relate to a horse's hypervigilance. A client's interpretation of a horse's movements, behaviors, and reactions determines the meaning of the metaphor. Horses can also give accurate and unbiased feedback, often mirroring both the physical and emotional states of the participant (Klontz, Bivens, Leinart, & Klontz, 2007).

Some areas of practice lend themselves well to a specially trained facilitator. The facilitator may or may not be a licensed counselor. Therefore, combining a provider and facilitator is a common model, as in an equine experience. A provider does not need to become the expert in all areas, but can instead pull in an expert, or use a facility with on-site expertise.

A provider wishing to become certified in one experiential area can also choose this option. Certifications offered include, but are not limited to: Registered Music Therapist, Registered Art Therapist, Registered Play Therapist, Registered Sandplay Therapist, Professional Association of Therapeutic Horsemanship, Eagala Equine-Assisted Psychotherapist, and Therapy Dogs International dog handler. Each of these experiential areas maintains its own organization and governing bodies, requires specialized training and supervision, and continues education requirements. Each of these areas hosts websites to support their mission and outline training requirements. The provider receives recognition for their competence and referrals on the organization's website. Credentialing however is not required to incorporate these activities into therapy for a licensed practitioner. Providers may pursue educational opportunities for the purpose of practice expertise rather than credentialing.

Access Ability

In selecting experiential activities, it is important for the therapist to know enough about the consumer, including any medical or physical issues, age factors, cognitive functioning, sensitivities, likes and dislikes to create or adapt opportunities that are appropriate and accessible to the individual or group. Additionally, the organization of the activity space must be based on the needs and abilities of those served. Paying attention to these details will allow the consumer to access the space and activity in order to maximize the experience.

How does one create access-able space? Pre-planning and design creativity are key to the experiential therapist's success. Prior to introducing any activity, careful consideration to access includes planning for physical access such as ramps, raised beds (for horticultural activities), weather conditions (including sensitivity to sunlight), ventilation (paying attention to sensitivities to smells), and safety issues (particularly for age and cognitive considerations). Easily accessible spaces support a trusting relationship between consumer and provider and allow for greater meaning-making, growth, and change (Haller & Capra, 2017). This next section will explore how experiential therapy can be applied to a specific case.

Introduction to the Case of Sam

Sam's unique case is an amalgam of consumers, thoughtfully prepared to protect the confidentiality of each without compromising either the intent of the work or the therapeutic achievements. Sam's case is neither a full social history nor a diagnostic formulation. It is meant as a teaching case and will conclude with a suggested care plan.

Sam presents as a single, trans* individual who works part-time as a bartender while completing his (preferred pronouns his, him, and their) undergraduate degree in nonprofit management. Sam shared he is 22 years old, will graduate with his undergraduate degree on time, and with honors next year. Sam identifies as First Nations with his tribal connections in the Lakota Nation but is not presently practicing or participating in tribal activities.

Sam was referred to therapy by his physician at the local health center. Sam shared that he feels he "is ready to transition to my true self." Sam was able to easily articulate how he has been on this "quest" for that last 3 years to become the truest version of himself. So far, this "quest" has consisted of becoming connected to a local LGBTQX community clinic, participating in their psycho-educational programming for trans* individuals seeking to transition, and beginning his regimen of hormone replacement medications. He shared that he "now needs to do the hard work" of working on his self-concept, reconciling his disconnections in his social relationships, and embracing his strengths.

Sam shared he has been on hormone replacement medications for the last 3 years and has worked through the bulk of the side effects associated with his physical, emotional, and reproductive system changes (Feigerlová, Pascal, Ganne, Klein, & Guerci, 2019). Sam brought to the session a copy of his medical records, recent physical, and a summary of his current blood work. All of which support that Sam is doing well, is compliant with his medical care, and in excellent health. It is critically important that the medical care of transgendered persons be accessible, be patient-centered, and that satisfaction with their providers generates compliance (Thomas et al., 2017).

Family Dynamics

Sam shared his biological parents married young and divorced when he was in fourth grade. Sam shared he moved off the reservation with his mother and relocated to an urban environment after the divorce. Sam reports that he knew he was transgender before his parents divorced. He shared as a child he thought he was to blame for their divorce, but he now believes the divorce was more about his biological father's alcohol abuse. Sam talks with his biological father monthly and sees his mother about every 2 weeks when he goes home to visit. Sam shared that he has positive memories of visiting the reservation and has strong friendships that he maintains from his youth.

Sam shared both his parents are aware and supportive of his desire to transition. Sam has a large extended family that he is surrounded by when he visits the reservation as well as back home where he lives with his mother. He reports no history of legal problems—outside of a few tickets for speeding when he first learned to drive, no behavioral problems at school, no past academic issues at school, and no significant issues with his peer group. He does acknowledge that he tends to be quiet, reserved, and a bit of a loner in social situations. He attributes this social disconnection to his tendency to get mentally preoccupied with thoughts about being rejected and how others might negatively experience his "otherness."

Care Plan

Ultimately, Sam's goal for seeking services centers on affirming a positive self-concept. He shared that he is motivated for services and recognizes there is hard work ahead of him. He identified that he struggles with reconciling disconnections in his social relationships. Sam wants to recognize and embrace his strengths. Whether a care plan is developed as an integrative paragraph, or delineated in the manner below, the choice of style is more about what is required by the provider's setting, than the content. The content is mutually determined by the therapeutic working alliance of consumer and provider and informed by the consumer's reason(s) for seeking services (Shateri & Lavasani, 2018). The provider bears the responsibility for shaping the tasks and objectives in a manner aligned with their scope of practice, theoretical knowledge, and professional skills (Brubacher, 2017).

Goal: Affirm a positive self-concept.
>   Objective 1. Do the hard work.
>   Task A Schedule and attend all therapy sessions
>   Task B Actively engage in the therapeutic process/activities
>   Task C Trust the process and intent of the experiential therapy activities
>
>   Objective 2. Reconcile disconnections in his social relationships.
>   Task A Articulate patterns of behaviors, thoughts, and feelings among peers
>   Task B Develop three social activities to participate in weekly
>   Task C Allow yourself to learn new social skills free from scrutiny
>
>   Objective 3. Recognize your own self-worth.
>   Task A Identify his strengths/aptitudes
>   Task B Develop five interchangeable positive self-talk messages
>   Task C Recognize a strength when in the moment

Once the care plan is developed, the provider moves to facilitate the various tasks and processes. And the therapeutic work begins. Given how Sam has defined his desire to seek therapy at this time—as "a quest," this metaphor can be applied and enhanced by experiential therapy activities. The section below will review a few experiential activities, share Sam's reflections on his work, and highlight the provider's own thought on the process.

Theoretical Integration

The use of a myriad of challenge by choice activities will foster the depth of reflection and insight that Sam is seeking and can help clarify areas of disconnection that he has the power to change. In relation to his care plan, and in partnership with his provider, three experiential activities were considered: an art therapy activity entitled Life-As-A-Road, an outdoor experiential ropes course activity, and an equine therapy activity. Sam chose equine therapy and named his experience "Embraced by Grace."

Embraced by Grace

Equine Therapy uses the relationship with a horse as the catalyst for change. Horses have qualities that uniquely qualify them for a special relationship; impressive size, unique personalities that can match consumers, unconditional regard, and prey instincts. It is not uncommon to hear consumers share comments like:

> "... the horse doesn't care what you make. You know, the horse doesn't care that you are a million-dollar producer, or if you're a stay-at-home mom, or anything. The horse doesn't know, doesn't care. So, you have a level playing field there" (Legge, 2016, p. 1938).

Sam's equine activity began in a warmly decorated meeting room adjacent to the barn at the therapeutic farm. Sam sat at the large wood table and noticed the surrounding plants and horse pictures. This was obviously a place where animals were highly valued. The therapist and equine instructor both joined him there and discussed what the components of his session would look like. A variety of laminated horse pictures lay across the table, with the horses bearing a variety of expressions. They each picked a picture that demonstrated the emotion they felt at that exact moment.

Sam explained that he picked the horse whose expression was a bit shy and reserved looking, because that is how he felt. Even though he was excited for this moment, he had not met a horse in a very long time and felt quite apprehensive about what this experience might entail. Both professionals assured Sam that they would stay with him during his day, guiding him, and he could take a deep breath, relax, and just experience the activities.

Sam reflected that "When I first met Grace at the stable, it was like we chose each other. She made me feel special and she understood me ... almost like she could see right through me. We did the activities together and started to trust each other. I could tell that trust was hard for her too, like she had been rejected too. I felt no judgment from her. I know that it was because she trusted me that I could brush her and why she followed me through the obstacle course. Grace helped me see myself. It was with Grace that I first became aware of the emphasis I put on what others thought of me. I realized that the important thing for me was to like and accept myself just as I am. Only then would I be able to have close relationships and be confident in my life."

Provider Reflections

Animals like Grace exhibit unconditional positive regard for the humans who respectfully interact with them. This positive regard provides the perfect opportunity for human vulnerability. Consumers will come from backgrounds where people have failed to meet their needs, whether it be abuse, neglect, bullying, family instability, or general lack of recognition. For Sam, this was his father's alcohol abuse, physical separation from his father, and the struggle to accept his transgender identity, events that left him emotionally protected.

The power of the relationship with a horse includes the presentation of the metaphor of the consumer's human relationships. For Sam, he had a history of rejection experiences, and entered all his relationships expecting more rejection. The same theme presented when he met Grace, interpreting her behaviors as rejection instead of caution. In this safe space with Grace, Sam explored his rejection past and difficulty trusting others. Instead of moving away from Grace when he felt her resist, he tried moving inward. For example, when she did not want her hooves cleaned, he calmed her with his presence, and she relaxed. As his awareness increased of how he interpreted the behavior of others, his transformation process began. As he was progressing in therapy, he was growing outside of therapy. Sam presented as more socially confident, and was more comfortable with his physical presentation. He attempted to repair his relationship with his father, and was moving past the feelings of rejection experienced with peers, and when his parents divorced.

Cultural Considerations

Experiential therapy can serve as a valuable tool in integrating a culturally sensitive and responsive method of delivering services (Lewis, 2017). Experiential therapy is based on the humanistic orientation which has historically believed that what fundamentally makes human relatedness therapeutic is the quality of the working relationship along with unconditional positive regard, genuineness, and presence (Rogers, 1951) and that the work "addresses the continual need for multicultural competence by allowing consumers to explore their worlds and issues from their unique cultural perspective without judgement" (Davis & Pereira, 2014, p. 263).

Sam's intersectional identity is a multi-faceted cultural experience for him. Time and attention should be paid by practitioners to understand his experiences, allow the consumer to teach the practitioner what is not known—by remaining culturally humble, and practitioners should seek out best practice strategies in intersectionality (Carbado, 2013). There are many factors that impact Sam's life. He identifies as a member of two distinct cultural groups: transgendered and First Nations—resulting in an intersectional experience of identity (Buchholz, 2015). These identities merge into a whole, which shapes and informs how Sam engages in his life (Samuolis, Barcellos, LaFlam, Belson, & Berard, 2015).

Sam's First Nations ancestry is an important therapeutic consideration. Most evidence-based practice research is conducted with non-diverse populations, demonstrating little basis for use with Native groups (Coleman, 2019; Leske et al., 2016; Wilson, Heaslip, & Jackson, 2018). This fact puts providers working with Indigenous people at a disadvantage for understanding the impact of a therapy type, such as experiential therapy, on a member of First Nations (Nebelkopf et al., 2011). Indigenous people have traditions of unity with the environment demonstrated through ceremony, song, custom, dance, food preparation, herbal wisdom, and storytelling (Mauro & Hardison, 2000). Incorporating these traditions and deep cultural history may be important for the consumer.

In addition, Sam views himself as trans* and as a member of the LGBT community. Trans* exists as an umbrella term for persons that identify as non-binary, gender variant, gender queer, and/or transgendered (Killerman, 2014). The term transgendered is often used by those unfamiliar with the community to mean the disconnect between their sex assigned at birth and current gender identity (Blake, 2017). However, providers familiar with the LGBT community often distinguish trans* by recognizing the significance of the above terms. For example, non-binary refers to a gender identity that exists outside of the gender binary of masculine and feminine (Brill & Kenney, 2016), which relates to gender variance—a lack of identification with pre-constructed gender norms (Killerman, 2014). Gender queer is a term associated with the emancipation of gender and the lack of labeling is intentional (Donatone & Rachlin, 2013). It is important for experiential therapy providers to recognize and respond to the terms and meanings of the words used by their consumers to define their unique identity.

It is critical to understand the uniqueness of Sam's intersectional identity to avoid marginalizing and/or compartmentalizing our consumers (Galupo, Mitchell, & Davis, 2015). As such, experiential therapy activities and the thrust of Sam's reason for seeking services must align in his overall plan of care.

Conclusion

Experiential theory is supported by the strong philosophical underpinnings of humanistic theories, honoring the choices and subjective realities of the consumer, accessed through the creative, experiencing process. Experiences are metaphors for the consumer's real life. Metaphoric transfer allows for growth in experiential therapy to be transferred to the consumer's real-life situations. The process-guiding dialogue of reflection following activities, between consumer and provider, is key to awareness. It is through this new awareness that change can happen.

The consumer is honored on all levels. As in the case of Sam, the social and cultural experiences of the consumer are valued as the lens through which the consumer experiences. Flexibility in the development of creative activities allows for individual choice and difference and the opportunity to bring in the consumer's unique metaphors.

Experiential therapy's high level of emotional arousal creates a fast and bold approach to consumer work. The social work field is more aware of the theory of change behind this process and accepting experiential therapy as a stand-alone therapy model (Borden, 2013; Foels & Bethel, 2018; Froggett, Ramvi, & Davies, 2015). Our professional challenge now becomes connecting consumers to experiential service options, respecting choice, and dignity of our consumers.

The broader professional push for the use of evidence-based research methods, along with limited available research, has restricted the incorporation of experiential therapy in practice (Watson & McMullen, 2005). It is important for practitioners to be cognizant of evaluating and substantiating their use of this modality and sharing their findings with the wider community. Thus, the case is being made for a strong future for experiential theory's place in social work practice.

Discussion Questions

Sam's case highlights the unique adaptability and versatility of experiential therapy to meet the consumer where they are. Sam requested that his services thoughtfully consider his faith, his physical health, and the bigger gestalt of his "quest to transition into my true self." As such, experiential therapy is poised to be responsive to the goals and requests of clients. Please take a moment and think through Sam's needs and wants in relation to his transition. Then thoughtfully answer the following discussion questions in your own words.

1. How do you define your style of social work practice?
2. Could Sam's quest for self-worth be achieved with a different theory and/or therapy? Be able to explain your answer in detail.
3. How do you envision using an experiential therapy model in your own area of practice?
4. How would you create a therapeutic environment that would be conducive to experiential therapy?
5. How do you see the human–animal relationship as beneficial to Sam's healing, in a unique way that may not have been achieved in a human relationship?
6. Identify presenting consumer problems that you believe would be a good match for experiential therapy. Explain and support your choices.

References

Allen, B., & Hoskowitz, N. A. (2017). Structured trauma-focused CBT and unstructured play/experiential techniques in the treatment of sexually abused children: A field study with practicing clinicians. *Child Maltreatment, 22*(2), 112–120.

Baggerly, J., & Parker, M. (2005). Child-centered group play therapy with African American boys at the elementary school level. *Journal of Counseling & Development, 83*(4), 387–396.

Bailis, D. S., Fleming, J. A., & Segall, A. (2005). Self-determination and functional persuasion to encourage physical activity. *Psychology & Health, 20*(6), 691–708.

Barker, B., Cannell, C., Naylor, S., Pearl, K., Stewart, E., & Oka, M. (2019). Let's play: Using systemic and experiential techniques in the play therapy instruction of MFT masters' students. *American Journal of Family Therapy, 47*(1), 1–18.

Beetz, A. M. (2017). Theories and possible processes of action in animal assisted interventions. *Applied Developmental Science, 21*(2), 139–149.

Berdondini, L., Elliott, R., & Shearer, J. (2012). Collaboration in experiential therapy. *Journal of Clinical Psychology, 68*(2), 159–167.

Blake, V. (2017). Being with the emergence of transgendered identity. *Transactional Analysis Journal, 47*(4), 232–243.

Borden, W. (2013). Experiments in adapting to need: Pragmatism as orienting perspective in clinical social work. *Journal of Social Work Practice, 27*(3), 259–271.

Brill, S. A., & Kenney, L. (2016). *The transgender teen: A handbook for parents and professionals supporting transgender and non-binary teens* (1st ed.). Jersey City, NJ: Cleis Press.

Brubacher, L. (2017). Emotionally focused individual therapy: An attachment-based experiential/systemic perspective. *Person-Centered & Experiential Psychotherapies, 16*(1), 50–67.

Buchholz, L. (2015). Transgender care moves into the mainstream. *JAMA: The Journal of the American Medical Association, 314*(17), 1785–1787.

Carbado, D. W. (2013). Colorblind intersectionality. *Signs: Journal of Women in Culture and Society, 38*(4), 811–845.

Coleman, D. E. (2019). Evidence based nursing practice: The challenges of health care and cultural diversity. *Journal of Hospital Librarianship, 19*(4), 330–338.

Cozolino, L. J. (2010). *The neuroscience of psychotherapy: Healing the social brain*. New York: W.W. Norton & Co.

Davis, E., & Pereira, J. (2014). Child-centered play therapy: A creative approach to culturally competent counseling. *Journal of Creativity in Mental Health, 9*, 262–274.

Donatone, B., & Rachlin, K. (2013). An intake template for transgender, transsexual, genderqueer, gender nonconforming, and gender variant college students seeking mental health services. *Journal of College Student Psychotherapy, 27*(3), 200–211.

Edwards, J. (2017). Trauma-informed care in the creative arts therapies. *The Arts in Psychotherapy, 54*, A1–A2.

Feigerlová, E., Pascal, V., Ganne, D. M., Klein, M., & Guerci, B. (2019). Fertility desires and reproductive needs of transgender people: Challenges and considerations for clinical practice. *Clinical Endocrinology, 91*(1), 10–21.

Foels, L. E., & Bethel, J. C. (2018). Revitalizing social work education using the arts. *Social Work with Groups, 41*(1/2), 74–88.

Froggett, L., Ramvi, E., & Davies, L. (2015). Thinking from experience in psychosocial practice: Reclaiming and teaching 'use of self'. *Journal of Social Work Practice, 29*(2), 133–150.

Fukui, S., Starnino, V. R., Susana, M., Davidson, L. J., Cook, K., Rapp, C. A., & Gowdy, E. A. (2011). Effect of wellness recovery action plan (WRAP) participation on psychiatric symptoms, sense of hope, and recovery. *Psychiatric Rehabilitation Journal, 34*(3), 214–222.

Galupo, M. P., Mitchell, R. C., & Davis, K. S. (2015). Sexual minority self-identification: Multiple identities and complexity. *Psychology of Sexual Orientation and Gender Diversity, 2*(4), 355–364.

Glazer, H. R., & Marcum, D. (2003). Expressing grief through storytelling. *Journal of Humanistic Counseling Education and Development, 42*(2), 131.

Grenier, M., Fitch, N., & Colin Young, J. (2018). Using the climbing wall to promote full access through universal design. *Palaestra, 32*(4), 41–46.

Haller, R., & Capra, C. (2017). *Horticultural therapy methods: Connecting people and plants in health care, human services and therapeutic programs* (2nd ed.). Boca Raton, FL: Taylor and Francis.

Harris, H. (2017). The social dimensions of therapeutic horticulture. *Health & Social Care in the Community, 25*(4), 1328–1336.

Helbig-Lang, S., & Petermann, F. (2010). Tolerate or eliminate? A systematic review on the effects of safety behavior across anxiety disorders. *Clinical Psychology: Science and Practice, 17*(3), 218–233.

Herrick, S. S. C., & Duncan, L. R. (2018). A qualitative exploration of LGBTQ+ and intersecting identities within physical activity contexts. *Journal of Sport & Exercise Psychology, 40*(6), 325–335.

Jones, M. G., Rice, S. M., & Cotton, S. M. (2019). Incorporating animal-assisted therapy in mental health treatments for adolescents: A systematic review of canine assisted psychotherapy. *PLoS One, 14*(1), 1–27.

Killerman, S. (2014). Breaking through the binary: Gender as a continuum. *Issues, 107*, 9–12.

Klontz, B., Bivens, A., Leinart, D., & Klontz, T. (2007). The effectiveness of equine-assisted experiential therapy: Results of an open clinical trial. *Society and Animals, 15*(3), 257–267.

Kordeš, U., & Demšar, E. (2018). Excavating belief about past experience: Experiential dynamics of the reflective act. *Constructivist Foundations, 13*(2), 219–229.

Lariviere, M., Couture, R., Ritchie, S. D., Cote, D., Oddson, B., & Wright, J. (2012). Behavioural assessment of wilderness therapy participants: Exploring the consistency of observational data. *The Journal of Experimental Education, 35*(1), 290–302.

Legge, M. M. (2016). The role of animal-assisted interventions in anti-oppressive social work practice. *British Journal of Social Work, 46*(7), 1926–1941.

Leske, S., Harris, M. G., Charlson, F. J., Ferrari, A. J., Baxter, A. J., Logan, J. M., et al. (2016). Systematic review of interventions for Indigenous adults with mental and substance use disorders in Australia, Canada, New Zealand and the United States. *The Australian and New Zealand Journal of Psychiatry, 50*(11), 1040–1054.

Lewis, C. P. (2017). The road to trans-inclusive health care: Policy implications and the critical role of social work. *Health & Social Work, 42*(1), 60–62.

Makinson, R. A., & Young, J. S. (2012). Cognitive behavioral therapy and the treatment of post-traumatic stress disorder: Where counseling and neuroscience meet. *Journal of Counseling & Development, 90*(2), 131–140.

Malin, A. J., & Pos, A. E. (2015). The impact of early empathy on alliance building, emotional processing, and outcome during experiential treatment of depression. *Psychotherapy Research, 25*(4), 445–459.

Martin, M. E. (2015). *Introduction to social work: Through the eyes of practice settings.* New York, NY: Pearson.

Mauro, F., & Hardison, P. D. (2000). Traditional knowledge of indigenous and local communities: International debate and policy initiatives. *Ecological Applications, 10*(5), 1263–1269.

McNish, B. (2013). Spirit of healing group: Safety in storytelling. *BU Journal of Graduate Studies in Education, 5*(2), 41–45.

Messina, I., Sambin, M., Beschoner, P., & Viviani, R. (2016). Changing views of emotion regulation and neurobiological models of the mechanism of action of psychotherapy. *Cognitive, Affective, & Behavioral Neuroscience, 16*(4), 571–587.

Mullings, B. (2017). *A Literature review of the evidence for the effectiveness of experiential psychotherapies.* Melbourne: PACFA.

National Association of Social Workers. (2017). *NASW code of ethics.* Retrieved December 1, 2019, from http://www.socialworkers.org/About/Ethics/Code-of-Ethics-English.

Nebelkopf, E., King, J., Wright, S., Schweigman, K., Lucero, E., Habte-Michael, T., & Cervantes, T. (2011). Editors' introduction: Growing roots: Native American evidence-based practices. *Journal of Psychoactive Drugs, 43*(4), 263–268.

Nye, A., Connell, J., Haake, R., & Barkham, M. (2019). Person-centered experiential therapy (PCET) training within a UK NHS IAPT service: Experiences of selected counsellors in the PRaCTICED trial. *British Journal of Guidance and Counselling, 47*(5), 619–634.

Rogers, C. R. (1951). *Client-centered therapy: Its current practice, implications, and theory.* Boston: Houghton Mifflin.

Samuolis, J., Barcellos, M., LaFlam, J., Belson, D., & Berard, J. (2015). Mental health issues and their relation to identity distress in college students. *Identity, 15*(1), 66–73.

Schoel, J., Prouty, D., & Radcliffe, P. (1988). *Islands of healing.* Hamilton, MA: Project Adventure.

Shateri, Z. E., & Lavasani, F. F. (2018). Therapeutic alliance and early change in depression: Benefits of enhancing working alliance at the initial sessions of short-term supportive--expressive psychodynamic psychotherapy. *Archives of Psychiatry and Psychotherapy, 20*(1), 17–25.

Shipman, D., & Martin, T. (2019). Clinical and supervisory considerations for transgender therapists: Implications for working with clients. *Journal of Marital and Family Therapy, 45*(1), 92–105.

Simms, J. (2017). Transformative practice. *Counseling Psychology Review, 32*(2), 46–56.

Thomas, R., Pega, F., Khosla, R., Verster, A., Hana, T., & Say, L. (2017). Ensuring an inclusive global health agenda for transgender people. *Bulletin of the World Health Organization, 95*(2), 154–156.

Thwaits, B., & Mosher, M. (Eds.). (2016). *A photographic journey of hope and healing: Under the surface.* Webster, WI: Northwest Passage, Ltd.

Tremblay, M., Kingsley, B., & Gokiert, R. (2019). Engaging vulnerable youth in community-based participatory research: Opportunities and challenges. *Journal of Community Engagement and Higher Education, 10*(3), 52–60.

Tucker, A. R., Norton, C. L., Itin, C., Hobson, J., & Alvarez, M. A. (2016). Adventure therapy: Nondeliberative group work in action. *Social Work with Groups, 39*(2–3), 194–207.

Watson, J. C., & McMullen, E. J. (2005). An Examination of therapist and client behavior high and low alliance in sessions in cognitive behavioral therapy and process experiential therapy. *Psychotherapy: Theory, Research, Practice, Training, 42*(3), 297–310.

Wilson, D., Heaslip, V., & Jackson, D. (2018). Improving equity and cultural responsiveness with marginalized communities: Understanding competing worldviews. *Journal of Clinical Nursing, 27*(19–20), 3810–3819.

Woolf, S., & Fisher, P. (2015). The role of dance movement psychotherapy for expression and integration of the self in palliative care. *International Journal of Palliative Nursing, 21*(7), 340–348.

Zepke, N., & Leach, L. (2002). Contextualized meaning making: One way of rethinking experiential learning and self-directed learning? *Studies in Continuing Education, 24*(2), 205–217.

Appendix

Life as a Road Exercise

Purpose: To create a therapeutic discussion which promotes the ability to (1) reflect on life lessons learned, (2) disclose pertinent history for purposes of discussion, and (3) to develop a sense of value to one's experiences and potential future experiences.

Directions: This exercise can be used across a wide variety of group, family, and individual settings. It offers a chance for expression of self, generates discussion, fosters a sense of shared purpose, and allows a practitioner an opportunity to learn from their consumer within the consumer's experienced life context.

Sample:

I would like you to take a minute and think of your life. Think of the journey that you have been on until now. I want you to conceptualize/view your life as if it was like driving on a road. How is your life like a road?

How have you traveled so far? What has come along your path? How has your path changed over time?

What scenery is around your road? Landscape: Mountains? Rivers? Forests? Country? City? Small town? Oceans? Hills? Jungles? Suburban? Animals? Houses? Buildings? People?

What is your road made up of? Gravel, dirt, brick, cement, asphalt, grass, or other subject matter?

What direction are you traveling within your life? N S E W, up, down, vertical, horizontal. Are there any patterns in your road; such as, but not limited, square blocks or city streets, country winding roads, cul-de-sacs, dead-ends, or turnabouts?

What signs are on your road? Slippery when wet, speed limits, Men in trees, construction signs, caution, and/or directional?

Are there things on your road? What are you traveling in? Are there other persons traveling on your road? Other vehicles? Items within your road: speed bumps, pot-holes, roadkill, and/or obstacles. Is your road a one lane, two lane, four lane, and/or multiple lane super-highway?

© Springer Nature Switzerland AG 2021
R. P. Dealey, M. R. Evans (eds.), *Discovering Theory in Clinical Practice*,
https://doi.org/10.1007/978-3-030-57310-2

Discussion Questions:

What direction are you traveling? What are you going towards? Where have you come from? Where are you in your journey? Where are you on your road? What patterns exist for you? Have you ever driven the same path twice? What have you learned about yourself from this experience?

Create your own KEY:

Indicate a symbol for experiences of grief, loss, bereavement, death, and dying. Add additional symbols as you see fit to illustrate your "LIFE AS A ROAD."

Ropes Course Activities

Low Ropes Course: Hula Hoop Activity:

Using 10 hula hoops, arrange them on the ground in a large open space or field, in a line or zig zag fashion. The facilitator assigns an age group to each hoop, so that the 10 hoops span a consumer's life. For example, if they are 20 years old, each hoop will represent 2 years of their life. As the consumer enters each hoop, they are to identify a memory or event from that life period that influenced who they are today. The complete accuracy of the memory is not challenged, but rather focus on a view of themes. A "witness" will be the listener and walk along with the consumer. The witness can be the facilitator, provider, or a fellow consumer. The witness will ask a reflection question to the consumer at each hoop following the telling of the memory. The purpose of the activity is to identify life memories and themes, so that a consumer can better understand themselves, a starting point for each consumer.

Potential Reflection Questions: In which hoop did your life trajectory change the most? What life theme followed you in every hoop? Which hoop would you choose to experience again?

High Ropes Course:

A high ropes course is generally built as part of an outdoor community recreational site or youth camp site, with a mission to support and engage at-risk community members. Providers who want to include high ropes course experiences in their work with consumers will generally partner with such an organization and use their course. Facilitators must be trained in safety and equipment use. Facilities go through extensive annual inspections. Course obstacles include rope ladders to enter the course, zip lines to exit the course, walking across logs, navigating swings, and various rope configuration obstacles. Courses are generally near 25 feet off the ground and consumers are harnessed in safety equipment. Elements of fear and trust are pervasive throughout the experience.

Potential Reflection Questions: How do you respond to fear in your life? What are the "safety nets" in your life away from this course? Identify a time in your life when you "went for it" even though it felt risky.

Equine Activities

Emotional Language Activity:

Print in color a variety of animal faces that express a wide array of emotional expressions. Laminate the animal pictures. Line up pictures on a table and allow consumers to choose a picture that represents their current emotional state. Faces can be used before and after another activity to represent emotional change. This activity provides emotional expression and encourages relationships with animals.

Potential Reflection Questions: What emotion does your picture represent? What do you think caused the animal to make that face?

Choose Your Animal Activity:

Allow consumers to choose an animal with whom they relate from a variety of animals, such as a group of horses, or a group of small animals.

Potential Reflection Questions: What characteristics do you have in common with this animal? What do you think is this animal's life story before they came to live here?

Animal Grooming Activity:

Educate consumers on grooming of the animal and safety around animals. Allow consumers to participate in grooming activities. Grooming activities develop nurturing behaviors, care-taking behaviors, trust building, and responsibility for others.

Potential Reflection Questions: How have you taken care of an animal or person before? How do you experience being taken care of?

Obstacle Course:

Build an obstacle course of activities for consumers to lead the horse through. The consumer is generally on foot. Animals are very difficult to move or direct unless trust and respect exist. Leading a horse around cones or over a bridge prop are examples. Other leading challenges include leading a horse to his stall. This activity builds relationships among consumer and animal, requires cooperation among the two, emphasizes trust, builds patience, and builds tolerance for choices of another.

Potential Reflection Questions: How did you feel when your horse followed you or did not follow you? How did you show up in the process?

Sensory Riding Trail:

Build a trail that stimulates all the rider's senses (see, hear, smell, touch, talk). Consider including hills, bridges, flowers, chimes, and touch stations. Slopes and turns will challenge the rider's balance. Sensory trails also provide peaceful walking for the horse and side-walkers.

Potential Reflection Questions: Which sensory experience was most pleasant for you? Which sensory experience was least pleasant for you?

Index

© Springer Nature Switzerland AG 2021
R. P. Dealey, M. R. Evans (eds.), *Discovering Theory in Clinical Practice*,
https://doi.org/10.1007/978-3-030-57310-2

Printed by Printforce, the Netherlands